Penguin Books

The Innovator's Handbook

Vincent Nolan is Chairman of Synectics Ltd and a
director of the International Synectics Corporation,
which has been researching the innovation process
and applying the findings to the needs of major
businesses throughout the world since 1960. Before
starting the Synectics business in Britain in 1971, he
was Head of Management Services and Assistant
Director, New Business Development, for Rank Xerox
Ltd. Previously he had worked for thirteen years as a
management consultant with PE Consultants and
Metra Consulting Group.

THE
INNOVATOR'S
HANDBOOK

The Skills of Innovative Management

Problem Solving, Communication and Teamwork

Vincent Nolan
Chairman, Synectics Ltd

PENGUIN BOOKS

PENGUIN BOOKS

Published by the Penguin Group
27 Wrights Lane, London W8 5TZ, England
Viking Penguin Inc., 40 West 23rd Street, New York, New York 10010, USA
Penguin Books Australia Ltd, Ringwood, Victoria, Australia
Penguin Books Canada Ltd, 2801 John Street, Markham, Ontario, Canada L3R 1B4
Penguin Books (NZ) Ltd, 182–190 Wairau Road, Auckland 10, New Zealand

Penguin Books Ltd, Registered Offices: Harmondsworth, Middlesex, England

Problem Solving, *Communication* and *Teamwork* first published
as separate volumes by Sphere Books 1987
This omnibus edition, under the title *The Innovator's Handbook*,
published in Penguin Books 1989
10 9 8 7 6 5 4 3 2 1

Made and printed in Great Britain by
Richard Clay Ltd, Bungay, Suffolk

Contents

Acknowledgements

The material in this book is derived largely from my experience of using and teaching the Synectics body of knowledge over the last fifteen years. This knowledge is based on videotape recordings of people at work and idenfication, in microscopic detail, of the practices that correlate with successful performance, in different types of situation.

In one sense, therefore, I am indebted to all Synectics practitioners past and present, and the client groups with whom they have worked (200,000 people at the last count!). Certainly the 5,000 (at a guess) with whom I have worked personally over the last fifteen years have provided me with rich material and insights.

In particular I am grateful to George Prince, a founder of Synectics Inc. and current Chairman of the Synectics Corporation, for his unstinting encouragement and sharing of his own discoveries; also to Rick Harriman, President of Synectics Inc., and my co-directors in Synectics Ltd – John Alexander, Jason Snelling and Sandy Dunlop – for their support and understanding.

Three experienced independent consultants – Reg Hamilton, Terry Simons and Eddie Bows – responded generously to requests for help in their particular areas of expertise. I have tried to acknowledge their specific contributions in the relevant parts of the text, along with those of other individuals, whenever I have been able to remember who first made the point to me.

However, what I have written represents very much my personal view of the world and should not be read as an 'official' Synectics text. Everybody who encounters the Synectics body of knowledge takes from it what is useful to them – here I am presenting what has proved useful to me.

I am also grateful to Brough Girling, who as my agent guided me through the strange world of book publishing.

Finally I would like especially to thank Lynn Hobson, who has typed every word of all three books, with cheerful calm and composure, in addition to her normal duties – all at a time when she was coping with her new responsibilities as Manager of Operations Staff in Synectics Ltd. Next time, Lynn, I promise I will learn to use the word processor myself!

Addition to Acknowledgements

For this 'omnibus' edition, I wish to express my thanks to Ewan Park of Mecca Leisure Holidays for bringing to my attention the Machiavelli quotation at the beginning of the book, and to George Long of Esso Engineering for permission to include my account of the launch of his Quality Programme.

Vincent Nolan

Introduction: The Management of Innovation

'There is nothing more difficult to carry out, nor more doubtful of success, nor more dangerous to handle, than to initiate a new order of things.'

Machiavelli

Many managers would identify with Machiavelli. From experience, they know that to innovate, to 'initiate a new order of things', to do something that has not been done before, is difficult and hazardous. It involves change, and change will almost certainly encounter resistance. It involves uncertainty, and with uncertainty comes anxiety. It involves the risk that things will not turn out as expected, the risk of 'failure'.

Not surprisingly, such managers tend to be wary of innovation. Intellectually, they are all in favour of it. They recognise that the future of the business, in a rapidly changing world, depends on its ability to innovate. They want it to happen – without doing something new themselves. Yet, 'if you do what you always do, you get what you always got' (according to the experts of Neuro Linguistic Programming) and it's hard to argue with that (though I will be suggesting a qualification later).

Nevertheless, and in spite of all the experience to the contrary, I believe Machiavelli is out of date. Innovation *is* manageable, provided you know how to; you need the appropriate skills. And these skills are essentially different from those needed to manage established routine operations. They are the skills of managing uncertainty and risk.

Paradoxically, at a time when the need to innovate has never been more widely recognised, the norms and values which are honoured and rewarded in business are those appropriate to the efficient running of an established routine business. 'Many of the actions and attitudes essential if subordinates are to maintain an innovative posture are, for the manager, counter-intuitive and counter to conservative training. Counter, in fact, to many of the expectations transmitted by the boss'* (and the company culture).

* George Prince, Chairman of Synectics Corporation, January 1986

1

To be logical, analytical, orderly, decisive, 'right first time', and aggressively single-minded are valuable qualities for dealing with one part of a manager's role – the efficient running of today's business. To create the business of tomorrow, i.e. to innovate, and encourage innovation from others, calls for quite different qualities and behaviours, and these are the subject matter of this book.

Innovative management skills are complementary to the skills of running an established operation, not a replacement for them. The successful managers of the future will require a much wider repertoire of skills than their predecessors. They will also need the ability to select the appropriate skills for the situation and to communicate explicitly to those they are working with what is expected from them, in each particular situation.

Probably the most important difference between innovative and routine management lies in the attitudes toward and the handling of risks. The risks of innovation are of two quite different kinds: alongside the risks of something actually going wrong in the real world, is the *emotional* risk of being criticised or blamed, feeling foolish or embarrassed.

The interaction of two types of risk (which for convenience I will label 'subjective' and 'objective') enables us to identify four different categories of risky situations, as follows:

Low Subjective/: Feels low risk, and is in fact low risk, because the
Low Objective   familiar methods are still appropriate – call it
   ROUTINE.

High Subjective/: Feels risky, because it is something I have not
Low Objective   done before, but even if it turns out badly, the
   outcome is tolerable and affordable, because it is
   a low risk experiment – call it EXPERIMENTAL.

Low Subjective/: Feels safe, because it is familiar, but in fact it is
High Objective   high risk, because the situation has changed and
   the old ways are no longer appropriate. Call it the
   OSTRICH position.

High Subjective/: Feels risky, and is in fact high risk. It's a
High Objective   GAMBLE.

The well managed business operates mainly in the lower half of the diagram below, moving between the Routine and the Experimental (spiced, perhaps with the occasional, affordable, Gamble). It makes

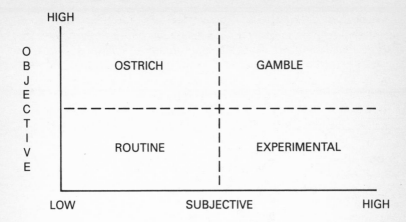

money from its Routine activities; it innovates and safeguards its future through the results of its Experimental work.

Similarly the individual manager will maintain a mix of routine and experimental activities, the routine providing a base of productive output, and the experimental pushing out the frontiers of knowledge and new possibilities. The balance between the two will vary according to the nature of the job, but both need to be present. The most creative of jobs requires a foundation of routine skills – the Creative Director of a large advertising agency once told me that 90% of his department's work was made up of routine craft skills. Similarly, the most repetitive of jobs needs to have some outlet for experiment and change if the person doing it is not to become bored and frustrated; without it, the job is better automated.

By contrast the business or individual who never experiments and continues to do things 'the way we've always done it' feels safe and comfortable but is in fact taking a big risk of being caught out by changing circumstances. They are liable to wake up one day and find that the established methods are no longer working (the Ostrich experience, the one situation where the NLP maxim no longer applies – you do what you always have done, and you *don't* get what you always got!).

There then tends to be a panic reaction, an urgent need for drastic new action, without a bank of experimental learnings, and experimental skills, to draw upon. The result is often a Gamble – a great leap forward, into major new initiatives, untried and untested, with no groundwork of knowledge or experience. Sometimes it can come off, but the odds are against it – predictably, the great leap forward falls flat on its face.

The great paradox of innovation is that the biggest risk of all is *not* to innovate, *never* to do anything new, even at the experimental level. Yet it feels safe and comfortable to stick to the tried and tested.

Experiments are vital for several reasons:

· They identify new possibilities, some of which will probably be an improvement on what we are currently doing. Even if they are not, we have ensured that we are not missing anything – a valuable insurance in a changing world.
· A multiplicity of small risks is actuarially safer than one or two big ones – the risks are spread.
· The experiments are steps on a learning curve; the new knowledge obtained from each one can be used to minimise the risks of the next one.
· They keep the innovative muscles in trim; they provide practise in creating newness, taking new initiatives, and handling the consequences. People who are used to doing new things are able to respond positively to unexpected new developments. Businesses which lurch from the Ostrich position to the Great Leap Forward remind me of people who take no exercise and then attempt a marathon!

The key to encouraging experimentation is to create an environment that encourages the maximum subjective risk, and the minimum objective risk. Bold, speculative, even outrageous *thinking* is the mainspring of innovation. It needs to be converted into prudent *action*, in the form of multiple, affordable experiments.

And these experiments must be viewed as vehicles for learning, not tests of performance. 'There is no such thing as a failed experiment' as the great inventor, Buckmaster Fuller, pointed out, 'only experiments with unexpected outcomes.' Because the outcome is unexpected, the experiment is rich in potential learning. Too often, in the business environment, it is viewed as a 'failure', to be covered up, swept under the carpet and forgotten as quickly as possible. Instead of being applauded for its courage and imagination and studied for the new insights it must contain.

Because innovators are constantly learning from their experiments, they are likely to be (perhaps surprisingly) very good at conservation, as well as innovation. They will evaluate their experiments in terms of the benefits they achieve, in relation to the benefits of the status quo. They become conscious of the strengths of what currently exists, rather than taking them for granted. Indeed their experiments may well start from a balanced evaluation of the present position, in terms of what needs to be retained, as well as what needs to be changed.

By contrast, when the Ostrich type organisation finally bestirs itself to take the Great Leap Forward, it is likely to take the view 'we've been doing it all wrong – scrap everything and start afresh', and throw away lots of babies with the bath water (a bit like many of the town centre developments of the 60s).

Part of the difference lies in the method of thinking. Instead of the binary, black and white, good/bad frame of mind that views newness and routine as opposites and mutually exclusive, the innovator sees them as complementary parts of the whole, which need to be kept in a dynamic evolving equilibrium. The innovator does not think in black and white, he thinks in colour, adding the richness of what might be made to exist, to the background that exists already.

There is no better place to start the process of innovation than your own behaviour as a manager. There's a great temptation, especially for the experienced 'successful' manager, to assume that the way we have experienced the world is the way the world has to be; and likewise that the methods we use and which have made us successful are necessarily the best methods available.

In the last quarter of a century, much new information has become available, particularly from research by my company, Synectics Corporation, using videotape recordings of working situations. It demonstrates that conventionally accepted ways of working grossly underutilise the talents of people at work. The world does not have to be as we have experienced it; it can be very much better, more productive, more rewarding, more satisfying and more enjoyable.

But to take advantage of this opportunity may mean abandoning some cherished beliefs and established practices. It may mean experimenting with doing things in ways that you have not used before, when you cannot be sure that they will work any better than – or even as well as – your habitual methods. That's the essence of innovation – doing new things with the risk that they may not work as expected. If the business is to be innovative, the managers in it must be innovative in their own ways of working, and they must understand from personal experience the dynamics of the innovation process.

They need to be particularly aware of, and sympathetic towards, the emotional risks of doing new things, the risks of feeling foolish, getting it wrong, being criticised or ridiculed. They need to know how to protect the fragile self-esteem of the individual as he or she experiments and learns from new experiences. The manager who is also experimenting and learning is well placed to provide the necessary support and understanding to others.

The focus of the book is therefore on the skills of innovative management. I have no macro-economic theory of innovation; such theories do not actually change anything in the real world. I am concerned with the things that the individual manager can do, in the two areas of:

- managing innovatively, doing their own job in new ways, and
- managing for innovation, creating an environment in which creativity and innovative behaviour by others are encouraged and rewarded.

The two aspects are closely linked; managers who want innovation must provide leadership by modelling the behaviour they want to encourage. So they must be prepared to take *personal* risks, and be seen to take them, in spite of the potential embarrassment (*because* of it, in fact).

Recently I was privileged to witness an intriguing example of innovative leadership. George Long, the General Manager of Esso Engineering Europe Ltd, was launching a Quality Improvement Programme in his organisation, where morale was still suffering from the effect of substantial redundancies in recent years. He concluded his short opening address by doing something he had never done before – singing a song in public, unaccompanied, and getting the audience to sing with him (appropriately, 'accentuate the positive, eliminate the negative . . .').

The effect was dramatic: at the second launch conference, his deputy accompanied him on the violin, and the management team produced a sketch parodying their own deliberations before the launch. The message was well and truly delivered – take the risk of doing new things, even at the risk of personal embarrassment. (Interestingly, when the idea first came up at the rehearsal of the launch, several of George's colleagues were aghast, and begged him to drop the song. George persisted, with my strong support. After the event, everyone agreed that he was right).

In addition to the appropriate experimental, risk-taking posture, the innovative manager also needs the relevant skills. I have divided the skills into three categories:

Problem Solving – to release the creativity that produces new ideas and new solutions, the raw material of innovation. According to John Sculley,* 'If innovation is our only chance, then only a respect for individual

* John Sculley: Odyssey Pepsi to Apple

creativity will lead to innovation. We desperately need new tools to help us become more creative.'

Communication – to share understanding, knowledge and ideas throughout the organisation, and to exploit the opportunities created by new communication and information technologies.

Teamwork – to generate the commitment, enthusiasm, tolerance and emotional support that is needed to sustain an innovative project through its vicissitudes.

Each of these categories is dealt with in a separate section (the material was originally published as stand-alone books, each complete in itself). Inevitably, there is some repetition between the sections, because the subject is in fact indivisible. There are strong links between the topics, and skills in the three areas are mutually reinforcing.

- The experience of successfully solving problems together creates bonds which strengthen teamwork, through shared risks and shared achievement.
- Skill in developing a wide variety of alternative solutions allows teams to work on a win/win basis – no one needs to subordinate their interests to those of the team (except occasionally).
- Problem solving develops open-mindedness, and open minds communicate better than closed minds!
- Good-quality communications prevent misunderstandings and build trust within the team.
- Problem-solving experience demonstrates that we all see the world differently (as a result of our different life experiences) and this diversity is a source of richness in ideas, leading to a high level of tolerance and appreciation for diversity between team members.
- A good team environment encourages open and honest exchange of information and ideas, and the emotionally safe climate in which problem solving and innovation prosper.
- as John Sculley says 'new communication and information technologies not only give us new things to think about, but new tools to think *with*'.

In an innovative business, the quality of communication, problem solving and teamwork needs to be of an altogether higher order than in routine operations. Probably the most demanding task is to sustain commitment to the innovation over the often extended period it takes to produce results. It always seems to take longer and cost more than expected, and as the problems and difficulties manifest themselves, the cynics, the sceptics and the guardians of the status quo have a field day.

My colleagues John Philipp and Sandy Dunlop, adapting an idea from Darryl Connor, depict this phenomenon of the 'long dark night of the innovator' in the graph below.

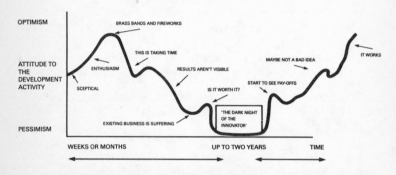

THE ANATOMY OF INNOVATION
- A MAP OF THE ORGANISATIONAL ENERGY DURING ANY MAJOR TRANSITION PROGRAMME.

THE 'WAY' INNOVATION IS HANDLED IS CRITICAL IN RETAINING ENTHUSIASM AND COMMITMENT, AND IN OVERCOMING THE INEVITABLE PROBLEMS THAT ARISE.

It takes courage to stay with the vision during this period, to persevere, to maintain enthusiasm and commitment. The role of management is to supply that courage – to EN-COURAGE in the full sense of that word, where the EN prefix means 'to put into'.

I trust that the methods and insights offered in this book will EN-COURAGE you to become an innovative (or a more innovative) person and manager, and that you will EN-JOY the process!

Vincent Nolan
November 1988

Problem
Solving

Contents

1. Problem solving: scope and limitations

Scope

'Problem solving' is the art of finding ways to get from where you are to where you want to be (assuming you do not already know how). The 'problem', therefore, is the *gap* between the present situation and a more desirable one.

This concept of a problem and problem solving is a broad one. It includes the exploiting of opportunities, and the creation of opportunities, as well as the more everyday sense of dealing with an unsatisfactory situation. Problem-solving methods do much more than solve problems! Problem solving in this sense includes, but is not limited to, a famous but restrictive definition of a problem as a 'deviation from the norm' (propagated by Kepner and Tregoe in *The Rational Manager*). That definition covers circumstances where something has gone wrong and the objective is to put it right. Given correct diagnosis of the fault, it's usually easy to rectify it.

But there are many cases where no norm yet exists – it still needs to be created. And even when there is a norm, and the problem is the deviation from it, fixing the fault is not the only way to deal with the situation. There are always alternatives to be considered, some of which may be preferable to correcting the fault. That kind of problem-solving is dealt with in one chapter of this book (chapter 7); the other chapters deal with other types of problem solving and their far-reaching implications.

Problem-solving skills enable you to get what you want; they are, therefore, the key to success for both individuals and organisations. They contribute to success in many aspects of business, the most important of which are outlined below.

Achieving objectives

People who are good at solving problems can develop a variety of alternative ways to achieve their objectives. If one way doesn't work, they can invent another and continue experimenting until they find one that does. Progressively, they discover that they can set and meet increasingly demanding objectives.

Innovation

Problem solvers will be good innovators, because their problem-solving skills make them alert to opportunities and imaginative when they invent ways to exploit them. Problem solving is the cutting edge of innovation.

Teamwork

They are good team members, because they can usually find mutually acceptable ways to deal with a situation – a skill which enables them to resolve conflicts constructively and work effectively with others. They also make good colleagues because they are open-minded, willing to accept that other people may see the world differently from them, and prepared to explore the new ideas which flow from different perspectives.

Negotiation

The same qualities help them to be good negotiators, approaching a negotiation as a shared problem which both parties have an interest in solving in a mutually acceptable way. Again their ability to invent a variety of alternative ways of handling the problem will increase the probability of a successful negotiation. (They will also need other qualities for those negotiations where a mutually acceptable solution cannot be found.)

Management of change

Similarly, good problem solvers will be skilful in the management of change. They are accustomed to dealing with newness, because they will constantly be taking new initiatives, trying out new things. They will not be disconcerted by external change, because they are confident of their ability to find ways to deal with the new, a confidence based on practice and familiarity. They will see change not as a threat, but as an opportunity and a challenge to their problem-solving abilities – unlike the manager who is stuck in routine and incapable of coping with anything new.

Decision Making

Decision making is usually perceived as a totally different activity from problem solving, and in principle it is. It consists of making the best choice from the known options, whereas problem solving is the process of creating the options. But the two are very closely linked, and the greater the skill in problem solving, the easier the decision making becomes. Decisions are usually difficult when none of the options is entirely satisfactory. The good problem solver will be able to invent additional options and/or improve some of the existing ones. It is often the case that one of the options can be improved far more than the others and becomes the clear leader, in which case the decision makes itself.

Good problem solving can create a different kind of difficulty in decision making, when it produces attractive options which are mutually exclusive or which exceed the capacity to implement them. When this happens, the decision making is hardly critical. There is an *embarras de richesses* and any choice gives a satisfactory result. You have to be philosophical about the options you leave aside: a good problem solver will tend to have more solutions than he or she has the capacity to implement, and there is no point in having regrets or feeling guilty about the ones you have to neglect!

Learning and research

The connection between problem solving and learning is also a close one. Both are processes of discovery, and the conditions conducive to good problem solving are also good for learning. Our academic training conditions us to think of learning in terms of acquiring existing knowledge, particularly at the level of information. For the individual this is still a process of discovery, even though what he or she discovers is not new to the world at large.

When it comes to developing skills, as opposed to acquiring information, the learning process is more obviously one of discovery. You can only learn to ride a bicycle, play the piano or programme a computer by actually doing it, and discovering what is involved. Success comes from a series of experiments, each one new to the learner, building on the experience of the previous ones. The rate of learning depends critically on how these experiments are handled and how the results are evaluated – an exact parallel with the handling of the experiments generated by innovative problem solving.

For the acquisition of new knowledge – which is to say, research – the links are even closer. New knowledge comes from doing new things and obtaining new experience from them. The good problem solver will have a lot of practice in doing new things (either new to him or her personally, or new to the world as a whole), and consequently will have lots of opportunities to acquire and generate new knowledge.

Potential problems

It is not only current problems which can be addressed in a problem-solving way; the same skills can be brought to bear on problems which may arise in the future, to develop contingency plans for them. (When emergencies arise, there is not usually time to invent a way of dealing with them; they often need an instant response. The time to invent that solution is when the problem does not yet exist.)

To identify potential problems – 'what could go wrong' – is itself an imaginative exercise and calls for the same mindsets and skills as the invention of solutions. It is a valuable counterweight to the excitement and possible euphoria that can arise when a highly original, new solution is invented. It highlights the risks involved in the new solution, with a view to finding ways to deal with those risks, rather than using them as a reason for not going ahead with the solution.

Alternatives to successful activities

When things are going well, it is natural to assume that there are no problems and therefore no need to engage in problem solving. Natural, but dangerous, because the successful practices are not necessarily the best available. I believe it is worthwhile to try periodically to invent better alternatives, even though the attempt may well be 'unsuccessful', in that nothing better may emerge.

The attempt will have been a success in two senses. First, it will have ensured that no superior option has been overlooked, and it is therefore valuable as an insurance. Second, it will have exercised the problem-solving muscles of the people involved, so that they do not get stuck in the rut of thinking only in a routine way.

One of the hazards of a successful enterprise is getting locked into the practices that made it successful and never looking beyond them. In time, the ability to invent new solutions atrophies from lack of use. The business is in danger of being overtaken by unforeseen external developments and lacks the skills to respond quickly and imaginatively. Successful practices should not be changed lightly, but they should be re-examined regularly. And the re-examination will often throw up detailed minor improvements as a side-benefit.

Limitations

You will have gathered that I am an enthusiast for innovative problem solving. To put that enthusiasm into perspective, it is necessary to take a cool look at the possible dangers which can be associated with problem solving when it is carried out inappropriately or unskilfully.

Taking unacceptable risks

Risk taking is an inherent part of problem solving. By definition there must be uncertainty attached to anything new, because we have no previous experience of it – if we had, it would not be new. Where there is uncertainty, there is risk.

In the creative-thinking part of problem solving, a high level of risk taking is actively encouraged, because thinking itself is an inherently safe activity. Thoughts, words, pictures – the stuff of ideas – do not themselves change anything. Consequently we can safely think the unthinkable: our ideas may be illegal, immoral, fattening or downright crazy and still contribute nothing but good to the problem-solving process (for reasons described later). The only risk attached to them is a subjective one – the fear of being criticised or ridiculed or of feeling foolish.

When the ideas are being converted to possible actions, a totally different set of considerations come into play. Whereas thoughts do not change anything in the real world, actions most certainly do. So we need to consider the possible consequences of new actions very carefully indeed. With any significant new steps it is essential to consider imaginatively *what might go wrong*, and then decide whether the risks identified are 'affordable' – could we survive the consequences of that happening? If the answer is 'no', it is prudent to go back into the thinking process to find a modification or safeguard which will make the risk acceptable.

The euphoria associated with inventing new solutions can be such as to cloud judgement of the risks involved in the new solutions. There is much to be said for a cooling-off period between the invention of a new solution and final commitment to its implementation, so that the risks can be examined in the cold grey light of dawn.

Change for its own sake

Because change is exciting, there is a temptation to change things that are already working well, often without any net benefits. This usually happens when the problem-solving process has been misdirected – directed not at the area of need, but at the area in which it is easiest to find new solutions.

A good safeguard is to make a balanced appraisal of the existing situation before starting on problem solving. The balanced appraisal will identify all the good features of the present situation, as well as the areas that need improvement. Problem solving can then be directed at those areas, with the explicit understanding that any new solution must retain the strengths of the present situation, or offer such outstanding benefits that their loss is more than offset.

It is all too easy to start problem solving by attacking the perceived areas of weakness, and then come up with solutions which deal with them brilliantly and at the same time inadvertently destroy or lose the unacknowledged strengths of the existing situation – the 'baby with the bathwater' syndrome.

Wheel-spinning

Generating ideas and developing possible solutions is a most enjoyable process – intellectually stimulating, exciting, amusing, occasionally mind-blowing. It is tempting to stay in this mode indefinitely without ever getting to the point of facing harsh realities and committing to some new action.

To prevent this from happening, high-quality problem solving starts from the identification of the person or people who are willing and able to take new action, and they become the focal point of the process. As much time is devoted to developing and checking out of new courses of action as to the initial speculative thinking to open up the problem to new approaches and new ideas.

Overload

'You can have too many good ideas,' I recently had to tell the chairman of one of my favourite clients. He is a brilliant source of exciting, original and entirely practicable new ideas. Unfortunately he has far more ideas than his organisation can possibly do justice to. His colleagues, despite their respect for him and their genuine enthusiasm for his ideas, finish up feeling frustrated and guilty because they do not have the capacity to implement more than a small proportion of the ideas.

The supply of novel solutions needs to be kept in balance with the capacity to implement them; in the event of a surplus there has to be a clear ordering of priorities and an acceptance that the lowest priorities will probably not be implemented.

The Grasshopper syndrome

Because problem solving encourages lateral thinking, there is a danger that it can result in 'lateral action' – a series of unconnected initiatives with no coherent unifying direction. Each one is a 'stand alone' experiment, and there is no mutual reinforcement or synergy between them.

Innovation needs a context of clearly formulated strategies and policies so that separate initiatives contribute to a common purpose and build one upon the other.

Unsolicited ideas

There is a world of difference between inventing a new solution to implement yourself and developing one for someone else. Unless the other party has indicated that he or she is looking for new solutions, there is a good chance that that person will hear your ideas as a criticism of what he or she is currently doing, and an interference to boot. The response to the perceived implied criticism is likely to be defensive, and you can easily find yourself drawn into a game of 'Why don't you . . .'/'Yes, but . . .'

We need clear contracts covering the exchange of ideas. When the recipient has asked for the ideas, there is no problem. When the recipient has not, the idea-giver needs to check whether the recipient wants to hear an idea or not, and if so, on what basis. It may be that he or she is prepared to listen out of interest, with no intention of doing anything with the idea – in which case we know what sort of response to expect.

Or that person may not want to hear the idea at all – a perfectly legitimate position to be in, because new ideas can be a distraction from single-minded concentration on what someone is currently doing. In that case it is better not to offer the idea at all; it will certainly fall on deaf ears and cause irritation rather than gratitude.

Which leaves the idea-giver with a dilemma. He or she is naturally excited by his or her own idea (which of us is not?) and wants to share it with the world. It takes a good deal of self-restraint to refrain from forcing it down the throat of the unwilling recipient, and it is useful to have some kind of safety valve.

One of my colleagues, Jason Snelling, has come up with his own solution to this problem. He has set up a (notional) Unsolicited Ideas Department, to which he attributes any ideas that he needs to get off his chest. The understanding is that the recipient is under no obligation to process or even acknowledge the idea. The 'department' exists solely to satisfy the needs of the idea-giver, and no judgement or criticism of the recipient is intended, or taken.

A similar outlet is provided by the Ideas Bank concept. Here anyone with an idea for which there is no immediate use enters it in an Ideas Bank. When ideas are being sought, the Ideas Bank can be used as a source material and a triggering device.

I believe that once the idea-producing mechanisms are liberated, you will always have a surplus of ideas, in the sense of more attractive courses of action available than there is capacity to implement them. At first I found this worrying; I felt a vague sense of guilt at not exploiting all the opportunities open to me, and I observe a similar anxiety among managers when they first experience the power of idea-getting strategies – how can they possibly do justice to the wealth of ideas they have produced?

Yet if we have enough new courses of action to achieve our objectives, plus a pool of unused ideas in reserve, it makes little sense to worry about the ones that got away. I console myself with the thought that nature is notoriously redundant; only a small proportion of the seeds produced grow into plants. Ideas are the seeds of action, and it seems sensible to expect only a proportion of them to grow into new courses of action which are actually implemented.

In passing, it is worth noting that the traditional Suggestions Scheme is an institution built on unsolicited ideas – hence their general ineffectiveness and unpopularity (there are some shining exceptions). I have long believed that some guidance from management on the areas where new ideas are needed would greatly improve the productiveness of Suggestions Schemes, by increasing the proportion of solicited to unsolicited ideas.

I have offered this thought to many managers of Suggestions Schemes, and it has never been taken up – it is, after all, itself an unsolicited idea!

Preconditions for problem solving

Given that problem solving is 'the art of finding ways of getting from where you are to where you want to be', it is clearly not appropriate to use problem-solving methods when there is no gap between the two – where you are *is* where you want to be – or when you already have a perfectly satisfactory way to get from one to the other. On the face of it, this is so obvious that it should not be stated, yet as we shall see, it is often ignored in practice.

So before getting involved in problem solving it is necessary to do some planning, to establish whether the necessary preconditions exist. Here are some things to look for in the planning phase:

— Who owns the problem – who is sufficiently dissatisfied with the present situation to consider it as a problem that needs to be solved? Who, in other words, is motivated to solve it?

— Is that person willing to *do* something new about it? It may be that although he or she is dissatisfied, the person is looking for sympathy rather than ideas for action.

— Is that person expecting someone else to take action rather than him or her? And in that case, does the other party see it as a problem – is the other party motivated to take some new action?

— What is the problem owner's power to act? What sorts of action is he or she in a position to take? Does he or she command resources? If so, what are they? Under what constraints does he or she operate?

— Does the problem owner already have a solution, and is he or she satisfied with it? Some managers invite ideas when they already have a solution, in the mistaken belief that they will get greater commitment to the solution if the idea appears to have come up from their team. This game is called 'Guess what's in my mind', and actually destroys commitment rather than building it, because the game is essentially dishonest.

— Does the problem owner want to find a new solution, or does he or she want to prove that no solution exists? If the latter is the case, he or she will find reasons to reject every idea, to 'prove' that no solution exists, and the effort will have been a total waste of time (I have been caught like this a couple of times).

Before I run a problem-solving meeting, I make a point of meeting each of the people involved privately to satisfy myself that the preconditions for genuine problem solving exist – namely, that I have one or more problem owners looking for new action that they can take, and that it is within their power to take that action.

It may be that the problem owner already has a solution but is interested in finding a better one, if it exists. In this case, his or her existing solution needs to be declared at the outset, so that the group does not waste time reinventing the known solution (and feeling understandably resentful when they find out what has happened).

Or the problem owner may have come to a solution privately and wish to check out that solution with his or her colleagues. This is very common in those organisations where to admit to having a problem is seen as a confession of failure. Managers do their problem solving privately, without the benefit of their colleagues' ideas. If the meeting is starting from a solution, the problem-solving format needs to be adapted to the situation. What is needed is feedback to the proposed solution, with a view to solving any problems it in turn may create.

I also use the opportunity of the planning meeting to encourage the problem owner to explore the context of the problem, to check whether the problem as he or she initially perceives it is the point that person really wants to start from. Every problem statement can be seen as a part of a hierarchy of problems or objectives, and it can be very useful to identify such higher- and lower-level problems, and to consider them as alternative starting-points.

The mechanisms to do this are quite simple. We take the problem as originally stated, and assume it was a solution, not a problem. We can then use it to identify the higher-level problem it would solve. The process can be repeated with the new problem statement to identify the next level problem, and so on.

Similarly, assuming the original problem statement to be a solution, we can ask what would be the benefits of that solution, and in this way identify sub-sets of the initial problem. At the end of the process of exploring 'backwards and forwards' from the original problem statement, we are likely to have half a dozen alternative problem statements. The problem owner then judges which one is the most fruitful point to start from.

The problem owner may well choose his or her original statement, but will have done so with some additional perspective, and if his or her view of the problem changes as he or she gets into the problem-solving process (as it may well do), he or she will be less surprised and disturbed by the change than might otherwise have been the case.

The backwards/forwards planning process is best illustrated by an example.

Backwards/forwards planning: Example

A maintenance engineer in a canning factory posed the problem:

— 'How to check whether the chain which carried the conveyor through the steriliser was properly balanced, without stopping the conveyor.'

Suppose the engineer were able to do that, what problem would it solve? The need to stop the process for periodic inspection of the chain. So there is an alternative problem statement:

— 'How to avoid stopping the process for periodic inspection of the chain.'

And if we had a way of doing that — what higher-level problem would that solve?

— 'How to prevent loss of production through stoppages for inspection'

which might lead us to:

— 'How to ensure continuous running of the plant.'

Having gone backwards from the original problem statement, we can now go in the opposite direction by asking what benefits would flow from it, if it were a solution. (These need to be different from the higher-level problems already identified.) In this case the benefits might be:

— prevention of breakdowns causing the scrapping of products in the steriliser at the time;
— ability to take corrective action early;
— avoiding major repair costs.

In that case additional possible problem statements might be:

— 'How to prevent breakdowns'
— 'How to take corrective action at an early stage'
— 'How to avoid major repairs costs'.

The process of backwards/forwards planning is an antidote to the 'tunnel vision' which locks the problem owner in to his or her original view of the problem as the only possible way of looking at it. A similar effect is achieved by the generation of Springboards (see chapter 3), but there is merit in starting the process before the problem-solving meeting.

It is also useful in advance of the meeting to check with the problem owner the number and quality of possible solutions he or she is looking for. By *quality* I mean the tradeoff between newness and feasibility – the newer a solution, the more doubtful its feasibility. If the problem owner wants very original solutions, he or she would be wise to look for several of them. With a new idea, there can never be any certainty that it will work.

Additionally, the problem owner needs to appreciate that there is unlikely to be a single unique solution to the problem (unless we are dealing with a diagnostic type of problem – trying to discover the cause of a 'deviation from the norm'). In the real world, there is usually a package of useful things that can be done to improve the situation; only in the world of mathematics does there have to be one correct solution to the problem!

Logic and beyond

'The reasonable man', wrote George Bernard Shaw, 'adapts himself to the world as it is; the unreasonable man tries to change the world to what he wants it to be.' An acceptable enough distinction to a reasonable person like me (or you, I imagine). So what?

'Therefore', concludes Shaw, 'all progress depends on the unreasonable man.' That comes as quite a shock – is it really the case that we have to stop being reasonable to make progress?

The answer is: 'Yes – temporarily.' Shaw is quite right. To make progress, to innovate, requires us to set aside the assumptions, mindsets and ways of thinking of the reasonable person, to open our minds to new ideas and new possibilities. Bill Gordon puts it neatly: 'the ultimate solutions to problems are rational; the process of finding them is not.' (W. H. H. Gordon, *Synectics*.)

The limitations of logic in the context of finding new solutions are twofold. First, the connections between phenomena which provide the pathways for logical thought processes do not yet exist – obtaining new solutions depends on making connections which have not previously been made. As George Prince puts it, 'when solutions depend on connections yet to be made, logic must fail'.

Secondly, logical thinking always starts from a set of assumptions, some of which may be made explicitly, but others so habitual that we may not be conscious of them as assumptions. To illustrate this, here's a story which you may find puzzling if you have not come across it before.

A man takes his son out for a drive in the car. They are involved in a car crash. The father is killed outright and the son is badly injured. He is rushed to hospital. The surgeon comes in to the operating theatre, takes one look at the boy and says, 'I can't operate on that boy – he's my son.'

When I put this story to groups who have not previously heard it they are puzzled – how can the surgeon be the boy's father if the father has been killed in the car crash? They begin to speculate about stepfathers, illegitimate sons, spiritual fathers and so on.

The obvious answer* is not always obvious until it is pointed out. What prevents it from being obvious is the unconscious, unacknowledged assumption that the surgeon has to be a man. If we were to ask the same people, 'Are all surgeons men?' they would reply, 'No, there are some women surgeons.' They would not be aware, until presented with the story, that the contrary assumption was a mental block, preventing them from thinking of a possibility which, with hindsight, was obvious.

The habits of logical thinking are deeply ingrained by formal education, and it may need a conscious decision to relinquish them (temporarily) to free the mind to consider new possibilities. One way to do this is to seek out and explore 'nonsense' instead of rejecting it, for reasons elegantly explained by Gary Zukav:

. . . the importance of nonsense can hardly be overstated. The more clearly we experience something as nonsense, the more clearly we are experiencing the boundaries of our own self-imposed cognitive structures. 'Nonsense' is that which does not fit into the pre-arranged patterns we have superimposed on reality. There is no such thing as nonsense apart from a judgmental intellect which calls it that.

*The surgeon is the boy's mother.

. . . nonsense is only that which, viewed from our present point of view, is unintelligible. Nonsense is nonsense only when we have not yet found that point of view from which it makes sense.*

In the idea-getting strategies I shall be describing later, I will be encouraging you to express impossible wishes and 'absurd solutions', to help you break out of the strait-jacket of logical thinking. The practical managers I work with often have difficulty accepting this approach at first. 'What's the sense in producing a load of crap?' they ask. 'What you call crap', I tell them, 'is the fertiliser that enables new solutions to grow.'

The objective is to create a state of mind described by the Zen masters as 'beginner's mind'. 'In the beginner's mind, there are many possibilities, but in the expert's there are few', according to Suzuki Roshi, and this explains why new inventions so often come from outside the industries that would benefit from them. The Xerox copier, for example, was invented by a lone physicist and turned down by some twenty photographic and office equipment companies, including Kodak and IBM. No wonder that an expert is sometimes defined as a person who knows all the reasons why something will not work!

To be successful in problem solving you need to approach it in the appropriate frame of mind or mindset, according to the type of problem you are dealing with. At one end of the spectrum are the 'puzzles', the deviations from the norm when something is not working as it was designed to work. Intrinsically the solution is already known – it was built into the original design, which is why the unit worked in the first place. Solving the puzzle is a matter of diagnosing the fault and restoring the known solution. The process is properly logical and analytical, because the solution already exists.

At the other end is the invention of ways to achieve the apparently impossible. To put a man on the moon, to invent a heavier-than-air machine that will fly, to develop a camera that will provide an instant print – all these needed the creation of totally new connections and insights. Breakthroughs of this kind need the 'beginner's mind' mindset, in which the impossible equals that which has not yet been invented, and nonsense is that for which we have not yet found the point of view from which it makes sense.

Between these two extremes lies the mix of problems the manager is likely to encounter. They will require a mix of both kinds of mindset, the reasonable and the unreasonable, the rational and the non-rational. The key is to recognise which is appropriate when, and to move easily and comfortably between the two. To get locked in at the logical/analytical end of the spectrum is to cut yourself off from your ability to invent and innovate.

*Zukav, *The Dancing Wu Li Masters*.

The characteristics of the two types of activity are well described by George Prince in his 'Mindspring' theory:

Creative	Routine
High novelty	Well-established
Unknown	Known
Approximate	Precise
Irrelevant	Relevant
Uncertain	Certain
Confused	Clear
Wrong	Right
Uncomfortable	Comfortable
Insecure	Secure
Anxious	Safe
Exciting	Boring

Most of the qualities most highly valued in the business environment – precision, relevance, certainty, clarity and so on – are those associated with the 'routine' end of the spectrum. It takes a major gear change to get into the frame of mind which accepts confusion, ambiguity, irrelevance and other such 'nonsense' as potentially valuable contributions to the progress of the business. And yet it is highly necessary because, as George Prince puts it, 'precise thinking is a very limiting way of thinking, if you insist on thinking that way all the time'.

2. From where you are to where you want to be

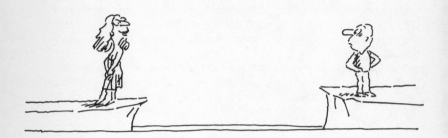

Wishful thinking

If problem solving is the art of finding ways to get from where you are to where you want to be, it would seem logical to start our description of the process by examining 'where you are' – what could be more logical than to start at the beginning?

Logical it may be, but not, in my view, appropriate. In this as in many other areas, creative problem solving stands logic on its head. The place to start is at the end, where you want to be. 'Necessity is the mother of invention', and the quality of the inventing depends more than anything else on how well the need is articulated.

To articulate the need in a really powerful way so that it becomes a magnet for new ideas and a real stimulus to our creative abilities, we have to re-learn how to wish for the impossible. I say re-learn because it is an ability we all had when we were small children. But education and social conditioning have taught us that wishing for the impossible is a bad thing – 'that's just wishful thinking', we are told scornfully. So we give it up; we wish only for the possible, and in so doing we starve our inventive muscles of the opportunity to get any exercise. Because the possible has already been invented – that's how we know it is possible. Every invention was once an impossible wish – a heavier-than-air machine that could fly, a carriage that would move without a horse to pull it, a device that allows me to talk to someone miles away, or on the other side of the world.

No doubt the idea was dismissed as wishful thinking at the time – I have in my office an article by an erudite engineer and scientist pouring scorn on the idea of a heavier-than-air machine that would fly, demonstrating entirely rationally, logically and indeed correctly in the existing state of knowledge *why* it was impossible (it was written about 1900). But the inventor is not deterred, knowing that the impossible wish is the necessary starting-point for the invention process.

If we do not wish for the impossible, our inventive muscles atrophy for lack of exercise, and we never invent anything. We never experience the excitement of making the impossible possible; and in the absence of such experience we are confirmed in our belief that it is sensible only to wish for what we know to be possible. A self-fulfilling cycle.

Such an attitude results in what I call the 'no problems problem'. In preparation for the training courses in problem solving run by my company, we ask prospective course members to identify four real problems for which they would like to have better solutions than they have currently available. The intention is to use these real problems for exercises on the course. The request causes a surprising amount of difficulty. Course members often tell us they have difficulty in identifying more than one or two problems. At the extreme, we had a gentleman who decided not to come on the course because he had no problems of his own and did not want to waste a week helping other people solve theirs!

This type of attitude can easily be dismissed as arrogance or complacency, but I see it more as a kind of resigned acceptance that things must be as they are ('that's the way it is', with the implied assumption 'that's the way it has to be'). Problems are not perceived as opportunities for problem solving but as part of the inevitable human condition, to be borne with fortitude rather than tackled with imagination.

In certain organisations, especially in aggressively managed businesses, to admit to having a problem is considered to be a sign of weakness. 'To seek assistance is considered a confession of inadequacy', according to Dr R. C. Parker, who spent many years as Research and Development director in industry, and subsequently published major studies on technological innovation.

The end-product of such attitudes on the part of individuals and organisations is that the opportunities for problem solving tend to be submerged and go unrecognised.

A powerful leader can change the attitudes by setting demanding objectives and by stimulating problem solving to discover ways to achieve the apparently impossible. Recently a new managing director was appointed to a company in a declining market, where they were losing market share because public taste was shifting from the type of product in which they were strongest to the type in which their competitor was leader. The decline in their fortunes was seen as inevitable and beyond their power to change. The new managing director refused to accept this attitude, laid down four apparently impossible objectives, and replaced all but one of his management team. By the end of the first year the company had achieved all four objectives. More important, the resigned acceptance of the inevitability of decline had been replaced with an aggressive drive to expand the business.

The first step to becoming good problem solvers is to break out of the vicious circle of low expectations and low achievement, and the mechanism is to start wishing for the apparently impossible – wish BIG.

It's not quite so easy as it sounds, particularly if you are not in the habit of wishing, so here are some mechanisms and guidelines to help you revitalise your wishing skills.

— Include yourself as the subject of the wish – formulate it along the lines, 'I wish I could find a way to . . .' In this way you will stimulate ideas for actions you yourself can take, and you will not be dependent on others for their implementation.

— If you find your wishes come in a form that depends on other people – for instance, 'I wish they would', or 'I wish I could persuade them to, or get them to' – ask yourself what problem it would solve for you if they did as you wished. For example, 'I wish I could persuade the publisher to extend the deadline for this book.' If I could, what problem would it solve for me? It would reduce the pressure of work. So my wish becomes 'I wish I could find ways in which I could reduce the pressure of work', and I am in business for ideas that I can implement myself, rather than depend on the kindness of the publishers. 'I wish I could' is a more powerful kind of wish than 'I wish they would'.

— Try to visualise the desired end state as ambitiously and imaginatively as you can. The image is a powerful motivator (provided it is really desirable – provided you have wished ambitiously enough) and can stimulate ideas.

— Write a 'Vision of the Future', a piece of science fiction set at some future date, based on the assumption that things have gone extremely well for you and you have succeeded beyond your wildest expectations. (You can do this on a long-term or short-term basis – five years away, a few months, or even the end of the day.) It will help you discover what is truly important to you and the achievements necessary to get what you want. Some of these achievements will be beyond your existing capabilities (if they are not, your vision has not been ambitious enough), and these are the starting-points for your problem solving.

— When you first restart active, explicit wishing, the wishes may tend to be rather superficial (the machinery, after all, may be a bit rusty). So it is worth probing a bit to find out what is behind the wish and get to a deeper level. It can be an interesting process of self-discovery. Try this two-minute experiment (to which I was introduced by Peter Frank):

1. Form an image in your mind's eye, of something very desirable to you – wish in picture form.
2. Now think why this image is so desirable – what would it get for you? As you think about this, let the image change or modify as it will . . .
3. Repeat the cycle a couple of times: as each new picture appears, think why it is attractive to you.

You may find that a couple of repeated cycles will bring quite a different image from the one with which you started, and one reflecting a much deeper and more fundamental wish than the original. If that has happened, you are now ready for the second half of the experiment:

4. Move the last image into the far distance (the reverse of zoom-lens effect).
5. Now start to make a path towards your distant image.

If this bit of the experiment has worked for you, you will begin to see some action you could be taking now, to take you in the direction of that distant objective.

Where you are

Having considered 'where you want to be', it is now necessary to discuss the other end of the problem-solving map, where you are now, to establish the 'gap' which is the dimension of the problem. Knowing where you are should not be difficult, but it is worth tackling systematically to ensure that no essential element of your present situation is overlooked inadvertently. It will also enable you to brief anyone who is helping you in a succinct and helpful way, without dumping on them your own preconceptions of the nature of the problem. Used properly, a clear description of the present situation can also stimulate the idea-getting process both for yourself and your helpers.

This may sound like the familiar injunction 'you've got to define the problem correctly', and I am definitely NOT saying that. I do not believe there is any such thing as a 'correct' definition of the problem (except for the fault-diagnosis kind of puzzle – and even then you only know that it is a correct definition when the solution has been reached!).

The widespread, and widely taught, belief that it is necessary to define a problem correctly before you can start solving it wastes a great deal of time and energy. It attempts to impose a spurious objectivity on something that is essentially subjective – the problem, to begin with, is what the problem owner perceives it to be. The problem owner may indeed need to change his or her perception to arrive at a solution, and to do that may also need to consider alternative 'definitions' of it; the opportunity to offer alternative ways of looking at the problem is an essential part of the problem-solving process.

But to attempt to identify a single 'correct' definition to the problem is unnecessary and sterile. It can promote endless debates beween the proponents of different definitions, without providing any means of settling the issue. It diverts the energy of the participants from solving the problem, and postpones the constructive generation of ideas, sometimes indefinitely. (I have observed groups spending the whole time allotted to solving a problem in debating its correct definition, without producing a single idea.)

The argument is also divisive, with the loser giving way from exhaustion rather than conviction and probably making no further constructive contribution as a result. If the loser happens to be the problem owner, the consequences are even worse; the whole point of the problem-solving exercise has been destroyed. Without the motivation of the problem owner, no action will result. What that person wants is an answer to the problem he or she perceives, not to one someone else perceives.

Even the arch-exponents of precision in problem solving, Messrs. Kepner and Tregoe, do *not* say that a problem has to be correctly defined. What they do say (in the context of problems which 'are deviations from the norm') is that 'a problem cannot be solved unless it is *precisely* described' – described, not defined, you will note.

I agree that, for problems of any kind, a 'good' description of the problem is a helpful starting-point. But what constitutes a 'good' description? There is a dilemma here, because the more fully the problem owner describes the problem, the more likely it is that he or she will close down options in the minds of those who are trying to help. The problem owner will be in danger of moving their 'beginners' minds' in the direction of becoming 'expert', and therefore less original and helpful. At the same time, the helpers need some information to get them started, and the problem owner does need to get his or her thinking straight.

From practical experience, I find the problem examination

checklist below helpful for the problem owner to structure his or her thinking about the problem.

Problem examination checklist

Thinking about and writing down responses against the headings in this checklist can be an effective way of beginning to 'define' a task.

Task as seen

A one-sentence 'headline' of the goal or wish:
   How to . . .
or
   How can I . . .

Analysis

(a) What is the present situation?
(b) Why has the problem arisen?
(c) Why should/must it be solved?
(d) Why is it a problem for me personally?
(e) What thoughts have I already had, or what efforts have I made, to solve the problem?
(f) Why are these thoughts/efforts insufficient or unworkable?
(g) What kind of action can I take/initiate for this problem?
(h) What would be the 'ideal world' solution?

For briefing a group of helpers, the following subset of the headings seems to be all that is required to get them started productively (and takes only three or four minutes):

— Background
— How it is a problem (for the owner)
— What has been already tried and thought of
— What is the problem owner's 'power to act'
— Ideal solution

Each of the headings is expanded below.

Background. A simple summary of the principal facts of the present situation, including how it has arisen (if that is deemed relevant). The background should not attempt to cover 'all the facts'; it simply provides a context for the problem.

How it is a problem. This is equivalent to the doctor's question 'Where does it hurt?' and is a key clue to the problem owner's interest and motivation. As such, it has to be personalised – 'How is it a problem *for you*, Problem Owner?' We are not interested in how it might be a problem for anyone else, or for the company as a whole, or for the world at large: we want to know how it affects YOU.

What has been already tried and thought of. We need to know about the past efforts and thoughts for two reasons. First, if we do not know them we will almost certainly reinvent them and then be disappointed to discover that they are not new. Secondly, the past efforts and existing ideas act as triggers for new ideas, ways of doing the same thing differently, or ways of doing the opposite, and so on. Problem owners often feel that by disclosing their past experience or current thinking they will bias the group and inhibit their creativity. In my experience this does not happen; I am strongly in favour of starting the group from where the problem owner is.

'Power to Act'. The heading asks the problem owner: 'What sorts of thing are you in a position to do yourself; and what sorts of thing are you not able, or willing, to do?' It is a description of the constraints under which the problem owner operates, and it sets the boundaries within which the solution will probably have to fall. (Not necessarily, however – the problem owner may have more power than he or she thinks, or we may invent ways to stretch the boundaries.) The question is often misunderstood as 'Are you powerful?' and gets a yes/no answer. But everyone has *some* power, and we need to know what that power is. Of course, if the problem owner really believes he or she has no power, or is not willing to do anything new, there is no point in pursuing the problem – clearly we cannot come up with a new course of action for that person.

Ideal solution. A big wish, which articulates where the problem owner wants to be; what that person would ask for if magic was available. Managers often have difficulty wishing for the impossible, and need to be encouraged to wish big. The *direction* in which they wish is an important signpost to where the solution will lie.

The style of the problem owner's briefing is just as important as its content, because the purpose is to stimulate the imagination of the group and trigger material from the group's experience which will help with the problem. Consequently, the more colourful and evocative the language in which the problem owner speaks, the richer will be the response he or she elicits. People who describe the problem with metaphors and images stimulate the listeners' imagination to come up with novel ideas.

Similarly, the emotional messages that person puts out in describing the problem have a major impact on the performance of the group. If he or she talks the language of gloom and despondency – 'There probably isn't a solution to this problem: if there was, bigger companies/better people than us would have solved it already', 'The odds are against us', 'We don't really have the resources', and so on – the group will be defeated before it starts.

Conversely, the group will respond to optimism and ambition. 'Let's see if we can really break the mould/come up with something really original', 'It would be great if we could find a way to . . .' – this language creates an environment in which the group will be challenged and stretched to come up with its most creative thinking.

Problem owners get the help they deserve. They start to deserve it with a briefing that is concise, evocative, demanding and above all honest. Nothing turns the members of a group off more quickly than the suspicion that they are being conned, that something important is being held back. For this reason alone, it is essential to come clean about existing ideas and what has been tried in the past. If there is some data which cannot be disclosed for reasons of confidentiality, the problem owner should say, 'This is not the whole story, but it is all that I am at liberty to disclose.'

3. Opening up the problem

Open-minded listening

The way in which you listen to somebody describing a problem has a major bearing on your ability to help solve it. (The same applies to the way you 'listen' to your own problems, a point to which I shall come back at the end of this section.)

Conventionally, we listen to understand what the problem is, and ask questions to get more detail and clarify aspects about which we are confused. Only when we feel we have a thorough grasp of the problem do we feel able to make a contribution, either by putting forward a solution or by suggesting an alternative definition of the problem. Such behaviour is based on the assumption that you have to understand the problem before you can offer a solution, with a sub-assumption that only feasible solutions are helpful. These entirely understandable assumptions are born of experience of a world in which ideas are instantly judged in terms of what is wrong with them. Any idea which is not a feasible solution is likely to be rejected, politely or forcibly.

This rejection (we know this from studying videotapes of many such episodes) is a painful experience for the idea giver. Rejection of my idea feels like rejection of myself as a person, a blow to my self-esteem. To avoid the rejection, we all become skilled at filtering and screening our ideas very carefully so that we only voice 'good' ideas – those we judge likely to be accepted as solutions. To make this judgement skilfully we need to know the criteria against which our ideas will be tested by the recipient. So we need a thorough understanding of the problem, as good as the problem owner's, because we are going to second-guess that person's reaction to our ideas before we put them forward.

Good problem-solving practice stands these assumptions, and the behaviour that goes with them, on their head. It introduces an alternative assumption: that *all* ideas are potentially valuable to the solution of the problem. (This is not to say that all ideas are feasible solutions!) Consequently I do not need to make judgements about which ideas are going to be useful and which are not. Therefore I do not need to have a thorough, or even a correct, understanding of the problem, to start contributing ideas.

In this case, I can approach the task of listening to the problem in a totally different way. What the problem owner is telling me about the problem will be valuable as a source of triggers for material in my own mind which will help me come up with ideas. I do not particularly need to retain or understand what that person is telling me, but I do need to keep track of my own thoughts as I listen, because these thoughts will be the raw material of my ideas. So as I listen I need to be making notes of all the associations, images and other connections my mind is making between what the problem owner is telling me and my own data bank of all my life's experience (not 'relevant' experience). So I need to be listening to my own stream of consciousness and the way it responds to what the problem owner is telling me. I need to accept my own stream of consciousness uncritically, without trying to judge whether it is relevant to the problem or not. In fact, I need to switch off my judgemental faculties altogether as I listen in this way.

This is a totally different way of listening from that to which most of us are accustomed. It is closer to daydreaming than to 'paying attention'. It feels risky, because if your understanding of the problem were to be tested, it might be found wanting (probably it would not, for reasons explained later). It takes a little practice to become good at it, if it is new to you. And it is very rewarding once you have mastered the knack because you will never be short of ideas.

To illustrate the process, here is the briefing for a problem, by my colleague, John Alexander. As you read it, make a list of all the associations and images that occur to you.

Briefing on the Recruitment Problem

Task as seen

How to find an easy and effective way of recruiting new staff.

Background/analysis

Over the last three or four months we have had a plan to recruit new staff to Synectics and have decided that we would not do anything explicit other than talking to friends and people that we saw until

1 January. That date has come and gone and I still have not done anything explicit to find the right kind of people to join us. Thinking about it, one of the reasons I haven't is that I am not really satisfied in my 'heart of hearts' with the conventional ways, such as putting an ad in a journal or magazine. I think something tells me that I should do something a little different from that, to get the kind of people we need.

It is a problem on a number of counts, really: the sheer effort I feel currently of getting my mind around what I have got to do with all the other things that are going on in my life; I keep looking for an easy way out, wanting an easy way of doing it, but it is also a problem because when I think of the ways of doing it I keep thinking, 'Well, I am going to have to see a lot of people and this is all going to take time.' I just wish I could short-circuit seeing a lot of wrong people in order to see the two or three right people that we are looking for.

The things that we have tried in the past have been:

— putting an ad in a professional journal;
— sending a copy of that out to people that we know, asking them to pass it on. (The last time we did that we didn't get anybody from the ad.)

I thought of putting a big ad in a national newspaper, somehow making it exciting and having a recruitment conference in Central London, and getting fifty or sixty people there in one go. Out of that, people would be self-selecting and we would be able to define clearly the kind of people we want, and somehow they would emerge through that kind of process. But I haven't done any more on that. I keep thinking the easy option for me is to do something like put an ad in, but I'm really not satisfied that is right.

My 'power to act': I can do anything that I decide to do, providing the amount of money I spend doing it is not excessive. I can use my time in the way that I choose, to get the result I am looking for.

If I had one wish: all the people that we have ever worked with, that were attracted to Synectics and had a feel for it, would wake up tomorrow morning and say, 'Hmm, think I'll give Synectics a call to see if there is an opportunity there for me to work with them.' That is what I would wish for.

My own list follows; if my list is longer and more varied than yours, it is because I have used the techniques often before!

In—out listening notes (recruitment problem)

Searching	Novelty	Emerging
Pole	Boxing	Aphrodite

Boy Scouts	Tug of War	Legitimate
Canvas	Subcontract	Banner
Tents	Computer	Career change
Network	Screen	Stand out
New year	Cinema	Original
Bond	Electric circuit	Reframe
Adhesives	Signals	Knock on door
Uniqueness	Fireworks	Telepathy

Having captured this material from my stream of consciousness, I now need to convert it into material that may be helpful to the problem owner. To do this, I have to make connections between my notes and the problem — or, more accurately, let the notes themselves suggest such connections. The connections may take the form of practical ideas; more likely they will be vaguer, less specific ideas, goals or wishes, metaphors, alternative ways of looking at the problem or ways of addressing a piece of the problem. To give them a common label, I will call them 'springboards', following Synectics terminology; springboards are discussed in detail in the next section.

They are all welcome: at this stage our objective is to open up the problem to new approaches, and a wide range of them. We do not know yet where any one of these lines of thought will take us, so we have no way of judging which are going to be useful and which are not.

In fact, *not* judging is the key to the whole operation — the listening, the connection-making, the formulation of the springboards, their expression and, particularly, their reception by the problem owner. The approach is only possible if there is a contract between the problem owner and his or her helpers that he or she will suspend judgement, as in brainstorming (see chapter 7), and accept every contribution as potentially helpful.

The skilful problem owner will go one step further and suspend judgement internally as well as publicly. He or she needs to listen to the springboards in the same 'stream of consciousness' way as that in which I suggested the helpers should listen. Then that person can allow their contributions to trigger new lines of thought in his or her own mind which he or she can share as springboards with the helpers, so that the generation of springboards becomes an interactive dialogue.

Listening in this way might seem to detract from understanding the problem: certainly its purpose is very different. But the notes I made of my own thoughts are linked by association with what triggered them in the problem owner's explanation of the problem, and that association enables me to remember what the problem owner was saying at the time. When I am demonstrating the technique, I am often challenged to paraphrase the problem, and I could do this quite easily with the benefit of the associations. In fact, the use of imagery and association are taught as ways of improving memory.*

In the final stage, we need to adapt this approach to problem solving to situations where you are working on your own, without the benefit of others to help you. How can you 'listen to yourself'?

It is quite feasible to do so literally, by tape-recording your own description of the problem (using the problem examination checklist or the subset of briefing headings). As you play back the tape, practise open-minded listening as though you were listening to somebody else. I know people who do this quite successfully. Personally, I believe you can dispense with the tape-recorder. Simply write down the information required by the checklist and, as you do so, make notes on a separate pad of anything that crosses your mind (again without judgement as to its relevance). You may need to re-read the checklist to get yourself a second batch of associations.

The habit of censoring ideas is deeply ingrained, to the extent that we often filter material out of our conscious mind without being aware that we are doing so. Do not be disappointed if your stream of consciousness is a bit stagnant to begin with. Persevere with the practice and if necessary help it along with some of the 'right brain' exercises described in chapter 4.

Springboards

The concept of springboards draws together three threads which we have already discussed – wishing for the impossible, defining (or rather *not* defining) the problem and open-minded listening.

Essentially, a springboard is a constructive response to a problem, without being itself a solution. As such, it may take one of many forms – an alternative definition of the problem, a challenge, a wish, a goal, an embryonic idea, a metaphor, an image. Virtually anything is acceptable, provided it is constructively orientated to helping the problem owner (it is the spirit of the springboard that matters more than its form or content).

The rationale for grouping together such disparate elements is simply that this is the way the mind seems to work naturally. As we listen to a problem description, our responses can fall into all the categories listed above. It makes sense to capture them as they arise, provided we can do so in a format that is helpful to the problem owner. In the development of the Synectics process (of

* See, for example, Peter Russell, *Brain Book*, p. 163.

which they are a part), springboards grew out of a novel way of handling the 'define the problem' debate. Instead of spending time on fruitless argument as to what was the 'correct' definition of the problem, it was decided to accept all alternative definitions as legitimate and potentially valuable ways of looking at the problem. The problem owner's original definition was labelled 'Problem as given'; each of the helpers in the group was invited to put forward a personal definition, labelled 'Problem as understood'.

Each of the problem statements was found to be useful in triggering fresh reactions from the rest of the group, which resulted very quickly in a rich array of fresh perspectives on the problem. Each of these was liable in turn to trigger ideas, embryonic or more fully developed, which also needed to be logged. The whole rich mixture was eventually labelled springboards, a highly appropriate metaphor for what were effectively taking-off points for exploration of the problem area and its possible solutions.

The most useful language for springboards has been found to be that of goals and wishes. Participants are encouraged to preface their springboards with 'I wish' or 'How to', a shorthand for 'It would be nice if we could but I don't know how to'.

This language (at first sight a little strange and uncomfortable) has a number of advantages:

— it explicitly encourages wishes, which opens up space for invention;

— it is forward-looking and action-orientated (it has to be followed by a verb);

— it permits and encourages speculation – a goal or a wish can be as unrealistic as you like;

— it does not need to be defended;

— it invites ideas.

On the downside, it is not a particularly suitable language for developed ideas, which may also come up at the same stage of the meeting (it does not make sense to say 'How to pay commission to the sales force' if you already know how to). In that case, simply drop the 'I wish/How to' format and come up with the idea as it stands – 'Pay commission to the sales force'.

The springboards offer the problem owner a smorgasbord of opportunities and, as with a smorgasbord, you are not expected to sample every one of them. The problem owner should be listening to them with an open mind, and should allow them to trigger new lines of thought which he or she should feed into the discussion in the form of his or her own springboards. The 'I wish' format is particularly appropriate for the problem owner's springboards, as it is a way to direct the helpers' attention where their thoughts would be most valuable.

Equally, the helpers need to give special attention to the problem owners' springboards as further input of information from that person, clues as to how his or her thinking is developing, and cues for additional springboards from them. Helpers may find themselves out of sympathy with the direction in which a problem owner is moving, and while it is acceptable to *offer* the problem owner an alternative direction in the form of another springboard, there is no point in trying to push him or her down that road. It takes real self-discipline to stick to the role of helper, and help the problem owner to solve the problem in his or her own way, rather than persuade him or her to do what you would do, if it was your problem. It is not yours, and what might be a good solution for you is no good for that person if he or she does not want to do it!

It is worthwhile to convert the material we generated in the open-minded listening exercise into springboards. Go back either to your own list of associations, or to the one generated by my colleague and me, and let the words trigger springboards for that problem. Now make a list. Use the 'I wish/How to' format as you find appropriate, and let one springboard trigger another. Here is our list of springboards.

Springboards for recruiting problem generated by in—out listening

I select a few of the words on my list, going for those which seem to have least relevance to the problem, and let them suggest approaches to the problem: For example:

Aphrodite. She emerged from the waves, I think. And that makes me think of the Sirens luring Ulysses on to the rocks (if it was Ulysses – no matter). So 'How to have the people we want emerge in response to our siren call'.

John says the Aphrodite image triggers him to think of the sea and the fish finding plankton in the crevices of rocks, which prompts 'How to find recruits in unusual places'.

Adhesives. I think of the weak glue that led to the development of 3M's detachable notelets: it suggests making use of failures. 'How to attract misfits – people with latent talent who are frustrated in their present job'.

John says adhesives makes him think of ticks sticking to the backs of animals, and prompts 'How to recruit on the backs of other people', which suggests 'Ask our clients to put us in touch with any candidates they reject who might be suitable for us'.

Tug of War. Suggests immediately 'How to get the whole team to help', which triggers 'Offer an incentive – much better to pay the money we spend on advertising, etc., to our own people'.

Fireworks. Makes John think of lighting the blue touch paper to produce a spectacular effect in front of an audience, so 'How to find a touch paper to create excitement'; 'How to put on a company fireworks display – maybe a display of our achievements'.

Cinema. Prompts 'How to give our company a fascinating face that haunts people', and 'How to find people with fascinating faces'.

Career change. We could put on a public conference on using creative problem solving to find a career change; it might attract some of the people we are looking for.

And so on. The springboards range from the abstract to the fairly practical: they are doing their job in opening up the problem to new approaches.

Although the generation of springboards uses the 'brainstorming' principle of suspending judgement (see chapter 7), it should not be confused with brainstorming itself. Springboards are, or should be, qualitatively different from the *ideas* generated in a brainstorming session – they should be more wishful and speculative, extend to alternative problem definitions, include more metaphor and analogy and generally be at a more generic/policy level than the more actionable ideas to be expected in a brainstorming session. And the criteria for selecting springboards to develop from are different from those used for screening ideas after a brainstorming session, as we shall see later in this chapter.

I am sometimes asked, 'How many springboards should we generate?' Enough to open up some new angles or approaches to the problem, is the general principle – how many that is will obviously vary according to the problem and the context.

A useful rule of thumb is to allow not more than half the time available in the session to briefing and springboard generation. At least as much time is needed to generate actionable ideas from some of the springboards and develop them into feasible new solutions. In a one-hour session it would be reasonable to expect thirty to fifty springboards in the first half-hour. Quality is more valuable than quantity, quality here being a question of originality, wishfulness and stimulation rather than immediate feasibility.

Beware of continuing to generate springboards as long as they are still flowing; the process is open-ended and in principle there is no end to the number of springboards that could be generated for any particular problem. If we are working with a group for a couple of days on a major problem, we might start by generating 100 to 150 springboards in the first hour. The rest of the two days would be spent working with clusters of springboards to develop new solutions from them.

Selection of Springboards

Having generated your springboards, whether there are twenty or 200, you are now faced with the need to select the ones to pursue – clearly it would be impracticable to pursue all of them. It is not such a critical decision as it may feel; the springboards can be viewed as pathways leading into unexplored territory, and it may well be that a number of different pathways will lead to the same solution (you can get to the same solution from many different routes/trains of thought).

Even so, there are different types of springboard and different criteria for selecting them:

— There may be, among the springboards, feasible solutions/new courses of action that are attractive to the problem owner and which can be adopted without modification or development. (Strictly speaking, these are not springboards as such but practical ideas; they often come up in the springboard phase and are worth capturing without being pedantic as to whether or not they qualify as springboards. They are often known solutions which the problem owner has not heard before.)

— Some springboards may be embryonic solutions which need development or refinement to overcome drawbacks and make them feasible. Here the problem owner can, as it were, see light at the end of the tunnel, and would like to get to it by finding ways round the obstacles.

— Pure springboards may be novel, intriguing, appealing, but are in no way feasible as they stand. They may be wishes, images, alternative ways of looking at the problem; where they will lead is anybody's guess. It's to be hoped that they might lead to an original, feasible solution.

The last category is potentially the most rewarding one to pursue. It also feels the most risky, as indeed it is. In problem solving, as in investment, the maxim 'If you don't speculate, you don't accumulate' applies. (Except that with investment, if you *do* speculate, you may lose your shirt – but the investment advisers don't usually tell you this! In problem solving, the worst case is only that you have spent some time exploring an avenue that did not take you anywhere.)

So it is with the pure, speculative springboards. They may lead you to a highly original and attractive solution or to a dead end. There is no way of knowing in advance. But the risk is small, ten or fifteen minutes of your time. And even if you do not get to a solution, you will have learned some things that are useful to you. For example, if a springboard leads you to an idea you do not want, your reasons for not liking it will help to clarify what you do want.

The choice of a speculative springboard has to be an intuitive decision. If they are pathways into the unknown, and we do not know to where they will lead, there can be no data to enable you to make a rational choice. Choose the springboards that give you a good warm feeling. Maybe they amuse you, maybe they intrigue you, maybe they really surprised you when they came up. Perhaps it will be a wish of the kind, 'Boy, if we could find a way to do *that*, we really would have something marvellous.' If you trust your intuitive judgement in this way, you give yourself the chance of arriving at a truly novel and exciting solution. The solution you first come up with is rarely, in my experience, the best available. The 'instant solutions' are worth noting and keeping in reserve as a security against the search for more attractive solutions proving unsuccessful.

When a group is involved in problem solving, it is the problem owner, the person with primary decision-making and action-taking responsibility, who has the responsibility for choosing the springboards to pursue. However, it can be useful to involve the whole group in the selection, on the basis that their choice may be of interest to the problem owner, but he or she is not bound by it. The members of the group like to be involved in this way; they often have strong opinions, generally in favour of a brilliant springboard they have put forward themselves! It also keeps them usefully occupied while the problem owner is making a choice.

But there are dangers in group involvement in the selection of springboards. It can diffuse the responsibility for decision making and lead to 'group think' of the worst kind. A weak or indecisive problem owner can opt out of responsibility for making the choice by following majority opinion. At the same time, that person opts out of the responsibility of getting a solution from it – he or she has no personal commitment to the choice. As Rick Harriman puts it, 'what's everybody's is nobody's'. Interestingly, I find a strong tendency to want to work on this group basis in conservative organisations with a bias against innovation. Everyone is so concerned to protect themselves from criticism for making a 'wrong' choice that nobody is willing to make an individual choice in conditions of uncertainty – however small the actual risks attached to the choice.

However, the anxiety experienced by the problem owner in making that choice is real enough, and the person running the session needs to be sensitive to it. Faced with fifty, a hundred or perhaps more springboards generated rapidly in an hour or so, and then asked to select three or four to pursue further, the problem owner can easily feel bewildered or even overwhelmed. How can you possibly make the 'correct' choice from such a rich array? The session leader must understand the problem owner's predicament. Jon Prince compares it to doing open-heart surgery and then giving the patient a needle and thread to sew the hole up with! The problem owner needs some space and some guidance. He or she needs to be reassured that the choice is not critical; it is self-correcting through the 'idea development' stage, and a choice that proves unrewarding can always be abandoned without loss. It does not require any more justification than 'I like it', 'it feels good', or 'it intrigues me' or 'I'd never thought of it like that before'.

Resist the temptation to classify the springboards into groups of related ones. The rational, logical part of the mind makes a strong case for doing so – it makes the numbers more manageable, and makes it easier to make a rational choice. But we do not want a rational choice – we want an intuitive one. The urge to classify is an urge to get back to the safe ground of the known. The disturbing, new and unfamiliar thoughts become less threatening if they can be neatly filed away in familiar boxes. To do so would be to defeat the whole purpose of the springboards, which is to 'reframe' the problem by looking at it in entirely new ways. An important part of reframing is to break down the existing framework of thinking. Any attempt to classify, or even to label them, runs the risk of putting the new wine into old bottles.

At the level of information, as opposed to decision making, the group's choice of springboards can be valuable in its own right, as a kind of opinion poll to show the degree of diversity or common ground in the group. I had a fascinating experience of this kind when I was discussing the future relationship of my UK business to our American licensers, Synectics Inc. After a number of informal conversations over a couple of years, we finally decided to tackle it as a formal problem-solving exercise (taking our own medicine, as it were). Their president and I quickly generated a large number of springboards: we then independently selected the ones we found appealing. As I read out my selection, his reaction was, 'Mine are strikingly similar'. The high level of correspondence in our choices demonstrated vividly how close we were in our aims and objectives. From this foundation of shared objective we were able to put in motion a series of steps which culminated in the merging of the businesses six months later.

4. Idea-getting strategies

There will be times when you or the group you are working with are stuck for an idea; or the ideas you are getting are too hackneyed, boring or otherwise unoriginal. The 'self-censors' are in control, cutting off awareness of the flow of idea-forming material (the images and associations thrown up in the in—out listening process).

When this happens, you can use a number of techniques for outwitting the self-censor and getting the same benefits as the traditional 'sleeping on the problem', without the delay and with a greater probability of getting a result. The generic label for these techniques is 'excursion', and that is exactly what they are – a temporary holiday from the problem. What the techniques have in common is generating material that has no apparent connection with the problem, and then deliberately making a connection. The process was originally described by W. H. H. Gordon as 'making the familiar strange, and making the strange familiar'.

The easiest way to make the connection back to the problem (known as a 'force fit', or a 'loose fit', whichever you prefer) is through an absurd solution (sometimes called a 'get fired solution' – something so ridiculous that if you were to come up with it in a normal meeting, you would be in danger of getting fired!) An absurd solution is just that – it is absurd, crazy, ridiculous, so that you could not possibly do it; but *if* you could do it, it would help in some way with the problem, so it is a 'solution' in that sense. It will be connected with, or suggested by, the material generated in the excursion.

The value of absurd solutions is that they 'break the mould'; they enforce a different way of thinking about the problem and they counteract tunnel vision. Obviously they are not to be taken literally; they should be listened to as poetry, not prose. The conversion of the absurd solutions to more practical ideas should not be hurried; it should be allowed to proceed at its own pace. Absurd solutions are for playing with, building and modifying them till they begin to suggest a more practical, but still new, line of thought.

For a comprehensive listing of all the possible idea-getting techniques, you can consult the specialised text books, such as Van Oech's *A Whack on the Side of the Head* or (less satisfactorily) Van Gundy's *108 Ways to Get a Bright Idea*. Or, preferably, go back to the original sources: W. H. H. Gordon, *Synectics*; George Prince, *Practice of Creativity*; and Koberg and Bagnall, *The Universal Traveller*. Here I want simply to describe the half-dozen or so techniques I find myself using most frequently.

Word association

Starting from a word in the 'task as seen' headline, or a chosen springboard, make a list of perhaps a dozen to twenty words, by spontaneously associating each time with the word previously expressed. The associations should preferably be lateral rather than logical, since the object is to get distance from the problem. If the association is surprising or provokes laughter, so much the better.

Then select one of the words with the greatest distance from the problem, and use it to suggest an absurd solution to the problem. It is a good idea to repeat the process three or four times to give yourself more material to play with.

Here's an illustration. Assuming we are working on 'How to recruit new staff more quickly and economically', the word association might start from 'Recruit' and might proceed:

Soldier	*Girls*	*Church*
Sailor	*Dancers*	*Choir*
Collar	*Legs*	*Angels*
Grab	*Legwarmers*	*Wings*
Excavator	*Wool*	*Planes*
Miner	*Gathering*	*Woodworking*
Diamonds		

Looking back at the list, I might select *excavator*, *diamonds*, *wool* and *woodworking* as having no immediate or obvious connection with recruitment. The task now is to make a connection and come up with an absurd solution. From *excavator* the absurd solution might be: 'Use a device to scoop up a large number of people and dump them in a heap: recruit the one on top of the heap.'

From *diamonds* I think of glass-cutting, and the absurd solution is: 'Cut out an exact profile of the people we want and match it against the population so that only those who exactly fit come forward.'

From *wool* I think of knitting, so: 'Get the candidates to knit something against a pattern we supply – select the best ones.'

From *woodworking* I have an image of someone planing a piece of wood and shaping it, which gives me: 'Take on anybody and shape them to our own requirements by intensive training.'

These are not intended to be 'good' ideas, or practical solutions. Their purpose is to open up new lines of thought; I will come back to making use of them when we have a complete set derived from all the excursion techniques.

There is another application of word association which is worth mentioning here, though it has a slightly different purpose. In this case each association is with the same initial word, rather than the last one, so from *beer* I might have each of the following associations:

```
                    bitter
            gut          glass
      tankard                  pub
   home brew     BEER               keg
         brewer            mat
               stain
```

If you ask a group of people each to do this exercise privately, with about ten associations each, and then get them to read out their lists, you will usually find very little commonality. When you make a frequency distribution from the lists, you will find one or two words mentioned by the majority of the group, and a couple more mentioned by two or three people; the rest will be singles.

I find the exercise valuable as a demonstration of how differently people view the world and how diversely they think. Even when the starting word is one in which they have a common interest (as *beer* would be for a group from a brewing company) the same diversity prevails. It also demonstrates what a wide range of idea-forming material is available within the group, so you know the group need never be stuck for an idea.

Career excursion

One of the simplest of all excursions is to look at the problem through the eyes of someone completely different. You can do this by imagining you are in a totally different job – a coalminer, astronaut, deep-sea diver, football manager, ballet dancer. As you imagine yourself in that job, see what ideas occur to you that might help with the problem.

I think of myself as a football manager – how does he recruit? He may sign established players from other clubs, and pay a transfer fee, or – more appealing to me with my problem – he has a network of scouts who look out for promising talent in junior teams. It would be quite feasible for us to ask knowledgeable friends of ours in industry to do the same for us. It is worth trying – it is certainly low-cost and low-risk, but it may not produce results as fast as we would wish (so it is a practical idea, not an absurd solution).

Variations on the career excursion are to imagine you are some famous person – President Reagan, the Queen, Clive Sinclair, or the like – or even to take an animal's view of the problem, as a cat, dog, pig, worm – anything to get a different perspective.

The career excursion seems to be readily taken to by virtually everybody; it's a low-risk way of getting a fresh angle on the problem, and not a particularly powerful one.

Direct analogy

A direct analogy answers the question, 'Where else has this problem, or a similar problem, been solved?' Maybe our problem can be solved in the same way. A designer of bedding wanted to achieve a particular springing effect and found the answer in a privet hedge – the pattern of twigs and leaves achieved the effect the designer was looking for, and could be transferred directly to the plastic materials suitable for the bedding.

The richest source of analogous solutions seems to be the natural world. 'Nature seems to have solved just about every problem we can think of, if we only know where to look and are able to translate the idea from one context to another', writes Ronald Whitfield (in *Creativity in Industry*), and he quotes Bill Gordon's view that 'biology is the richest source of analogous problems and solutions'.

The same view is echoed by Gordon Edge, of PA Technology: 'if you want to solve a problem, see how it is solved in nature. Living forms always have the most economical answers, as a result of evolution.' His team has used the way a nocturnal moth's eye absorbs light and does not reflect it, by means of a delicate criss-cross pattern coating the eye, as the basis for an information storage system on an optical disk.

It is possible to tap into the analogies offered by nature at an 'endless variety of levels, from that which is apparent to the popular mind to that which is only known to the expert' (Gordon, *Synectics*). Whitfield mentions the homing skills of the pigeon, the camouflage of the flounder and the chameleon and the firefly's ability to produce cold light as examples of well-known natural solutions that can be used to suggest ideas to solve current problems.

In the case of the optical disk for information storage, the connection to the nocturnal moth was found by 'a lucky chain of coincidences', which recalls Pasteur's comment that 'chance favours the prepared mind', and George Prince's modification of it – 'the prepared mind makes its own chances'. We cannot all be experts in biology, zoology and so on, but we can take an interest in a wide variety of phenomena and trust our own minds to throw up clues that will lead us to the analogies we need.

When I ask my own mind for an analogy from nature for a rapid, economical and highly selective method of recruitment, I draw a blank – at least for the moment. Then I start to think of natural selection; it suggests I should take on anybody who applies but retain only those who make the grade in a specified time – survival of the fittest.

John's analogy is quite different. Fermentation processes, he says: think of the time it takes to produce a high-quality brew. Maybe we should be recruiting now for three years' time, and have a pool of candidates 'fermenting' (and possibly selecting themselves by some form of natural selection?). Something there we can store as an absurd solution.

Example excursion

An example excursion works by finding examples of a key concept taken from the problem statement or chosen springboard, from totally different environments or worlds. The examples are whatever occur to the participants as they think about the key concept in the context of the chosen world. They cannot be 'wrong', and the participants do not have to justify their example, though it helps if they explain the connection in their minds. The examples are then used to trigger absurd solutions.

Here's an illustration: on the recruitment problem, we might look for examples of recruitment from the worlds of 'geology' or 'electricity'. (Why geology or electricity? Simply because recruitment is a people problem and geology and electricity are inorganic, non-people worlds, which give us distance from the problem and stretch the mind to make new connections.)

Examples of 'recruitment' from geology or electricity:

— static electricity attracts ('recruits') particles;
— a geological fault 'recruits' earthquakes;
— lava from a volcano 'recruits'/absorbs everything in its path;
— electric light attracts insects;
— electromagnets pick up metal;
— the national grid 'recruits' consumers all over the country.

None of these examples could be justified literally as 'recruitment'; they are metaphors. The fact that they occurred to me as I thought about recruitment in the context of geology or electricity is sufficient reason for using them. (I should add that I have no expert knowledge of either geology or electricity – perhaps if I had, I could have come up with more elegant examples!)

The next step is to use one or more of the examples to give me absurd solutions. I take lava first because I was surprised when it came up. It suggests some kind of blanket coverage; it is also hot stuff, whch encapsulates and absorbs the things it covers. It makes me wish I had a giant vacuum cleaner to suck up the people I want – there's an absurd solution! It's a bit close to the excavator idea I had previously from the word association, so I will try one of the others.

I think of the light attracting insects, and this makes me think of the redlight district attracting punters. Suppose we were to become famous as a sort of red-light district for industry to attract the kind of performers we wanted (and the customers as well!). Not a very flattering line of thought, but we will put it in the store of absurd solutions, to come back to later. Here I am concerned only to illustrate the steps in the example analogy process; it is a device for stretching the mind and encouraging metaphorical thinking.

Personal analogy

A personal analogy is a process of identifying with the problem by imagining that you are the problem itself, or some part of it. Then explore the feelings you experience as you become the object.

For example, when I was working with a confectionery manufacturing company on ways to reduce their raw-material costs without affecting the quality of the product, I asked each member of the group to imagine they were one of the products in their range. Each one in turn talked about how they felt as the product. The rest of the group listened for triggers to get additional ideas. Every time I did this, with three separate groups, we got a rich flow of new ideas.

Personal analogy is most readily used on technical problems; identifying with an inanimate object and its imagined feelings really stretches the mind. I think it is the stretch that triggers the ideas. But there is no reason why we should not try it on a 'people problem' like recruitment. So I imagine I am one of the people I am trying to recruit – what does it feel like? I identify a sense of frustration with what I am currently doing, a feeling that there must be a more satisfying and rewarding way to earn my living. It is followed by a sense of delight and excitement in discovering this job that offers a very different, enjoyable and worthwhile activity, and gives me scope to carve out my own niche.

I think of a traveller discovering an oasis in the desert. Perhaps if we could make ourselves known as an oasis in the business desert, we could attract these thirsty travellers. How we might do that, I do not know at the moment; never mind, we will put it in the absurd solution store for the moment.

You can take the personal analogy one stage further, by having the group act out the problem in a tableau or charade. In one experimental session using drama workshop techniques, Sheelagh Duffy had the group acting out the operations of a production line, to stimulate ideas on how to prevent breakdowns in a particular part of the process. I recall that the experiment did produce some novel ideas, but my recollection of them is overshadowed by the look of shock and horror I saw on the face of another manager who happened to look into the room, without knowing what was happening, or why! There are risks in being truly experimental and innovative!

Imaging/visualising

Thinking in pictures is the way the right half of the brain works, and if we actively encourage the activity it can provide a rich source of idea-forming material – 'a picture is worth a thousand words'. The capacity to think visually tends to be discouraged in formal education, particularly at the higher academic levels. It is not uncommon to find managers who say they do not think in pictures; their verbal and numerate skills have been highly developed, at the expense of their imaginative abilities.

I have some sympathy with people in this position, since it was how I felt when I first encountered these techniques. I am eternally grateful to George Prince, who told me, 'Don't worry – just fake it!' This allowed me to use my imagination at the verbal level, like a radio rather than a television. As I did so, I gradually became aware of the pictures in my mind's eye, and their quality gradually improved. (My visualising abilities are still far below the level I would wish for, but that is another story!)

As an idea-getting excursion, imaging is a kind of structured daydreaming. Take a random word, or a word from a word-association exercise – any word so long as it has no apparent connection with the problem. Let the word trigger a picture in your mind's eye, and then let the picture take its own course, like a movie in the head. It may well take some bizarre twists and turns and become pure fantasy – so much the better if it does.

After a few minutes, stop the fantasy, replay it in your mind's eye and, as you do so, let it suggest ideas for the problem you were working on. These again can be as absurd as you like – the important thing is to capture them as they occur to you.

Let's try it on the recruitment problem. In front of me on the table is a cup. I decide to use the word 'cup' as the starting-point for my imaging excursion.

I immediately have a picture of the FA Cup being brandished aloft by the captain of the winning team. As he walks down the steps, waving to the crowd, he stumbles and is saved from falling by a pretty girl. He puts the cup down and picks up the girl instead, waving her aloft. As he does so he turns into a circus strong man, carrying a trapeze girl in a leopard skin. The team behind him are now a circus parade, complete with clowns and elephants. They form up round the entire centre circle, the elephant starts play with a huge squirt of water towards one goal; the clowns start playing with a passing movement using their hats like rugby balls . . . I could go on, but I'll spare you the rest. Anything can happen in your mind's eye, and generally does.

Now I have to go back over the scene to get some more absurd solutions. Perhaps we could put on a recruitment circus – some kind of entertaining display/seminar/exhibition to attract the kind of recruits we want. That elephant squirting water was a powerful image – what does that suggest? The image turns into a flame thrower . . . some kind of powerfully projected missile . . . I wish I had a guided-missile type of recruiting which would home in on the target people in some automatic way (because I do not know where these target people are).

So we have a couple more absurd solutions for the recruitment problem. Here I was using the imaging process on my own, very briefly. I use it frequently with problem-solving groups, with each person building in turn on another's contribution.

When people do it for the first time, the images tend to be cautious and heavily censored. A few people find it too threatening to join in at all; others want to 'legitimise' it by turning into a film set, and often try to curtail it by saying, 'And now the Director says "Cut".' The threat arises from sharing a part of our thinking that is normally kept private, at least from our colleagues at work – socially, or at home, it may be different. With a little practice and encouragement, most people get over their inhibitions fairly quickly and begin to enjoy the process. The fantasies become richer and more original. As a group leader, you can stimulate this trend by demanding that each contribution produces a discontinuity – a surprising twist to the story, like the conversion of my football team to a circus.

At a practical level, the value of the group imaging process lies in the mass of new idea-forming material it makes available, and that in itself is sufficient justification for using it. Psychologically, some even more important things are happening. Barriers are being lowered both within the minds of the people and between them.

To engage in an imaging excursion together is a powerful bonding experience – groups remember for a long time the stories they invented together, and the laughter and enjoyment that goes with it. They have taken some risks together and shared an unusual experience. Always, in my estimation, they work better after the imaging excursion than they did before. Minds have been opened to new connections, the group is more co-operative and more tolerant of each other's diverse points of view than they were previously. George Prince reports great improvements in listening ability (particularly among old people, who are notoriously bad listeners) following practice in imaging.

The benefits of imaging are not restricted to idea-stimulating excursions; it is an important component of the 'wishful thinking' process described earlier (chapter 2). Having a 'vision' of what you want means literally to think in pictures; while it is possible to have a verbal vision, it will be richer and more powerful if you actually have a picture in your mind of what you want to achieve. Visualisation is an important tool in many other areas, including psychotherapy, mental healing and sporting achievement. So developing your imaging skills to help you with problem solving can have pay-offs elsewhere too.

Street excursion

Taking a walk to help you solve a problem with which you are stuck is probably (along with 'sleeping on it') the most widely practised informal excursion technique. A street excursion puts a little bit more structure into the exercise, reduces the amount of time required and increases the probability of success.

As you take your walk, outside or within the building, look around till some particular sight catches your attention. Focus on this view, examine in detail its form, structure, texture, colours and so on. Take a mental picture of it. When you get back, start to make connections between your picture and the problem. Let it suggest some absurd solutions.

Right now it's too cold for a street excursion, so I look out at the snow-covered garden. What catches my eye is the upturned wheelbarrow, covered in snow. The two inverted V-shaped supports stick out of the snow, together with half the red wheel on which it runs. What is it trying to tell me about the recruitment problem?

It occurs to me that, had I not known the wheelbarrow was there, it would have been difficult to recognise it as a wheelbarrow. I wonder how easy it is for our potential recruits to get a clear picture of what we are like as an organisation for which to work. Perhaps we need a way to transmit a very clear and accurate picture of ourselves to potential recruits (not an absurd solution this one, but something I am pretty sure we need to do much better than we do currently). It reminds me of an advertisement I wrote for an office manager some years ago, which began with 'Picture yourself . . .' followed by a description of what she would be doing. It produced one outstanding candidate who was a great success in the job.

I have my own personal variation of the street excursion which I call the traffic jam excursion. If I get stuck in traffic for any length of time, I think of a topic for which I need some new ideas. Then I look around till something catches my attention and I use it to suggest novel ideas; I may or may not get something useful out of the exercise but, either way, it solves the problem of getting bored in the traffic jam!

Essential paradox/book title

A paradox is a contradiction as indeed is any situation requiring an inventive solution — it's an impossibility you want to make possible.

Try to capture the essence of the problem in a two-word paradox or 'book title'. Going back to the recruitment problem (my apologies if you are getting tired of it), the essence of the problem seems to be identifying and making contact with the few people of the kind we want, quickly and economically, without knowing where they are among a mass of possible candidates. The paradoxes that come to mind (you may have better ones) are:

— instant search (we have a lot to search through but we want them instantly);

— uninvited response (we would like the suitable ones to apply of their own accord);

— mass individuality;

— crowded uniqueness (something about the appropriate individuals standing out in a crowd);

— guided randomness (not quite sure why that came up — it doesn't matter);

— plentiful scarcity (I'm sure there are lots of suitable people around, but actual candidates are scarce);

From the paradoxes we can either go directly to absurd solutions, or we can link them with the 'direct analogy' and look for examples of the paradox. For instance, 'instant search' makes me think of computer dating – perhaps there is some agency that has a computerised database against which we could match our requirements.

'Guided randomness' makes me think of electrons – lots of them following individual paths but collectively making up an object, which follows the laws of physics. 'Predictable in the mass' seems to be the message, which suggest the predictable career patterns of most executives. What I want is to attract a few who want to depart from that pattern. If I had some way of catching them at the time they were ripe for a move . . . But only a few, not the great mass of them. Maybe I should contact university careers offices for people who left college five years ago and are dissatisfied with what they are doing?

'Plentiful scarcity' makes me think of famine in Africa at a time of food surpluses in Europe. I think of Bob Geldof – he would be an interesting candidate. How might we identify a few self-starters with great imagination like Geldof? Maybe we should try recruiting from pop groups!

Drawing/doodling/collage

If you look at people's pads after a meeting you will probably find a lot of them covered in drawings, patterns and doodles of one kind and another. I suspect the right halves of their brains are busy staving off boredom because they have nothing else to do.

You can put that energy to work for you as a problem-solving excursion. Simply draw anything you like, either individually or together in groups of two or three on flip-charts. One way to do it is to specify that each person draws a line in turn, each line to touch the previous line at some point, or continue on from the previous line.

The pictures which result are not expected to be works of art, and lack of ability to draw need not inhibit participation. In my view, the drawing is best done in silence, to prevent words intruding into an essentially visual exercise.

When the drawings are finished, pin them up and wander round the art gallery you have just created. Let the pictures speak to you suggesting connections, absurd solutions and starting-points for your problem (as in the 'street excursion').

Variations on the same theme include collage and a 'colour field' excursion. For a collage, collect objects at random and arrange them in some sort of pattern; then look at the objects and their relationships, and let these suggest ideas.

For a 'colour field' excursion, you need a box of assorted fabrics, coloured paper, masking tape, scissors, crayons or felt tip pens and anything else that might contribute to colourful pattern making. Invite the group members to use the materials to create their own picture on a sheet of flip-chart paper. It can be either an individual or small group exercise — my preference is for it to be done individually, and in silence.

I use the exercise more as a mood creator than a direct idea-getting strategy. It seems to have a calming effect, and it also accesses childlike qualities in otherwise hard-bitten managers. 'Haven't done anything like this since I was a kid' is the kind of comment that is often made. Our office cleaners say it looks as if a children's party had been going on!

These are valuable effects in that they are opening people's minds to new possibilities and changing the frame of mind in which people approach the task. I remember using this technique to start a meeting on a highly charged political issue; for the first fifteen minutes the seven or eight senior executives played with the materials and then admired, or were amused by, their creations. I kept the pictures on the walls throughout the subsequent discussions as a reminder of the experience, and as triggers for ideas. The discussions thereafter were constructive and tolerant, and I believe the excursion helped to create that atmosphere (though there is no way of knowing for certain).

It feels risky to ask people to do things which are very different from what they normally do, but my experience is that most people will have a go, if it is put to them as an experiment. They really have nothing to lose by trying something different for a few minutes. There is no need to promise them any specific results or benefits — they may or may not get anything from it, and if they do not, no harm has been done.

Writing sentences

Take a random word, and make yourself write sentences containing that word for a period of ten minutes. (You can write a lot of sentences in ten minutes, and it is hard work to keep going.) Go back over the list of sentences and use some of them to trigger absurd solutions to the problem — then develop those into more practical ideas.

I was introduced to this technique by my German associate, Professor Bernd Rohrbach, who actually specifies thirty minutes' writing. I have never had the stamina to keep it up longer than ten minutes; I have found that I get a rich supply of new ideas from ten minutes' worth of sentences.

As in the other excursion techniques, the exercise distracts the self-censor. I find the effort of continuing to write the sentences occupies my mind completely. The sentences release material from the subconscious that would otherwise be screened out by the self-censor. No doubt thirty minutes of writing would have even more dramatic effects; if you try it, I would be interested to hear the results.

5. Development of solutions

From absurd solutions to second generation ideas

In themselves, absurd solutions have no value — how could they, when they are made deliberately absurd? People often tell me they are 'crap', and I agree — but 'crap' is the fertiliser which helps new solutions to grow. The value of the absurd solutions lies in the trains of thought they trigger, leading to more practical ideas which still retain some newness.

It is a mistake to hurry this process. There is a strong temptation to grab at the first practical idea that comes up, almost out of relief at escaping from the anxiety-provoking world of absurdity. The first idea is rarely the richest or most original. George Prince uses the concept of 'hang time' to describe the process. (In American football, the length of time the ball hangs in the air from a kick is critical, to allow the kickers time to reach the point at which it will drop, before the opposition can start their attack.)

Having a stock of absurd solutions, as we now have from the various excursions, is a good way to ensure sufficient 'hang time'. We can play with each one in turn, see where it takes us, without pushing to develop any one to an immediate solution. Here goes.

From word association we had the excavator idea: 'Use a device to scoop up a large number of people and dump them in a heap: recruit the ones on top of the heap.' That suggests some kind of scooping and sieving operation. Perhaps we could write to every headhunter and employment agency to pick up a large number of candidates — then we would need some device to filter out the few we wanted.

From the idea of glass-cutting we had 'cut out an exact profile of the people we want and match it against the population . . .' If we were to write a very detailed and exacting specification of the people we want, that might act as the filter we needed for the previous idea.

From the idea of wool we had 'Get the candidate to knit something against a pattern we supply' – so that could be some kind of test. Or perhaps we should show a 'pattern' of the end-product – describe what a successful candidate would be doing and how he or she would be living, two or three years after joining us. Then ask candidates why and how they think they could match that pattern. From the direct analogy we had the idea of a pool of candidates fermenting over a period of time and selecting themselves by natural selection. It suggests that recruitment should be a continuing long-term process – we need to communicate that we are permanently on the look-out for likely candidates. 'I know,' says John, 'in our team brochure, where we have photos and biographies, we could have a blank space marked YOU?, with a specification of the candidates we want. And have a recruitment brochure which we could have available in our offices, and send to anyone who is interested. These are things we could do right away.'

As we talk about the pool of candidates, I think of nurseries, and remember that big football clubs use junior clubs as nurseries of talent. It would be nice if we had a nursery club – maybe in the business schools, perhaps?

Moving on to the absurd solutions from the example excursion, there was 'become famous as the red-light district for industry'. I think of escort agencies, and then of Avon ladies (sorry Avon, no offence meant). I wonder if we could use people working from home to help the recruiting – perhaps people we have worked with who have left work to start families?

'Or', says John, 'put recruiting ads in women's magazines like *Harpers* or *Cosmopolitan*, aimed at wives who want to get their husbands out of the rut of a boring job. Might attract the wives as well – and their husbands probably read the magazines too!'

The personal analogy gave me the image of presenting ourselves as an oasis in the business desert. 'We could use that as a picture in the recruitment brochure', says John.

And so we could go on, as long as we needed to. The material from the different trains of thought begins to coalesce in a package of actions we can take to move towards our objective. At the same time the exercise has shifted our thinking, from the immediate short-term problem to having a continuing long-term recruitment strategy. No doubt that *should* have been obvious to us at the outset, but in fact it was not.

Would we have got the same ideas without the excursions? There's no way of telling. And does it matter? The excursions have been enjoyable; they have not taken much time (they take much longer to describe than to do). And my experience is that the excursion material will stay in my mind and throw up more ideas on recruiting when I need them. (I can still remember the first excursions I did, fifteen years ago!)

The in–out listening process, which we applied also to the recruiting problem, is in fact a series of mini-excursions. As you become skilled in in–out listening, you may find you have less need for the formal excursion. Even so, it is worth continuing to use the excursion techniques, if only to keep the excursion muscles in good trim, as mental limbering-up exercises. And they are worth using on a group for the benefits to the group dynamics described earlier, without regard to their output in terms of new solutions.

Feel free to pick and choose the excursions according to your personal preferences, and combine them in any sequence you think might be useful. There is no one 'right' way to do an excursion – it is almost a contradiction in terms to think of a 'correct' excursion! You can, of course, invent your own. There is no reason why the invention methods we have been describing cannot be applied to the invention process. If you invent some new excursion techniques that work for you, I would be very pleased to hear about them.

Idea development

Idea development is the process by which an embryonic new idea, which is attractive but not yet feasible, is converted into a practical solution, without losing its originality or appeal. It is the missing link between the generation of ideas and the decisions to implement some of them.

Conventionally, a period of idea generation is followed by a process of screening into 'good' and 'bad' ideas. The result is usually a shortlist of good ideas, which on closer examination turn out not to be new. That is hardly surprising – the only way we can know whether an idea is 'good' or not is by previous experience, and if we have previous experience of it then the idea, by definition, cannot be new! There's no need to subject ideas to this binary good/bad judgement. Binary judgements are necessary for *actions* – we either do it or not. But *ideas* as such are only words and pictures – they do not change anything in the real world. So we do not need to make an instant judgement on them; we can explore them in a more gentle, open-minded way. They are neither good nor bad – just more or less interesting and appealing; they can be used as stepping-stones to a richer, more feasible proposal.

To accomplish this, we have to look at the idea in detail,

examining its features and its possibilities – both positive and negative – in a friendly, 'benefit of the doubt' frame of mind. It is an 'itemised' (detailed) evaluation rather than a net–out binary judgement – like looking at the individual items on the credit and debit side of a profit-and-loss account, rather than going immediately to the bottom line to see whether it is a net profit or loss.

A new idea is unlikely to be a feasible solution when it is first expressed; the newer the idea, the less likely it is to be feasible. So it needs protection from instant rejection. The protection has three components:

— a check that the idea has been correctly understood;
— identification of all the positive aspects of the idea;
— conversion of negatives into directions for improvement.

Each of these steps is so important in its own right, and has such far-reaching implications beyond the immediate problem-solving application, that they are discussed separately below.

Checking understanding

It is obvious that there is no sense in evaluating an idea (or anything else) that we have not understood. Yet people do it all the time, in my experience. Not knowingly, but unconsciously, because we *assume* we have understood.

When the assumption is put to the test we find that, as often as not, the idea has not been understood. For many years my colleagues and I have applied the principle *understand before evaluating* in problem-solving sessions which we run, by insisting that the recipient of the idea restates his or her understanding of it with a paraphrase, before making an evaluation. At least 50 per cent of the time, the paraphrase does not satisfy the idea giver that his or her idea has been correctly understood. (Independent communications researchers regard this 50 per cent success rate as a remarkable achievement. They find that in ordinary unstructured discussions, the success rate for communication is typically half as good – 25 per cent! The implications for communications generally are explored in my companion book, *Communications*.)

Paraphrasing the idea is worth doing simply to ensure that both parties are talking about the same thing. Endless time can be wasted in sorting out an evaluation based on a misunderstanding. But the value of the paraphrase goes deeper than mere functional efficiency. It creates a positive emotional link between the two parties. By taking the trouble to tell you my understanding of the idea, I am signalling that I value your contribution; it shows I *want* to understand it. I am also giving you information about myself, by expressing the idea in my language and from my perspective.

And the principle makes it safe to express any idea, however wild and speculative, because there is the assurance that it will be accepted as a potentially useful contribution to the discussion. It provides a useful 'cooling off' period, particularly when the initial reaction to the idea is negative; the relatively unemotional discipline of checking understanding acts as a safety valve, and quite often demonstrates that the emotional reaction was based on a misunderstanding of the idea.

Finding value in ideas

Every idea has *some* merit, and it is worth taking the trouble to search out all its possible benefits and articulate them. If you take nothing else away from this book apart from this principle, the time spent reading it will have been worth while.

This principle is the opposite of the way we all conventionally behave in our society. If you put forward a new idea, someone will immediately tell you what is wrong with it and why it will not work. It is the practical person's way of avoiding wasting time considering anything outside existing experience – a sort of 'management by exception', totally misapplied. We pay an enormous price for this cultural quirk. If ideas are going to be judged in terms of what is wrong with them, I will only voice ideas that I believe to be perfect (and I am unlikely to have many of those). I will spend a lot of my time processing and refining my ideas privately and only express them when I believe they are fireproof. If everyone is operating on this basis, there will not be many ideas around.

Moreover, the safest ideas to express will be those tried and tested by experience – old ideas, not new ones. Often they will be expressed at the broadest policy level, with which no one could possibly disagree – 'motherhood statements', in other words (how often have I heard people say, with an air of profound wisdom, 'We must find out what the consumer *really* wants', without proposing any new way of doing so!).

In this environment, not only is there a shortage of ideas, but a positive dearth of new ideas (and new thinking generally). Everybody develops a powerful 'self-censor' to keep themselves out of trouble. The self-censor becomes so automatic that it affects thinking as well as expression of ideas. The material thrown up by the subconscious mind as we listen to or think about a problem is filtered out of our awareness by the self-censor – it is judged to be irrelevant because the connection to the problem is not immediately apparent. The technique of in–out listening described in chapter 3 is one way of getting round the self-censor; we saw other idea-getting strategies to defeat the self-censor in chapter 4.

In addition to its effect on the supply of ideas, the practice of judging ideas in terms of what is wrong with them is equally damaging to interpersonal relationships and teamwork (as we know from examining thousands of such episodes on videotape). A typical sequence might be

Tom: I suggest . . . [gives idea]
Anne: No, that won't work, because . . . [points out flaw]
Tom: [Either] Yes, you're right. [accepts criticism]
[or] No, that's not so . . . [gets into an argument].

If we take the first case (where Tom accepts the criticism) and replay the tape to Tom and Anne, they will see it as a perfectly normal, polite and constructive exchange: 'It was a fair point, a valid cricitism', Tom will say.

However, if we follow Tom's subsequent behaviour on the tape, a very different story unfolds. Tom goes quiet for a time: his self-censor is working overtime to make sure it does not slip up again by letting something through that is vulnerable to Anne's criticism. He is also waiting for Anne to come up with an idea, and when Anne does so, Tom interjects in a flash – 'No, that would *never* work', or even, 'That's a stupid idea'.

When this episode is played back, there is no doubt what was happening. 'He attacked my idea,' says Anne, and no one can deny it. The attack was Tom's revenge for the rejection of his idea. Even though at a rational level he accepts the criticism as valid, at an emotional level he is sufficiently upset to need to get even.

When I describe this 'revenge cycle' phenomenon to managers, they all recognise it instantly – but it starts, without either party being aware of it, from apparently innocent, constructively intended 'criticism'. The discipline of explicitly acknowledging all the good points of the idea eliminates revenge cycles at source.

In the second case, where the two of them argue about whether the criticism is correct or not, the breakdown in relationship (and waste of time and energy) is more immediately obvious. If the idea is a new one, neither of them can possibly *know* (until it is tried out) what the outcome will be. What Anne is presumably trying to do is to draw attention to a possible risk or shortcoming in the idea, but she is speaking prematurely. Before doing so, she needs to have checked her understanding and identified all the positive features of the idea, so that her concern can be seen in perspective and heard as a constructively intended contribution.

Finding value in every idea, then, builds better relationships as well as keeping the ideas flowing. And for the evaluator it can be (should be) a process of discovery. As you start to specify good features of the idea, you will find that the first two or three come easily enough, and then there is a blank. Don't stop. Keep searching for additional positive features, giving the idea the benefit of the doubt: 'If we were to do this, what else might it achieve for us?' By stretching the mind to envisage a new situation, you will often make interesting discoveries and you may see the problem in a new light.

My German colleague, Professor Bernd Rohrbach, applies this principle with Teutonic rigour, particularly to ideas he does not like. 'When somebody offers me an idea I particularly dislike', he says, 'I take special trouble to search for all the good points I can possibly find in it – just in case that guy knows something I don't know!'

As well as leading to discoveries, particularly about our own values and objectives, itemising the good points will also trigger additional or alternative ways to achieve the same benefits. If the pluses of an idea are that it uses existing plant, uses material we already have in stock and is within the skills of existing staff – what other ideas can we find with similar qualities?

Notice how specifying the pluses and concerns specifies the characteristics of the solution that is being sought, and communicates this specification to the people who are supplying ideas. I have long believed that it is more valuable (though more difficult) to define the solution than to define the problem! Specifying in detail both the good points and the shortcomings of any idea provides a mechanism for progressively defining the characteristics of the solution.

Converting negatives to directions for improvement

What is wrong with an idea – its shortcomings, weaknesses, risks and dangers – is vital information. It tells us that we need to continue inventing in order to improve the idea or to replace it with a better one, and it stops us from going into action with any idea that could damage us. Information so vital must be presented at the right time and in the right way. As we have seen, the time is not right before these two steps have been taken:

— checking understanding, so that we can be sure that the negatives apply to the idea actually expressed and not to the idea we thought we heard;

— acknowledging all the good points of the idea, so that the negative is seen in perspective and the idea giver is not discouraged.

We have now to consider the right way to present the negative. Since its purpose is to draw attention to the need to improve the idea, that is exactly the way it needs to be expressed – as a direction for improvement, not as a criticism. The distinction is subtle but vital.

For example, the negative might be (and often is) 'That would be too expensive'. To find the direction for improvement, we have to ask the question, 'So what is it we need?' The answer could be

— an idea that costs less
— a way to reduce the cost of this idea
— a way to share the cost with others
— a way to increase our prices to cover the extra cost
— a way to pay for it without increasing prices.

Notice how the single negative can give rise to half a dozen different directions for improvement. It is the problem owner's responsibility to specify which of these directions he or she wants to pursue, and this is the key information which the helpers need to keep producing ideas which meet those objectives.

A direction for improvement is more informative and forward-looking than the negative from which it is derived. It is a signpost on the road to a solution. Given that it is a signpost, we only want one of them at any one time (we cannot go down two roads at once). So the problem owner needs to use the most important negative to give the direction for improvement: 'What I *most* need now is a way to . . .'

Other negatives can be dealt with sequentially after the first one has been resolved. They may no longer be relevant – as the first negative is overcome, the original idea may be changed or replaced; in its latest form it may no longer have any of the negatives of its previous existence.

In emotional terms, a direction for improvement has a totally different, and much more positive, impact from that of the negative. A direction for improvement immediately stimulates more ideas; if we need to find a way to reduce the cost, perhaps we could use cheaper materials, or simplify the design, and so on. If we are told only 'That's too expensive', the temptation is to give up, resign ourselves to the impossibility of changing anything. Although the direction for improvement may be *implicit* in the negative, it needs to be made *explicit*, so we know which direction to follow, and so we maintain the positive, constructive climate.

In fact, there is no need to articulate the negative at all; it is possible, and preferable, to go straight to the direction: 'What I need now is a way to . . .' But this takes practice; the habit of negative criticism is so deeply ingrained in our culture that you may find it necessary to take two steps – identifying the negative and converting it into a direction.

Example of idea development

The idea: Sitting at home writing this section on 'Idea Development', it occurred to me that it would be nice to work from home every day.

Paraphrase: You mean not go into the office at all except for client sessions and courses?

Check: Yes, that's right, I would go in for board meetings and staff meetings as well as client sessions.

Evaluation: pluses

— it saves travel time and costs
— fewer interruptions
— I can go for a run when I feel like it
— I don't need to keep office hours
— it makes more space available in the office
— I can have music while I work without disturbing anyone else
— I can eat and drink what I like when I like
— it stops me interfering with my colleagues
— it puts more responsibility on colleagues to make their own decisions (though they hardly need that)
— I will be in good shape when the office moves further afield
— it is good preparation for 'retirement'

Directions of improvement

I need to find a way to maintain informal contact with my colleagues.

Idea 1: I could schedule regular phone calls to them, and encourage them to phone me.

Evaluation: That takes care of the concern. What I need now is a way to ensure that I didn't give the impression I'm losing commitment to the business.

Idea 2: Tell them what I have in mind at the next staff meeting and get feedback from them as to whether this is a problem for them. OK, that takes care of that for the time being. What I need now is a way to handle the paperwork – files, correspondence and so on.

Idea 3: What about my own PC at home and a modem to link it to the office computer. Great idea: it would make me get up to date with computers, it would help us develop electronic mail, it would reduce the typing load, eventually it could link with other offices and colleagues working from home. Long term, it could save on office-space costs, if we adopted it more widely – some of my colleagues might like to do the same. We need to explore the cost-effectiveness, but my guess is that it's affordable.

 Any further concerns? No, that does it.

Closure: Let's check out your solution.

— Is it new? Yes, different from what I normally do now.
— Appealing? Yes – you bet!

— Feasible? I think so, subject to the computer cost and reaction of colleagues.

So what will be the next steps?
1. Tell board colleagues what I have in mind.
2. Get feedback from the next staff meeting.
3. Check out the cost of PC and modem.
4. Possibly propose it as a general policy for the business (subject to the reaction of colleagues).

Closure

The purpose of the 'idea development' process is to reach a solution, that is a course of action that is *new* (for the problem owner), *appealing* (so that he or she has sufficient energy and commitment to implement it personally), and *feasible* as far as can be judged with the information available. If these three criteria are satisfied, the problem owner needs to specify the *next steps*, so that that person and everyone else are clear as to what action is going to result.

In group problem solving, it is not usually necessary to dot all the '*i*'s of the solution; the time to stop is when the problem owner feels he or she does not need further help from the group. For the problem owner's own good, and for the satisfaction of group members, it is worth checking his or her solution against the criteria of *newness*, *appeal* and *feasibility*, and also to make the *next steps* explicit.

If you are responsible for running the session, be on your guard for the problem owner who gives false signals. Some may ask for more and more detailed development of the solution when they could quite easily do this for themselves outside the session. This is usually a symptom of putting off the commitment to action, and it is worth checking whether the problem owner's heart is really in this solution. If so, does he or she really need the group to work out the details?

Others will say they have a solution when there is no real commitment to implementing it. Here the next steps they specify are a good guide: if they are woolly and non-committal, and the tone of voice is half-hearted, you have grounds for suspicion. Distrust the problem owner who says his or her next action will be to 'think about it'; 'thinking' is not what is meant by 'action'!

These false signals usually arise when the preconditions for successful problem solving have not been satisfied: the problem owner is not genuinely looking for a novel solution which he or she can implement personally (see chapter 1). But they can still arise in spite of careful planning. One of my worst experiences was in developing new product concepts for a household-name company. The problem owner had specified that he wanted five concepts. At the end of the two-day session we had nine, each of which, we had checked with him was new, appealing and feasible. I thought we had comfortably met our brief.

To my astonishment, the problem owner said, 'Well, that was a complete waste of time!'

'But you have nine new concepts,' I said, 'and with each one we checked with you that they were new, appealing and feasible.'

'Yes,' he replied, 'but they weren't *really* new – just a little bit new. I wanted something really original.'

This experience prompted my colleagues and me to do some problem solving to prevent a recurrence. We realised that 'newness' was not just a binary concept – it makes sense to talk of highly novel or slightly novel, and the degree of newness could be an important ingredient in the quality of the solution. We decided to ask the problem owner to give a numerical rating to the possible solution – how new, how appealing, how feasible, in terms of a score of 0 to 10 for each characteristic. We found this NAF rating (as it came to be called) a simple and useful tool for articulating the problem owner's feelings about the quality of a solution.

The NAF rating can also be used to collect the opinions of the rest of the group, if these are thought to be relevant. Each member of the group writes down his or her own scores for newness, appeal and feasibility, and the results are assembled to give a quick snapshot of group opinion. If there are marked differences on any score, the reasons for them can be sought, and if these throw up weaknesses in the solution, further problem solving may be necessary to overcome them. We have also found the NAF rating valuable in the planning stage before a problem-solving meeting. By asking the problem owner to specify in advance the scores that his or her solutions need to achieve to be satisfactory, we can draw attention to the trade-offs which may have to be made, especially between newness and feasibility.

Generally speaking, the newer the solution, the less immediately feasible it is likely to be, and the higher the risks are likely to be – simply because, by definition, there is no previous experience to go by. At best, a highly original solution is likely to need a long period of investigation, research and testing before it can be implemented safely. So if the requirement is for solutions that can be implemented in the short term, then it is probably unrealistic or self-defeating to go for highly original solutions. Conversely, a research and development department drawing up a long-term research programme may well want several very novel projects of low feasibility in its portfolio (along with a mix of less novel, more feasible ones).

Going back to our definition of problem solving as the art of getting from where you are to where you want to be, the 'closure' process is a way of satisfying yourself that you (or the problem owner) have arrived, as far as you can judge. You will not finally know, of course, until you actually implement the solution, whether it will actually achieve what you want. The newer the solution, the greater the uncertainty, and the greater the need to have more strings to your bow in the form of some back-up solutions in case the preferred one does not work.

Summary: a structure for creative problem solving

It is now possible to pull together the elements of invention described in the previous chapters into a simple sequence of steps, which you can use either on your own or with colleagues.

1. Headline the task/problem/opportunity: *I need to find a way to . . . ; I wish I could . . .*
2. Describe the present position and where you want to get to, in the form of a big 'impossible' wish. The gap between the two is the ground to be covered. Mention what you have already tried and thought of, and be sure to indicate how the task affects you and how it fits into your action responsibility.
3. Suspending judgement, generate a list of 'springboards' – alternative problem 'definitions', wishes, starting-ideas, apparently irrelevant and crazy images, associations and the like. Note them as you go, preferably on a flip chart. (It helps to present them in headline form, and fill in the background as the headline is written up.)
4. Review the list of alternatives, identify any courses of action which are worth adopting without further development and then select an alternative which is novel and attractive but not yet feasible. Spell out what makes it attractive, and what needs to be done to make it feasible.
5. Ask for an idea aimed at making the approach feasible. (The idea itself does not have to be a solution, but it does have to be an 'action' idea, a 'go-do' as opposed to a policy statement or motherhood idea, such as 'all be nice to one another'.)
6. Paraphrase the idea and check that your understanding of it satisfies the person who put it forward. Identify all the useful features of the idea, and use the major negative feature to give direction for improving (or replacing) the idea. Invite a further idea

aimed at this new target, and process it in the same open-minded way.

7. Continue in this sequence until you have reached an idea that you think is worth implementing. Identify the action steps you intend to take. A finished idea needs to satisfy the criteria of being new, appealing and feasible.

Repeat steps 4 to 7 as necessary to develop as many new courses of action as you want (and as many as you have capacity to implement).

You can use this structure when working with a group, with a single colleague or on your own. The value of the structure when you are working with other people is that it ensures that everyone knows where they are and what is expected of them – they are on the same wavelength, as it were. My experience of working alone is that the structure imposes a discipline on my thinking which prevents me from ignoring stray thoughts or dismissing ideas which are not instant solutions. In both situations it saves time, by preventing rambling, anecdotes, second opinions and other such distractions.

Steps 1 to 3 in effect open up the topic to a wide variety of approaches, some of which are likely to 'reframe' it and provide novelty. Steps 4 to 7 use some of these starting-points to develop novel courses of action, which should, in your judgement, have a good enough chance of success (and constitute a small enough risk) to be worth trying.

The sequence, by the way, is known as the Synectics Problem-solving sequence, as the people at Synectics Inc. developed it.

Starting from a solution

One reason why disputes, conflicts, arguments and debates are so prevalent in our work culture is our practice of doing our creative problem solving privately and only sharing the end point of the process – the solution. When different individuals *think* about a problem privately and come to different conclusions, the stage is set for conflict and debate. The debate will be about which of the solutions is the best. The underlying (unconscious) assumption is that these are the only solutions available. Almost certainly, this assumption is wrong; a group problem-solving approach will usually develop additional options, some of which have a good chance of being superior to those produced by the individual/private problem solving.

We are accustomed to doing our creative problem solving

privately because, in the adversarial climate to which we are accustomed, it is emotionally dangerous to share the process. If we risk sharing the formative process by expressing the embryonic, 'half-baked' ideas with which we may be toying, we immediately expose ourselves to criticism, attack and even contempt.

I can still remember, fifteen years on, the scorn that was poured on a speculative thought which I expressed when I worked for Rank Xerox – that it might be valuable to develop a copy that could be erased. (Think of the paper it could save, not to mention the filing, shredding and so on.) 'What a stupid idea,' I was told. 'Think of the trouble we've had to make sure that our copies are permanent.' I still don't see why that invalidates the idea – and the fact that the incident still rankles after fifteen years illustrates the emotional impact of the experience.

So there is a vicious circle at work: the adversarial climate prompts us to do our problem solving privately and only voice the conclusions when we are satisfied they are totally defensible. When several people do this independently, a debate will ensue as to who is right and who is wrong. The debate, itself an adversarial win/lose process, reinforces the adversarial climate, which encourages us to do our problem solving privately, and so on.

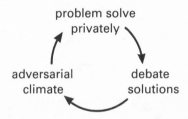

We can break out of the vicious circle by introducing group problem solving in one or both of these ways:

— go back to the problem that the solutions are addressing to invent some alternatives;
— go forward from the solutions in the way described in the procedure for a multi-problem-owner meeting (see chapter 6).

The first route requires a willingness on the part of the solution owners to acknowledge that theirs is *one* possible solution, not the only one (still less the 'right' solution). This is the precondition we mentioned earlier – that the solution owners are sufficiently open-minded to join in a search for alternatives. We can then ask them to say what problem it is a solution to – if it were implemented, what problem would it solve? The group (including the solution owners) can then invent alternative solutions to that problem. It is possible that none of the alternatives will be as attractive as the original, privately developed solution, in which case the solution owner has been proved right, but now has the willing support of his or her colleagues.

The second route requires the objector to a solution to check his or her understanding, identify all the positive aspects and then state the consequential problem it creates for him or her. The group, including the solution owner, then looks for ideas to overcome that problem. The same procedure is followed for each of the solutions under consideration.

The two routes are equally legitimate and mutually complementary. Which one to start with should be judged according to the strength of commitment of the solution owners to their existing solutions. When that commitment is strong, I will tend to use the second route, starting from the solutions. Otherwise, I prefer to go back to the original problem.

In going back to the original problem, it is not unusual to discover that the solutions on offer are actually addressing different problems, or different aspects of the problem. When this situation is clarified, the objector will often accept a solution as being valid in its own right, 'as far as it goes'. The objector needs an additional solution to deal with the part of the problem with which he or she is concerned.

I am not suggesting that there is anything wrong with problem solving privately (my colleagues will tell you I do a lot of it myself!). It is only dangerous when it leads you to become closed-minded about the conclusion – to think that because *you* are pleased with the solution, it is necessarily the best solution, the only solution or the right solution. It might be, and equally it might not be.

The alternative is to view it, and express it, as 'my best current thinking'* – which is exactly what it is. Colleagues to whom it is presented may well want to go back to the problem which it is addressing and try to invent better solutions. Or they may wish to take my solution and improve it by modifications which eliminate the consequential problems they see.

It is easy for me to join in this process if I can view my conclusion as an intermediate stage in the problem-solving process, and not necessarily the last word.

Collecting group opinions

I have emphasised the role of the problem owner as the key

* An admirable label coined by my colleague Jason Snelling.

72

decision-maker and direction-giver in a problem-solving session, and the responsibility of the other participants to suspend (or withhold) their own opinions and judgements. (I use the words 'judgements' and 'opinions' interchangeably, because they are in fact the same thing, a judgement being simply a better informed opinion!) I have also stressed the importance of handling one problem owner at a time, when there is more than one involved in the problem.

However, there are cases where it is necessary, or desirable, to collect the opinions of all members of the group. It may be that the solution affects all of them; or the problem owner wants to know how they all feel about it (solicited second opinions, rather than unsolicited). Or it may be useful to hear everyone's opinion about the current state of the project, or the business, as a prelude to tackling the aspects that need to be improved.

The mechanism I recommend for collecting group opinion is very simple. I ask each member of the group to write down privately what they see as the good features of the proposal, and their concerns about it. I then ask them to share this information, taking one good feature from each individual to start with, until all have been collected, and then doing the same with the concerns.

Before I collect the information, I lay down one key ground rule: *they do not have to agree!*

Each positive feature or concern is accepted as a truth about the person who puts it forward. There is no question about its being 'right' or 'wrong'; it is the way that person sees the world. Other group members may well see it differently; if so they can put up the opposite point of view, on the other side of the balance sheet.

I use the format and ground rule to eliminate debate and argument. This comes as a surprise to many people I work with, particularly those who are a product of higher education – scientists, engineers, marketing people, systems analysts and the like. For them, debating seems to be a way of life – not surprisingly, since it is actively encouraged and promoted by the education system and by our culture generally. In my view, it serves no useful purpose in the work environment; on the contrary, it takes up time and energy which can be much more usefully devoted to problem solving – which means finding ways to improve whatever is being debated. It also tends to polarise the group into two camps and set up a win/lose process. The debating never seems actually to *change* anyone's view; the winners are often the better debaters rather than those who have the better case, and the losers may well be alienated. They may have been argued down, but they will not have any commitment to the winners' viewpoint.

The views of the group, and the reasons for them, are obtained much more efficiently by the format I have described, and with a positive rather than negative impact on the climate and morale of the group. Identifying the positive features again articulates the common ground within the group, and puts differences into perspective.

The concerns are best expressed as wishes, or needs for improvement. To identify the negative is not enough; we need also a 'therefore' – what is the improvement or the change that is needed. Expressed in the form 'we need to find a way to . . . (improve, change, etc.)', it becomes the starting-point for problem solving and invites ideas.

Before we get into problem solving, we need to identify a problem owner for the concern. It is easy enough to say 'we' need to find a way to improve something; it is much tougher, and much more rewarding, for an individual to say: '*I* will take responsibility for improving it, if the rest of you can help me find a way to.'

Once a problem owner has been identified in this way, the problem solving can proceed along the lines already described. The 'group evaluation' technique can be valuable as a way of identifying opportunities for problem solving.

6. Problem solving with several problem owners

So far I have discussed problem solving from the point of view of a single problem owner looking for a new course of action which he or she might take to change a situation that is unsatisfactory, to exploit an opportunity or to achieve a demanding objective. While these circumstances may well apply in personal life, an individual's work circumstances are likely to be more complex, because other people will be involved.

The procedures and principles we have already examined still apply, but they need to be extended to cope with this additional complexity. In extending them, we encounter some of the most powerful and rewarding applications of the skills, namely the constructive resolution of conflict and the building of commitment in a team or organisation.

To obtain such benefits it is necesary to establish some clear principles about the way judgements are made and decisions are taken in the organisation. The concept of a 'problem owner' presupposes that the individual is able to make choices between ideas and to make decisions about what he or she will do or will not do. Clearly the individual cannot take these decisions in isolation: he or she has to consult with the other people involved. The extensions to the problem-solving model ensure that these consultations are handled constructively and progressively – provided it is clear which individual is responsible for which decisions.

In many organisations it is by no means clear who is responsible for what, and I will be suggesting an approach – the concept of *action responsibility* – which helps to clarify the issue. But first I want to describe how the model extends to deal with several problem owners, and the underlying principles which make it so effective.

Composition of the group

Ideally, the problem solving should include *all* the problem owners, so that a final conclusion can be reached in the meeting. If that is not possible the conclusions of the first meeting have to be taken forward to a further meeting which includes the missing problem owners, and follows the same procedures.

For a problem of this kind it is useful to include one or two 'neutrals', who can take a more detached view of the problem and contribute a more open-minded approach. The group should not exceed eight people; six or seven is preferable.

One problem owner at a time

It is essential to handle the problem from the point of view of one problem owner at a time, with the understanding that each one will have a turn, and no final conclusion will be reached till each of them is satisfied.

The problem owner has the key directing role: he or she specifies the problem, or aspect of the problem, to work on, selects the springboards that he or she judges to offer new approaches, evaluates the ideas, and decides when there is a solution. It is impossible to share this role; many of the choices are intuitive, and any attempt to share them is likely to result in an uneasy compromise at best – and a deadlock at worst. (I understand that the way to clear a log jam is to release one log; the same principle is at work here! Different people take different routes to a solution; there is no need to agree on the routes, only on the solution!)

Procedure

The procedure for the first problem owner is identical to that described in earlier chapters for the individual problem owner, except that when he or she has come to a possible solution, that is not the end of the story. That solution needs to be checked out with the other problem owners. If it creates problems for any of them in their area of responsibility, we need to switch to a second problem owner. *How* we make this switch is all important.

The second problem owner is asked to treat the first problem owner's solution as though it were an idea, not a solution, and to follow the standard three-step procedure for evaluating ideas, namely:

— check understanding by a paraphrase;
— find value in the idea, by specifying all its good points;
— convert negatives into directions for improvement.

The effects of following this discipline are remarkable. A paraphrase of an idea, as often as not, fails to satisfy the idea-giver that the idea has been properly understood – the 50 per cent success rate I referred to earlier. And where there is more than one problem owner, there is often a good deal of emotion and conflict involved. In these circumstances, the quality of listening tends to deteriorate. Participants often hear their own prejudices, rather than what is actually being said. By insisting on checking understanding through a paraphrase, we ensure that both the first and second problem owners are discussing the same idea. We make sure they are not at cross-purposes and do not get into an argument based on a misunderstanding.

In one case, I had to go through the ritual of paraphrase and check no fewer than four times before the two problem owners reached a common understanding about what was being proposed! What started off as a violent disagreement gradually calmed down as the misunderstandings were cleared up until finally the objector, having correctly understood the proposal at last, said, 'Oh, in that case I don't have any problem with it at all.'

That is an extreme example, but it is not uncommon for the removal of misunderstanding to be all that is needed to deal with the objection. When it is not, we move to the second step, finding value in the idea: we ask the objector to specify all the *good* features of the proposal to which he or she is objecting.

What the objector wants is usually the opposite – to attack the proposal, criticise it and tell us why he or she does *not* like it. The discipline of specifying the positive points compels the objector to treat the proposal in an open-minded way. And again the effects are remarkable. Once he or she gets down to it, the objector can usually find a lot of good in the proposal. By acknowledging it, he or she is identifying the common ground between the two parties and putting their disagreement into perspective. Very often the disagreement seems quite small in relation to the areas on which they do agree – a fact which has prompted me to formulate Nolan's Law of conflict: *90 per cent of the emotion is about 10 per cent of the content!*

It is actually in the interest of the objector to stretch the mind to discover all the good points which can be found in the proposal. He or she may actually learn something new by doing so, and will be demonstrating to the first problem owner that he or she is prepared to treat the proposal in a fair-minded way. This will encourage the proposer to do the same in return – to listen to the objections and join in the search for ways to deal with them. A co-operative bond is being forged.

Having identified all the good features of the proposal, the objector has earned the right to state his or her objection. We need to know what problem the proposal creates for that person, *in his or her area of responsibility*. (If the problem the objector foresees does not lie within his or her own area of responsibility, the objection is not valid – the objector is trespassing on some other problem owner's territory, and is not qualified to speak for the other party.)

We are making a vital distinction here between 'consequential problems' (something that will cause me difficulties in my job) and 'second opinions' ('If I were you I would not do that'). Sometimes the second opinions are couched in more objective-seeming language, such as 'That is not the right thing to do', or 'You should not do that'. Second opinions are a great source of trouble in organisations and teams; they waste time and energy. Occasionally, when someone is uncertain, a second opinion may be sought: 'What would you do, if you were me?' These occasions are relatively rare: the supply of second opinions greatly exceeds the demand! They are a glut on the market. They cause trouble because they seek to take away from the individual the right to make decisions about the way he or she does the job. They proclaim, in fact, 'I know better than you what is good for you'. They are insulting and patronising.

A consequential problem is a legitimate objection. No one wants to create problems unnecessarily for colleagues, and the first problem owner will be keen to find ways to solve the consequential problem. With the other members of the group, he or she will come up with ideas for getting round it, possibly by modifying the original solution, until the objector is satisfied. We can continue in the same sequential way to deal with the interests of the other problem owners involved. Any time a solution creates a consequential problem for one of the group, we will continue problem solving until it has been dealt with.

It always sounds a long-winded process when I talk about it or write about it. In practice it moves much faster, because of the constructive dynamics involved:

— First, there is a structure and a discipline that ensures that all the group members know what their role is and what kind of contribution is required from them, at each stage of the discussion.

— Second, only one person is making judgements at any one time, which ensures that the discussion is not being pulled in different directions (and as a result going nowhere).

— Third, care is taken to check understanding at the critical points, particularly when the role of problem owner is being switched from one individual to another.

— Fourth, the group members are talking about the areas of agreement – the common ground – as well as the areas of disagreement, thereby putting the disagreements in perspective.

— Fifth, problems are seen as opportunities for further invention, not reasons for rejection.

— Sixth, the inventive capacity of everyone involved is being used to create a rich array of alternatives at every stage; the discussion does not get bogged down in either/or choices.

— Last, and perhaps most important, all the members are 'minding their own business' in the sense of speaking for themselves and making decisions about their own area of responsibility, not everyone else's. (Second opinions are out!)

A meeting of this kind needs a process leader or facilitator who knows what he or she is doing and who is seen to be detached and objective by all the participants. To maintain neutrality, the process leader must keep out of the content of the discussion. That person must refrain from expressing any ideas or opinions of his or her own, and concentrate on managing the process. Though the role is not an easy one, it can be learned by suitable training and practice.

My colleagues and I spend a lot of our time running complex problem-solving meetings of this kind for our clients. We have a built-in advantage as outsiders (as well as being specialists) in that we are seen to be detached and uninvolved. We are outside both the politics and the hierarchy of the client organisation; we can be as firm with the chief executive as we are with more junior staff.

Internal process leaders lack these advantages, but if they do the job competently, their authority will be respected. And they do not need to be senior members of the organisation; if they are relatively junior, and competent in their specialised role, they will not be seen as a threat or as competition.

There is of course no guarantee that, even with the best possible process-leading skills and the most appropriate techniques, the problem will be solved or the conflict ended – as I have discovered myself more times than I like to remember.

Good planning can reduce the risk of getting into situations where there is no reasonable chance of success (see chapter 1, 'Preconditions for problem solving'). Planning involves talking to the key problem owners individually, to establish whether the preconditions exist for successful problem solving. These are:

— that the problem owners share common objectives – for example, the success of the busines or the organisation involved;

— that the problem owners are sufficiently open-minded at least to explore alternatives to their own point of view.

In a business environment, my experience is that these pre-conditions usually do exist. The overriding need for the business to survive and prosper usually provides sufficient common objectives, and it is politically unwise to be, or be seen to be, intransigent and closed-minded.

Only when interpersonal relationships have broken down irretrievably or when A and B dislike each other so intensely that they cannot actually listen to each other, does the problem-solving approach fail to get to first base. And this situation is not always easy to detect in the planning meetings; it may only emerge in the session itself. If that does happen, the only solution I know is to stop the session, confront the adversaries privately with what they are doing, and refuse to continue the session unless they change their behaviour – which is easier to do as an outsider than an insider! The ultimate resolution of these situations is for one or both of the antagonists to leave the organisation – and the more swiftly that happens, the better for the organisation.

Outside the business environment, huge and costly disputes drag on for interminable periods without any prospect of resolution – I have in mind the 1984–5 miners' strike, the 1985–6 teachers' pay dispute, the long-running battles over new technology in the newspaper industry, and the political problem of Northern Ireland. All of these are set up as adversarial trials of strength. They can only be concluded either by the collapse of the weaker party, or by a compromise born of exhaustion. Either outcome is usually unsatisfactory; the defeated party nurses its wounds and rebuilds its resources to renew the battle at a later date. The compromise solution leaves neither party truly satisfied, so there is little real commitment to make it work.

A problem-solving approach has the capacity to produce a 'creative consensus', which is quite different from a compromise. Unfortunately the language has been corrupted by politicians, especially Mrs Thatcher, in recent years, so that 'consensus' is spoken of as though it were the same thing as 'compromise'. It is not. A creative consensus is an outcome which pleases all parties: each can commit wholeheartedly to the action which must be taken to achieve it. One member may have reservations about the way other members of the group are tackling their part of the task, because that is not the way that individual would go about it, if he or she were doing that part. However, that individual is prepared to let them get on with their job in their way, if it does not affect his or her part of the job (that is, there is no attempt to impose a second opinion on them).

A compromise gives all the individuals a part of what they want, but leaves them more or less unsatisfied. A trial of strength is a win/lose contest: a compromise is a drawn game, without a winner or a loser. A creative consensus is win/win; all parties are satisfied.

A win/win outcome is made possible by the creativity and invention inherent in the problem-solving approach, which 'add value' to the situation. The added value has the potential to meet the needs of all the participants.

I was once asked to run a problem-solving meeting for management and shop stewards who were deadlocked in a pay dispute. The group (four managers, four shop stewards) invented a number of genuine productivity improvements which went a long way towards bridging the gap, and settled the dispute with only token industrial action. Moreover, by working together in a co-operative and constructive way, both parties increased their understanding and respect for one another. They asked for training in the techniques to enable them to continue to operate in this way on their own. I am not saying that all disputes can be resolved by problem solving. Often the preconditions described above do not exist – I have grave doubts whether Ian MacGregor of the National Coal Board and Arthur Scargill of the National Union of Mineworkers shared *any* common objectives. In Northern Ireland, the protagonists almost certainly do not.

But there are many other less dramatic disputes where the problem-solving approach could at least be tried *first*, to explore whether 'added value' can be invented to achieve a creative consensus. Even if it cannot (and there is no guarantee that it can), the parties will have been engaged in a constructive dialogue, which will have enhanced mutual understanding, respect and personal relationships.

This is an excellent basis from which to move from 'unsuccessful' problem solving to constructive negotiation. The principles of good negotiating have a lot in common with problem solving. In their excellent handbook on negotiating, *Getting to Yes*, Roger Fisher and William Ury of the Harvard Negotiating Project set out the following principles of good negotiating practice:

People: Separate the people from the problem . . . the participants should see themselves as working side by side, attacking the problem not each other

Interests: Focus on interests, not positions . . . behind opposed positions lie shared and compatible interests as well as conflicting ones

Options: Generate a variety of possibilities before deciding what to do . . . think up a wide range of possible solutions that advance shared interests and creatively reconcile differing interests

Criteria: Insist that the results be based on some objective standard . . . commit yourself to reaching a solution based on principle, not pressure.
These principles have a lot in common with, and are entirely consistent with, the principles of multi-group problem solving I have been describing.

Action responsibility

To use the concept of 'problem owner' raises a very interesting question: who does, in fact, own the problem? In discussing the preconditions for problem solving (chapter 1), I stressed the need to have one or more problem owners who were motivated – dissatisfied with the present situation – *and* had the ability and willingness to do something about it ('power to act').

In organisations there are usually a number of people involved in any problem, and the question of problem ownership easily becomes blurred. The concept of 'action responsibility' is a useful tool for clarifying the situation. It also takes us deep into the way that organisations work, or do not work – a subject explored more fully in the companion volume, *Teamwork*.

Action responsibility means that each of us is uniquely responsible for what we *do* ourselves. We do not have the same direct responsibility for what other people do. Managers indeed have responsibility for what their subordinates do, but they exercise it through the actions which they themselves take, not by doing the subordinates' job for them.

Ideally, decision-making responsibility should coincide with the action responsibility, so that people make their own decisions about how they do their job. In this way they have personal autonomy; they are likely to be highly motivated, and committed to making their own decisions work successfully.

Along with personal autonomy there has to be an understanding that the job must not be done in a way that creates problems for others in the organisation, including peers, subordinates and bosses. So if what I am proposing to do causes problems for anyone else, I need to start problem solving with them – either to find an alternative way to achieve my objectives, which does not cause these consequential problems, or to solve the consequential problems. The problem-solving meeting will follow the format described earlier in this chapter.

This procedure gives a manager sufficient scope to exercise control without imposing on the subordinate his or her own way of doing the job, which may well be different. The temptation is for the boss to regard the way he or she prefers as the 'right' way; in fact it is only one way among several possibilities, and although it may suit the boss best, it may not suit the subordinate who actually has to do the job. So if the subordinate's proposed course of action is not acceptable to the boss, the boss will use the format described:

— to check that he or she has correctly understood the proposal;

— to specify what aspects of it are acceptable;

— to state how it would need to be modified to deal with any consequential problems.

The boss will also be a resource in the problem-solving meeting, offering (not imposing) ideas (not solutions).

I accept that there are situations where this way of operating is not appropriate. The Armed Forces and similar hierarchical, disciplined organisations such as the Police and fire services operate on the basis of instant obedience to a superior's commands. 'I always do what my superior officer tells me do to,' an ex-Group Captain said to me once in industry, when he was doing something we both knew to be particularly idiotic. But even in these organisations, the principle of the superior giving orders for the subordinate to carry out is really only appropriate in *operational* situations. When the Fire Brigade is fighting a fire, instant execution of the commander's orders is essential. However, when the same team is discussing ways to improve operations – in the planning as opposed to the operational situation – the 'action responsibility' concept can apply.

Action responsibility makes it possible to operate on what I call the 'Mind your own business' principle – that ideas and opinions are offered only when they are wanted, which is to say when the problem owner wants help with a problem within his or her area of action responsibility. It is also the key to handling problems with multiple problem owners. An objector to a proposal or a solution has to deal with the question 'How is it a problem for you?'/'How does it affect your action responsibility?' If it does not, the objection is not a consequential problem; it is only a second opinion, which can be ignored safely.

To operate in this way you need to have clarity and agreement about the division of action responsibilities in the organisation. It is the action responsibility of the senior manager (the next level up in the hierarchy) to decide and communicate the allocation of responsibilities and ensure that all important functions are covered.

I find that some senior managers resist clarity and precision in these matters; they seem to prefer confusion and uncertainty, which they believe they can manipulate to their own advantage, playing off one subordinate against another. I believe they pay a heavy price for this style of managing, in terms of the de-motivation and lack of commitment of the people who work for them.

7. Problem-solving systems

The field of problem solving is littered with labels for techniques that are enthusiastically promoted by those who have a proprietorial interest in them. (As chairman of Synectics Ltd, I have to plead guilty to being one of the principal offenders!) The labels can cause a good deal of confusion; they can be used loosely to mean different things to different people and smart alecs will use them for one-upmanship. Business academics find them a fertile stamping-ground, producing learned treatises about the differences and similarities and relative suitability; they even conduct wholly bogus controlled experiments to 'prove' which is the best technique.

Out there in the real world, you can be a perfectly competent and successful problem solver without knowing any of the labels. There is no need to feel one down if someone says, 'We ought to use "morphological analysis" here, or "fundamental design method".' Just ask that person to spell out in plain English what is involved and you will have no difficulty following the method. Only the jargon gets in the way.

The various techniques have much in common, but the common ground tends to be obscured by the different languages used. They are also mostly 'common sense', in that there are sound reasons for using them where appropriate, which will be readily accepted when explained simply.

Most techniques provide a structured approach; separate steps in the process are identified and used in a methodical sequence. Structure is valuable in providing discipline for thinking privately; it is even more valuable when you are working with others, because it ensures that everyone is on the same wavelength, doing the same thing at the same time. (Many discussions I observe remind me of one person playing squash and the other badminton; neither of them has a good game!)

Here I want to describe briefly what is meant by the labels I most commonly encounter, with particular emphasis on the features they share. It is convenient to divide them into two broad categories:

— those suitable for problems which lie within, or close to, present levels of knowledge and achievement;

— those which lie well outside those levels.

Problems of the first category require predominantly logical analytical skills — Professor Revans suggests that they should be called puzzles rather than problems. Problems of the second require predominantly inventive, intuitive, creative skills. The distinction is far from absolute; both types of skill can be used in both categories of problem, but the mix is different.

In the first category, I include: Kepner–Tregoe; attribute listing; morphological analysis. In the second are: brainstorming; lateral thinking; Synectics.

Kepner–Tregoe

The key to the Kepner–Tregoe approach lies in the definition of a problem as a 'deviation from the norm'. That is a very narrow use of the word 'problem' — it implies that the solution already exists (to have achieved the norm in the first place). The solution has been 'lost' in some way, as, for instance, a component in a machine breaking down; we need to find out where the fault is, so that we can repair it.

Where this has happened, correcting the deviation is one way of handling the problem, not the only way. Suppose, for example, that my car will not start. One option is to find out why and to fix it. Alternatively I could look at the higher-level problem of why I want to start the car. The answer may be to go to the office. In that case, I might phone for a taxi, use a bus or train, hire a car or buy a new one, hitch-hike, ask a friend for a lift, decide to stay at home, have meetings by phone and so on. Even if I decide that fixing the car is the solution I want to pursue, I still have the choice of calling the AA or a garage, or getting help from a neighbour.

Once somebody starts to fix the car, the Kepner–Tregoe approach will be helpful. It consists of precise organisation of information about the problem, specifying what the deviation is and what it is not, and asking questions such as what, where, when, how much, how often and so on. When you've done that, the next step is to hypothesize possible causes, which means provisional statements of cause and effect. (Going back to the car that does not start, possible causes would be no fuel, flat battery, faulty spark plug, loose contacts, damp points, jammed starter motor, faulty carburettor and so forth.) We can then test each of these hypotheses and arrive at the correct diagnosis by a process of elimination.

Kepner and Tregoe stress the need to stay open-minded, in order to avoid jumping to a conclusion about a cause, and to test rigorously all the hypotheses, to ensure that they fit the specification of the problem completely. The more precise the problem specification, the more rigorous it will be as a test of the hypothesis. They also acknowledge the need to respect intuition and hunches, to encourage speculation about possible causes, even when the data is not yet available to support that speculation. The testing will provide the data.

The approach is extended to potential problems by asking 'What could go wrong?' The most important of these are assessed according to their seriousness and probability, and then dealt with in terms of their possible causes and the ways in which they can be either prevented or dealt with if they do occur.

It's all good stuff, and undoubtedly many managers speak appreciatively of the training they have had in these techniques (whether they explicitly use the approach in practice is another matter, but that is true of many forms of training). My own (prejudiced) view is that this approach, with its heavy emphasis on the logical and the rational, reinforces a bias that already exists in most managers from their formal education (particularly in the precise disciplines such as science, engineering and systems). It does nothing to encourage (indeed, it tends actively to discourage) creative and imaginative thinking, and completely ignores the human factors which are such an important component of most 'real world' problems. There is an implicit assumption that all rational people will come to the same conclusion – the one I have come to!

Having said that, if your problem really is a 'deviation from the norm' which you want to correct, the Kepner–Tregoe approach will serve you well.

Attribute listing

This is an analytical technique for identifying possible areas of improvement in a product. It starts from a factual description of each component of the product in physical terms, describes the functions of each component and then considers whether each attribute of each component might be improved. The systematic procedure ensures that no stone is left unturned in the search for opportunities for improvement. After the initial procedure, ideas can be considered for possible ways of improving the attribute.

Attribute listing can be used as a tool for 'value analysis', by relating the cost of each component to the function it performs. Aspects of the product which are disproportionately costly in relation to the value they provide can be identified, triggering a search for ways to reduce or eliminate the cost and improve the value.

Morphological analysis

Like attribute listing, morphological analysis is a systematic search for opportunities for improvement. It starts with a listing of the parameters of the problem, and then each one is subdivided into as many different forms as possible. The sub-sets are charted in the form of matrices and all combinations of the features considered. Quickly the number of combinations becomes very large. They are then screened to identify any which are novel and attractive.

Morphological analysis ensures that no stone is left unturned and, 'being largely mechanistic, by-passes blind spots, habit and prejudice' (Ronald Whitfield). It is also laborious and time-consuming. Some scientists of my acquaintance speak highly of it; its thoroughness probably appeals to their systematic minds. But it's not a method I find myself using.

Brainstorming

Brainstorming was the first formal idea-generation technique, developed some fifty years ago and by now more or less generally accepted as a useful (if dated) approach. It works by simply forbidding any judgement or evaluation as ideas are being expressed.

The effect is to produce a substantial flow of ideas in a short space of time. 'Quantity breeds quality' is the brainstorming claim, and it is true up to a point: the more ideas there are, the greater the chance of one or more of them, or a hybrid made up from parts of several ideas, providing a solution.

Looked at historically, brainstorming can be seen as a great breakthrough. It demonstrated decisively the inhibiting effect of judgement on the production of ideas – remove the risk of criticism and the ideas flow. And the sheer quantity of ideas is likely to open up new perspectives and new approaches, and so encourage thinking about the problem in new ways.

But there are important limitations to brainstorming. Although external critical judgement is forbidden, internal judgement (self-censoring) continues. Even at the conscious level, people continue to filter the ideas they express, for fear of making a fool of themselves. Consequently they censor the wild and crazy ideas, the very ones most likely to contain the seeds of novelty. And at the unconscious level, the brainstorming technique does nothing to release the ideas which are screened out of our awareness by the habit of self-censorship. More powerful aids, such as the excursion techniques described in chapter 4, plus practice in the in–out listening method (chapter 3), are needed to reinforce the brainstorming.

However, the biggest weakness of brainstorming as normally practised is the way in which judgement is reintroduced by screening the list of ideas into 'good' and 'bad' ideas. The shortlist of good ideas produced in this way will almost certainly not include any new ones! As we have seen, new ideas cannot be 'good' ones; we only know if an idea is a good one from experience of using it. If an idea is new, we have no experience to judge it by. The crude screen of 'good' and 'bad' ideas will screen out the new ones. As a result, the end-product of a brainstorming session is often disappointment. What was the point of generating that great list of ideas, if at the end of the day we finish up with a shortlist of 'good' ideas that are not new?

The missing link in brainstorming is the process of idea development (see chapter 5) which selects brainstormed ideas (or preferably 'springboards') on the basis of their *newness* and uses them as a starting-point or seed from which to develop a new and feasible solution. To go straight from the brainstormed ideas to the choice of solutions is unrealistic; it assumes that there will be instant novel solutions. With occasional exceptions such as advertising slogans (say, 'Players Please'), new solutions will not be instant; they require a period of incubation and transformation, which is provided by the 'idea development' process.

What we are left with from brainstorming is the underlying principle *suspend judgement to release ideas*. This is entirely valid and of fundamental importance. It underlies the technique of open-minded listening and needs to extend beyond 'ideas' as such to wishes, goals and problem definitions (as in the generation of springboards).

Lateral thinking

'Lateral Thinking' is a label coined by Edward de Bono to distinguish the thinking used for generating ideas from the 'vertical thinking' used in logical processes. It is a valuable distinction, and most useful to have such apt and convenient labels for the two different ways of thinking. The term 'lateral thinking' is now widely used by managers; it has done a good job in educating them to the fact that more than one way of thinking exists. (It's worth remembering that it was the *label* that de Bono invented, not the method of thinking! Some people seem to have the impression that de Bono invented lateral thinking, a claim I am sure he would not wish to make himself!)

The techniques suggested for lateral thinking have much in common with Synectics. De Bono's 'intermediate impossible' is similar to the 'absurd solution'; 'random juxtaposition' is like the excursion techniques, and there is a similar emphasis on positive thinking and suspended judgement through the introduction of the word *Po* as a substitute for the negative *no*. 'Po is to lateral thinking what No is to logical thinking. No is a rejection tool. Po is an insight restructuring tool.'*

Managers I meet seem to worry that they are not 'good' at lateral thinking. If you use the techniques described elsewhere in this book, you will in fact be practising lateral thinking, whether you choose to call it that or not!

Synectics

In a sense, most of this book (and its companion volumes in the 'Innovative Management Skills' series) is about Synectics, and I cannot objectively describe the Synectics 'system' in the same way as I have tried to describe the others. I will content myself instead with quoting an independent observer, Ronald Whitfield:

Synectics clearly offers a rich combination of disciplined problem clarification, 'method thinking' and support for individual risk-taking . . . it spans the whole spectrum of development methods for creative problem-solving and, in addition, it provides a team-building process which creates an environment where creativity is the central and coveted attribute.

He was writing in 1975; today I would take some of the emphasis off problem clarification, and add the key concepts of idea development (chapter 5) and problem ownership as distinctive attributes of Synectics, as well as the excursions which Whitfield identifies as its novel feature.

It's worth adding that Synectics was developed by detailed analysis of tape-recordings of the thinking processes of inventors as they invented new solutions. Processes which correlated with successful invention were encouraged, and alternatives were sought for processes which seemed to block progress. It is thus an empirically based body of knowledge, which is constantly being refined and extended as the research continues.

* Edward de Bono, *Lateral Thinking*.

8. Strategy for managing the creative resource

Creativity has in times gone by been seen as a gift from the gods, bestowed on the chosen few. Tests have purported to show that only 2 per cent of the population is 'highly creative'. Two streams of research – one scientific (neurophysiological), the other empirical (particularly Synectics) – have demonstrated that creativity is a natural human attribute available to all normal people. In most of us it is grossly under-utilised, as a result of the conditioning processes of our society, education systems and business organisations. The 'highly creative' minority are those who have escaped or successfully resisted the conditioning processes which cause most of us to repress our creativity.

Scientific research into the structure and use of the brain has demonstrated that we use only a tiny proportion of the mental capacity available to us. It has also demonstrated that the two halves of the brain specialise in different kinds of activity – the left brain in logical, analytical, sequential, rational and predominantly verbal activities, the right brain in holistic, visual and intuitive processes. It is clear that our educational systems and organisational values give a disproportionate encouragement to leftbrain skills.

The empirical research conducted by Synectics, using tape-recordings or videotapes of problem-solving discussions among inventors (and later among business managers), identified the activities and processes associated with creativity. They turned out to be predominanatly right-brain activities (though this was long before we knew about the specialisation of the two halves of the brain) such as visualisation, drawing and the use of metaphor and analogy.

So the latent creative ability can be rediscovered, released and put to work to the benefit of both the individual and the organisation for which he or she works. On a temporary, short-term basis this can be done quickly and easily for most individuals – as experience of a brainstorming session will illustrate. Take any group of 'non-creative' people, put them in an environment where critical judgement is forbidden and speculation encouraged, and suddenly you have lots of ideas, some of them original and novel.

But this is only the tip of the iceberg. Although the brainstorming environment has encouraged the expression of ideas that would not otherwise have been voiced for fear of public criticism, there is still a 'self censor' at work, operating at both the conscious and unconscious levels.

Consciously, people will refrain from putting forward their ideas because they consider them too ridiculous (or illegal or immoral or irrelevant) even for a brainstorming session. A skilful session facilitator can overcome this restriction by a variety of permission-giving techqniques, to encourage the expression of these potentially very valuable 'nonsense' ideas.

At the unconscious level, however, the self-censor or internal critic has a much tighter hold, such that it appears to be able to block the flow of creative material even before it reaches the conscious mind. By 'creative material' I mean the stream of images, associations, experiences that cross my mind as I think about a subject for which I want new ideas (or listen to someone else talk about such a subject). It is only when I cease to 'concentrate' on the problem and do something completely different that my self-censor seems to take a break, and my sub-conscious mind can get to work. Sometimes it makes enough progress to sneak a new idea past the self-censor, and I have one of my creative moments. Which is why many people develop the strategy of sleeping on a problem, or going for a walk; or doing something completely unrelated to the task (driving the car, mowing the grass, sitting in the bath – all times when the mind is allowed to wander in its own undirected way, like a dog let off the lead).

This 'accidental' creativity is a poor substitute for using our creative abilities deliberately and skilfully whenever we wish to. We do not leave any other resource in our business to the whims of chance or accident. We expect to manage the resources of our organisation, and creativity is a key resource, which needs to be managed like any other. So, given that there is a vast creative resource inherent in the people we work with – not only our colleagues, but also our customers and suppliers in the widest sense – how do we manage it, to achieve the objectives of our organisation?

I propose a five-step strategy for managing the creative resource –

— The first key step is to make this conscious *shift in our attitude* to creativity:
to view creativity as a resource to be managed rather than a random, accidental phenomenon.

— Along with this shift goes a *different attitude towards people:*
to stop thinking in terms of 'creative' and 'non-creative' people, and see everybody as a potential creative resource.

— Next we need
to make the resource *visible* – to take the wraps off it, to make everyone in the business realise they can be creative.

The fourth step is
to direct the creativity at the needs of business, especially the major *strategic* needs of business.

Finally we need
to create and maintain a *culture* in the organisation which fosters and values creativity – appropriately applied creativity – equally with other skills such as technical competence, quality assurance, financial wisdom and analytical ability.

I would like to explore what is involved in each of these components of the strategy for managing the creative resource.

To view creativity as a resource to be managed, not an accidental phenomenon

This is essentially a change of mindset, a change in the way we view the world. It is a vital step, because the assumptions we make – often unconsciously – about the way the world is, condition our behaviour and our interpretation of our experience.

It may well be that the traditional view of creativity is grounded in experience. People who are not aware of their own creative abilities, and those of other people, will have experienced creativity as an accidental phenomenon. Naturally they assume that this is how it must be – an understandable but faulty assumption. So they take no steps to seek out creative solutions, or even to consider whether creative solutions might be possible. It's a classic self-fulfilling expectation – if I believe I cannot draw, I do not try to draw, so I do not acquire the skill, which 'proves' what I always believed: I cannot draw.

So it is with creativity: managers who believe that neither they nor their people are creative will not look for new solutions and will not find them. Their talk will be full of words such as 'impossible', 'inevitable', 'no way'. They will fear change and try to resist it, instead of using the same energy to initiate change and profit from it.

Moreover, when creativity is seen as an accidental phenomenon, it can be feared as something uncontrollable and unpredictable, like lightning, which may strike where it is least expected. In fact, creativity is very controllable; the act of creation is only strange when we do not understand it. There is a wonderful unpredictability about the ideas it generates, but it is entirely a matter of choice which ones we implement.

Along with this fear of creativity goes a fear of 'creative people', a view that these different creatures will disrupt the organisation and put its very survival at risk. Again, this fear has a basis in experience. So-called 'creative people' do tend to wear jeans and sandals (or trainers) and open-necked shirts, long hair and beards, and otherwise flaunt their defiance of the conventions of the business world. They do so, I believe, because they have had to fight against the pressures to conform in order to preserve their creative skills from the forces that induce the great majority of us to keep ours under lock and key.

However, once we see creativity as a resource possessed by everyone, we need no longer worry about 'creative people' damaging the organisation (though we still need to ensure that creativity is properly directed). Perhaps as the rest of us become aware of our creative skills there will be less need to signal creative indpendence by non-conformist behaviour – or will we all start wearing sandals?

Which brings us to the next step in our strategy . . .

To stop thinking in terms of 'creative' and 'noncreative' people, and see everybody as a potential creative source

This is a similar change in mindset, and again it has to be acknowledged that the conventional belief that there is a minority of highly creative geniuses amid the mass of the uncreative is probably based on experience. Most of us only meet a few highly creative people: the rest never manifest any creativity.

Creativity is a little bit like running. Twenty years ago a reasonable observer might have concluded that only a small minority of adults (as opposed to children) could run – that small minority would be given a special label, athletes. Today the conclusion has to be that anyone in reasonable health who wants to run two or three miles can do so – given a bit of practice – and lots of people do.

Moreover, the belief in the existence of a creative minority is actively promoted by the (self-appointed) creative minority! Advertising agencies, for example, present themselves as the specialists in creativity who can relieve their clients of the burden and the risk of thinking creatively. Within the agencies you will find that one department, the self-styled Creative Department, claims creativity as its prerogative and its monopoly.

Yet I know from my own experience of the last fifteen years that everybody has creative talent and can quickly learn to use it. Give me any bunch of people – scientists, accountants, engineers, housewives, shop stewards, clerks or factory workers – and within a week I will have them producing lots of original ideas and converting them into new courses of action. When I do this for advertising agencies, I sometimes encounter resistance from the Creative Department, who start by denying that creativity can be taught and end up by accusing me of revealing the professional secrets of their trade! They need not feel threatened – their craft skills in copywriting, graphics, television and so on will keep them in employment, and their creativity will be better appreciated and understood by clients and colleagues who are in touch with their own creative skills.

Once we get away from thinking in terms of 'creative' and 'non-creative' people, we can divert our energies away from searching for creative people to using the creativity that exists right under our nose, in the people we already have.

To make the creative resource visible

Unfortunately the belief in a creative minority is so widespread that most people believe that they themselves are not creative. To make the creative resource visible, it's necessary to put everyone in touch with their own latent creative ability.

This isn't difficult, but it does call for the investment of time and money. There are well-established training courses, such as those run by my own company, which will in the course of a few days enable virtually any willing participant to rediscover his or her creative abilities and provide the tools to find creative solutions when he or she needs them. (I do emphasise *willing* participants: as with any other type of learning, a determined non-learner will always succeed in not learning. We encounter very few of these, but they do exist.)

The most valuable place to start this training is of course at the top of the organisation, with the chief executive and the management team. The experience of the course will reinforce the first two stages of the strategy – the shift in attitude towards creativity and towards people. It will also be a demonstration from the top of two key elements of creativity – open-mindedness and willingness to learn. Many senior executives proclaim themselve too busy to take time off to attend training courses. At least, that is the ostensible explanation: successful people tend to believe that they are successful because of the way they operate, and that therefore they have nothing new to learn.

I prefer to believe they are successful because of some of the things they do, and *in spite of* other things they do (or do not do). In an area like creativity, where a great deal of new knowledge has become available in the last twenty-five years, any manager who has not been exposed to it is putting himself or herself at a serious disadvantage.

Finally, it's important to start at the top of the organisation because that is where the creativity can be applied to the most critical areas, the strategic needs of the business. Almost by definition, the lower down the hierarchy, the smaller will be the area to which the individual can apply creative skills. This is an argument for *starting* at the top: it is still necessary to continue down the organisation.

To direct the creativity at the needs of the business

If management is to control the creative resource it has released through the training, it must provide the outlets and targets for creative activity. (Otherwise it will go underground and find subversive outlets!) The first area for the top managers of the business to apply their own creativity to once they have learned the necessary skills is their vision for the future of the business and the strategies to achieve it.

A truly creative strategy will not be a 'me too' extrapolation of the business as it has been. It will be a truly wishful expression of the business the management intends to create. 'Wishing for the impossible' is the key creative skill that most executives have to re-learn after years of being conditioned to believe that wishful thinking is a bad thing. It is the impossible objective that stimulates the invention of ways to achieve it; the possible has already been invented – that's how we know it's possible.

A truly creative strategy will generate demanding goals for the organisation to achieve. These, too, will seem impossible at first sight; in fact they *will* be impossible, until the people in the organisation have used their newly developed creative skills to invent ways to achieve them. The goals will cover the whole business calling for new products, greater productivity, quality improvement, overhead cost reduction, original uses of information technology, and so on. They may call for task forces and project teams drawn from many disciplines and functions.

Down the organisation, the targets for creativity might generate quality circles and suggestion schemes for tapping into the creative contribution of all employees. There is nothing new about suggestion schemes, of course, but the traditional suggestion scheme is not *directed*. The suggestions have the disadvantage of being 'unsolicited ideas' being offered to managers who do not want them. Unsolicited ideas tend to be heard as criticisms of current practice and to get rejected.

In a targeted suggestions scheme, managers specify the areas where ideas are needed; constructive detailed feedback is given on all ideas. For those which are not accepted for implementation, guidance is given on how they need to be improved to meet the objectives.

To create and maintain a culture which fosters creativity

This stage takes us full circle back to the reasons why creativity is suppressed in the first place. There is no point in releasing the creativity of the people in the organisation and directing it towards demanding targets, if at the same time the organisation continues to maintain values and norms that are hostile to creativity.

Organisations do not consciously and deliberately set out to be hostile to creativity. They do so inadvertently, by applying critical standards that are appropriate to established, routine activities, to new activities and new ideas as well. If a manager always has to be right, must never make a mistake, must prove with verifiable evidence that what he or she proposes to do is justified – that manager will not take the risk of being creative.

With something new there is no experience to go by; there is a strong probability that new initiatives will have unforeseen outcomes, positive and negative. The whole approach has to be experimental: 'Let's try it and see what happens. In the light of what we learn, we will do it differently next time.' With an experiment, *any* result is a success, in that it provides the information for learning and change.

So many managers say, 'We tried it, and it didn't work. Therefore it's no good – forget it.' So the experiment is wasted and creativity is discouraged. It is far more logical to remember that we thought the idea was good enough to try. We need to find a way to retain the attractive features of the idea and at the same time to understand *why* it did not work, and find ways to change it to get over the problem next time. The experiment then becomes a step on the learning curve.

This distinction is vital; it determines the whole attitude to risk-taking. Innovation (the end-product of creativity) is inherently uncertain and risky. The responsible innovator makes sure that risks are affordable, which is to say they will not damage the business significantly in the worst case, but that person has to take the risk that the innovation will not work. The attitude to risk affects the attitude to ideas. In a risk-averse culture, ideas are judged as though they were actions (they are not, of course – they are only words and pictures). If anyone can see a flaw in the idea it is dismissed instantly, out of hand – 'That won't work, because . . .'

We know from our studies of videotaped discussions that this rejection is so painful for the idea giver that he or she takes great care to avoid a repetition. In future he or she will only express 'good'

96

ideas, those that cannot be criticised. So these have to be old ideas, not new ones.

The caution in expressing ideas develops the powerful self-censor, which extends to thinking as well as to expression of ideas, such that new ideas and idea-forming material are screened out of the conscious mind and only occur randomly, when they by-pass the censor (while 'sleeping on the problem' for example). We are back where we started.

The training in creative skills, and their use on the major needs of the business, go some way to creating an awareness of the influence of the organisation's culture and may even begin to change it. They need to be reinforced by a conscious and explicit policy from top management to apply different and appropriate standards of judgement to *established* and to *innovative* activities.

'What is honoured in a country is what is practised there' – for creativity to be practised in an organisation it needs to be honoured, not just in the chairman's annual report, but in the everyday behaviour of the senior management. To change *that* is perhaps the biggest single challenge of those who want to release and use the creative talent of their organisation.

References

Edward de Bono, *Lateral Thinking*, Pelican, 1977.

Gordon Edge, *Sunday Times Colour Magazine*, 2 February 1986.

Roger Fisher and William Ury, *Getting to Yes*, Hutchinson, 1983.

W. H. H. Gordon, *Synectics*, Harper and Row, 1960.

Arthur B. van Gundy, *108 Ways to Get a Bright Idea*, Prentice Hall, 1983.

Rick Harriman, quoted from conversation with the author.

C. H. Kepner and B. B. Tregoe, *The Rational Manager*, McGraw, 1965.

Don Koberg and Jim Bagnall, *Universal Traveller*, Kaufmann, 1981.

Van Oech, *A Whack on the Side of the Head*, Angus and Robertson, 1985.

R. C. Parker, 'Creativity: A Case History', *Engineering*, February 1975.

George Prince, *Practice of Creativity*, Harper and Row, 1975.

Professor Revans, quoted in Bill Critchley and David Casey, 'Second Thoughts about Team Building', *Management Education and Development*, vol. 15, pt. 2, pp. 163–75.

Professor Bernd Rohrbach, quoted from conversation with the author.

Suzuki Roshi, *Zen Mind, Beginners' Mind*, Weatherill, 1970.

Peter Russell, *Brain Book*, Routledge, 1979.

Ronald Whitfield, *Creativity in Industry*, Pelican, 1975.

Gary Zukav, *The Dancing Wu Li Masters*, Fontana, 1980.

Communication

Contents

1. Communication: the everyday miracle

The scope for improvement

We all do it, all the time — exchange our thoughts, ideas, opinions, feelings with other people, at work, at home and in every other part of our life. The communication process is so commonplace that it becomes second nature: we do it without thinking about it; we take it for granted, like breathing.

Yet when we stop to think about it, the process is seen to be much more complex, and much less efficient, than we had assumed. (The same could be said about breathing.) And if we take the trouble to understand the communication process and work at improving our communication skills, we can greatly increase the efficiency of our communicating, with benefit to the productiveness of our work and the enjoyment of our relationships. (An athlete or singer would make similar comments about good breathing; a writer on yoga says, 'If only we would learn to breathe properly: the rewards are incalculable'.*)

Because communication pervades nearly everything we do, even small improvements in the effectiveness of our communicating are likely to have disproportionately large benefits. At work, most jobs have some communication component; most managerial, administrative and professional jobs depend very largely on successful communication. Whole industries such as television, newspapers and magazines, book publishing, advertising and public

* Andre van Lysebeth, *Yoga Self-taught*, Unwin Paperbacks, 1978.

relations are virtually communications industries. Teaching, and the academic world generally, is largely about communicating.

Both at work and outside it, the quality of our personal relationships depends heavily on the quality of our communications. The ability to make contact with others, to understand them and enable them to understand us, is a communication skill of the highest order, particularly because it deals with the intangible rather than the tangible, with feelings rather than facts. This is a dimension I do not intend to address in any depth here. My focus is communication at work; though to the extent that the quality of interpersonal relationships affects the quality of our working life – and therefore our effectiveness at work – we will need to give some consideration to communication at the emotional level too.

Dr Fritz Schumacher, in *A Guide to the Perplexed*, points out that the essential problem of communication is that we 'implicitly rely on other people's *visible* signals to convey to us a correct picture of their *invisible* thoughts'. He goes on to describe the four steps involved when there is a genuine wish on the part of one person to convey his thoughts to another:

— First, the speaker must know, with some precision, what is the thought he wishes to convey;

— second, he must find visible (including audible) symbols – gestures, bodily movements, words, intonation, etc. – which in his judgement are able to 'externalise' his 'internal' thought; this may be called 'the first translation';

— third, the listener must have a faultless reception of these visible (etc.) symbols, which means not only that he must accurately hear what is being said, knowing the language used, but also that he must accurately observe the non-verbal symbols (such as gesture and intonation) that are being employed;

— fourth, the listener must then in some way integrate the numerous symbols he has received and turn them into thought; this may be called 'the second translation'.

He concludes that 'it's not difficult to see how much can go wrong at each stage of this four stage process, particularly with the two "translations" ' Yet in spite of the difficulties, we do communicate successfully to some extent: as Schumacher says, 'miraculously, in real life, perfect communication *is* possible, and not infrequent'.

How frequent will vary from individual to individual according to his or her skill as a communicator, but as a generalisation we can say that it is far less frequent than we commonly assume. In fact, we behave as though the success of our communication can be taken for granted. You will hear people say things like, 'He must know – I told him myself'; as though the fact of telling, of itself, ensures the communication. The telling is just one of the four components of the communication process identified by Schumacher – and any one of the four can go wrong.

So although the miracle does happen every day, it is dangerous to assume that it happens every time, or even most times: as someone else (I do not know who) has neatly put it, 'the greatest danger in communication is the assumption that it has taken place'. The probability, according to communications researchers, is that it has not. For example, Professor Wiio, of the Helsinki School of Economics, told me that in his research into communications of all kinds, he came to the conclusion that typical success rates in communication were around 5 per cent! A statistician would regard a 5 per cent success rate as not statistically significant, a random event. So Professor Wiio concludes (with tongue slightly in cheek) that 'successful communication happens by chance'.

His research was concerned with communication through the media – television, radio, newspapers, etc. So his 5 per cent success rate becomes more understandable. Surely the success rate in face-to-face communication is much higher? Yes, indeed it is – five times higher, that is, 25 per cent (according to the Sperry company's research into listening). Which still means that the odds are three-to-one *against* any particular communication being successful – that is, the message received being the one the sender meant to convey. Or that only one in four of a group of people will hear the message you are presenting to them.

You can increase the odds by repetition (as I have done above). Speakers are often exhorted to 'tell them what you're going to say, say it, then tell them what you have said'. Most of us speak with a good deal of repetition, perhaps because we know intuitively, or from experience, that it is often necessary to do so to make the communication effective.

So although the miracle of successful communication does happen, it is safer to view it as the exception rather than the rule. When accurate reception is critical, it's worth going to some trouble to check that what has been heard is what was meant.

The good news is that communication success rates can be increased substantially – at least doubled – by quite simple methods described in this book. This bold assertion is based on my own experience of working with several thousand people over the last fifteen years.

When I and my colleagues are running problem-solving meetings we apply the principle of 'understand before evaluating'. We do not allow anyone to express a judgement on an idea until they have checked their understanding of it with the idea-giver by a paraphrase. They must tell the idea-giver what their understanding of the idea is and the idea-giver must confirm that that is what he or she meant.

As we applied this rule, we began to realise that *as often as not* the idea-giver was not satisfied that the paraphrase correctly expressed the idea; the idea-giver needed to amplify, amend, modify or even correct completely the idea as understood, to bring it into line with the idea he or she had originally intended to express.

We were getting, in fact, a success rate of approximately 50 per cent. I was acutely disappointed, since we had gone to a great deal of trouble to create a favourable environment for good communication and had introduced a number of techniques to enhance the effectiveness of communication.

It was only after my discussions with Professor Wiio and other communications researchers that I realised that our 50 per cent success rate was an outstanding success – *double* the average success rate, in fact. And 50 per cent is by no means a maximum: well-trained groups consistently score higher than 50 per cent once they have learned that successful communication cannot be taken for granted, but needs to be worked at.

The semantic trap

The word 'communicate' is itself a semantic trap. As an active verb it purports to give information about the subject of the verb, the communicator. But by definition communication is a two-party activity; it requires a receiver as well as a transmitter. Two of Dr Schumacher's four steps in the communication process are carried out by the transmitter and two by the receiver: communication is a shared responsibility.

So, sitting alone on a desert island, I cannot communicate (except with myself). I may write my message, put it in the bottle and toss it into the sea, but until it is picked up by a passing ship or a beachcomber on another coast, I have not 'communicated'. Nor have I even then; my message has to make sense to whoever takes it out of the bottle. Bad luck if it's a Chinaman who cannot read English!

Indeed, given that communication is a two-party activity and the activity of each party is quite different (transmitting and receiving), it is highly misleading to package the two together in a single portmanteau verb 'to communicate'. (There are other two-party verbs in our language with similar potential for misunderstanding: to 'sell', for example, implies someone else buying; to 'persuade' or to 'convince' imply someone else accepting the argument.)

The distinction I am making is not just an interesting academic point about linguistics, because the way we use the verb 'communicate' colours our whole way of thinking and talking about the communication process. It is equated with transmitting only, with speaking and writing. The receiving end – listening, looking and reading – tends to be ignored and neglected, or dealt with in isolation.

I was recently asked to comment on the draft syllabus of a university course in communication. The word 'listening' appeared once only in a 300-word document and other aspects of the receiving process were given equally scant attention. The whole bias was to the transmitting processes and the media through which they are carried out.

Even as eminent an authority as Peter Drucker falls into the same trap: 'effective communication has four parts – something we have known since Plato and Aristotle. One has to know what to say, when to say it, to whom to say it and how to say it. If one of those four elements is missing, there cannot be communication.' His conclusion is true, but his (and Plato's and Aristotle's) four elements relate to the transmission process only. They are a necessary but not sufficient condition for effective communication; the equally important elements of the receiving process are implied but not articulated.

If we were to make a similar breakdown of the elements of the receiving process, we might specify:

— a recipient willing to give attention and credence to the transmitter;

— a recipient able to hear and understand the message as it is intended;

— a recipient able to connect the new input with previous knowledge and experience it in such a way that it 'makes sense' to him or her.

Many transmissions are made to multiple receivers – somebody speaking in a meeting has several potential listeners, a memo may have multiple copies, a lecture speech or broadcast may have hundreds or thousands of recipients, as may a report, a magazine or book. It follows that, quantitatively, *receiving, not transmitting, is the largest part of any individual's communication activity*. This conclusion is at odds with the way we commonly use and interpret the word 'communicate' to imply the transmitting process only.

Consequently the greatest scope, quantitatively, for improving your communication skills is to improve your listening, observing, reading and watching abilities, as a priority over your speaking, writing, etc. I believe this is true qualitatively also, because the most effective transmissions are those that fit in with and connect to the receiving processes of the recipients. Awareness of your own receiving processes will help you to tune in to the receiving processes of those you wish to reach with your transmissions. And the receiving skills are a relatively neglected area, compared with the attention given to speaking and writing skills. You are more likely to have had training in speaking and writing than in listening and reading.

I was once invited to observe a company chairman's monthly 'communications meeting' with the two principal trade-union representatives in his factory. For twenty minutes he spoke lucidly in a friendly, relaxed manner about the state of the business, the order book, some possible future problems. The trade unionists sat in silence, impassive. At the end, the chairman asked, 'Any questions?'

one of the union people raised a point of detail which the chairman answered, and the meeting ended.

As a presentation exercise, the chairman would probably have got top marks: he had been clear, concise, relaxed and efficient. If he had been talking to investment analysts or his senior managers, it might well have been a very successful 'communications' meeting. But as a communication exercise with the trade unionists, it failed at first base. There had been no meeting of minds. The chairman had assumed that to communicate he had only to transmit. In my view he would have done far better to invite the union representatives to tell him about the views and feelings of their members and the information that was of interest to them – in other words, he would have set himself up as a receiver, not a transmitter. Then there might have been a dialogue; an exchange of information that was of mutual interest and benefit.

Of course, if he had thought in those terms, he wouldn't have held the meeting in his enormous plush office around a heavy, expensive boardroom table; he would have gone to them, or found a neutral location where both parties could have been comfortable. (Not long afterwards, by the way, the union was out on strike again.)

Intent and effect

Looked at in this way we can begin to see a single communication as two, or more, events, not one: one event for the transmitter and one for each receiver. Only when the two events coincide, when what someone has heard is what I meant to say, has communication begun to happen.

But correct hearing and understanding of the content of the message is not enough for full communication. There also needs to be a matching between my purpose in telling that person (my 'intent') and the effect the message has on him or her.

The mismatch between 'intent' and 'effect' is a common cause of communication failure. It is particularly evident, for example, with 'constructive criticism'. Most of us would claim that our criticism is always constructive, drawing attention to what needs to be improved. For the recipient it is invariably painful, and the pain tends to drown out the constructive intent.

If we look at the 'intent' and 'effect' of a communication as two separate realities, we begin to make sense of otherwise baffling breakdowns in communication. They correspond to Schumacher's two translations: the transmitter may not be sufficiently adept in translating his or her intent into the appropriate words and gestures. Equally, the receiver's interpretation of what he or she sees and hears is conditioned by assumptions and frame of mind (particularly attitudes to the speaker).

The consequences of such breakdowns can be far reaching and cumulative. They immediately affect the personal relationships between the parties concerned and often provoke counter action or retaliation to deal with a negative effect. The retaliation is likely in its turn to have a negative effect, this time more intentional. Though the origins of the retaliation may be understandable, and justifiable, in terms of the negative effect of the first 'communication' (or more properly miscommunication), it will be totally mystifying and unjustified to the recipient, who is aware only of the constructive intent of the first transmission.

Any one such misunderstanding (unless resolved) affects the parties' views of each other; they may approach the next encounter in a wary, suspicious frame of mind, which increases the probability of misinterpreting the transmissions again. Good relationships depend on good communications; awareness of the potential gap between the intent and the effect can help to prevent misunderstandings and clear them up quickly when they do arise.

Extending the argument from the individual transaction to the collective communications within a working group, we can see how the quality of the communications is a major factor in creating the 'climate' or culture of the group. The prevailing climate will in turn affect the quality of communications in a self-reinforcing way.

I personally believe that much of the tension, hostility, non-cooperation and lack of commitment that exist in many organisations can be traced to failures in basic communications, to the gap between 'intent' and 'effect'. It is not a matter of human perversity or original sin; it is simple clumsiness, an inability to express our constructive intentions in ways that have a corresponding constructive effect.

As you start to bridge that gap, you begin to change the culture of the working environment, and the process becomes self-reinforcing in a positive direction. People begin to see each other in a positive light, listen with positive expectations, begin to hear the constructive intent, and start to respond to it. The process starts with the care and attention you bring to the individual communication.

A book as a communication exercise

There is a nice irony in writing a book about communication. A book itself is an exercise in communication, or attempted communication: the thoughts I wish to convey, translated into words and pictures that in my judgement are able to 'externalise my internal thoughts' (to paraphrase Dr Schumacher) and then launched into the ocean of competing transmissions, to be picked up and perused by the unseen, unknown reader at the bookstall, in the library or elsewhere.

The communication is only complete when you, the reader, have a faultless reception of my words and pictures and are in some way able to integrate them into your own thoughts (Dr Schumacher's 'second translation'). It is a daunting process. It is probably no accident that a moment ago I had the image of a man on a desert island tossing his message in a bottle into the sea, hoping it might be picked up!

The irony is that only if my transmitting skills are of a high order, and my judgements about the interests and backgrounds of my potential readers are broadly accurate, will what I want to communicate about communication actually get communicated and not just expressed! Moreover, if what I have to say about written communication in the book is to have any credibility I have to write in a way that is a model of my own precepts. Otherwise it will be a case of 'do as I say, not as I do'.

Because the book has to connect with an unknown, unseen readership, I have to make some assumptions about you, the potential reader. I will spell them out here, so that you can judge whether this might be for you or not:

My assumptions about you, the reader, are that

— although you have been communicating all your life, you have not previously given much thought or attention to the communication process (you are not a specialist in the field);

— you are interested in the possibility of improving your own effectiveness as a communicator, particularly as it relates to your work, although anything it contributes outside your work will also be welcome;

— you don't have a lot of time to spend ploughing through a lot of material that is not strictly essential for achieving that objective (improving your communication effectiveness);

— you are prepared in principle to try out some new approaches to your ways of communicating, without advance proof that they will necessarily work for you;

— you would like to be entertained as well as instructed as you read the book.

You don't have to fit totally with my assumptions. If you are broadly in sympathy with them, then we're in business — the business of shared responsibility communication.

2. Communication and the manager

The communication pattern of your job

If 'management' is the art of 'achieving results through other people' (or something of the kind – for our purposes it does not really matter which particular definition you adopt), communication is a key part of the job. A mental picture of a manager managing conjures up an image of someone interacting with others directly, speaking and listening, or indirectly, reading and writing. The only other activity that person engages in, as a manager, is thinking, with or without the aid of pencil and paper or computer terminal.

One estimate puts the proportion of the typical manager's time devoted to 'communication' at 70 per cent. If anything, I think that is on the low side: most managers I know do not spend 30 per cent of their working time on their own, neither reading, writing, dictating, nor on the phone.

More important than the general picture is your own individual communication pattern. Think back over your last working day and recall all the communication events in it. Then list (if you can!) each phone call, incoming and outgoing, each meeting, formal and informal, each document you read or scanned, each one you generated (letter, memo, telex, etc.). If it was a typical day, you will probably have a pretty lengthy and varied list – that is, if you can remember them all. Enough, I hope, to confirm that communicating, in the two senses of transmitting and receiving, is a major part of your job. It follows that if you can make significant improvements in your communicating skill and effectiveness, it should help you to do your job better.

If you are really dedicated to improving your communication skills, it is worth going a stage further and keeping a detailed communications log, over a week or two (or however long you feel is necessary to give a representative sample of your work pattern). The checklist below suggests the headings you might use for your log. Analysis of the data will show which are the predominant communication modes in your activity.

It is also possible to add a judgement of the quality of your performance for each mode of activity, to highlight where the greatest scope for improvement lies. Unfortunately this judgement has to be subjective; because of the two-sided nature of the communication process, both parties need to be involved in any reliable judgement of its success. You may think you have written a beautifully clear and lucid memo, but if the recipient has not understood it, or has not even read it, your memo has failed as a *communication* (as opposed to an *expression* of your views).

An alternative is to use your communication log to identify the principal partners in your communications process, and to review with them the quality of some sample communications. Make it clear that it is *your* part of the process you want to examine; they may be willing to help you do that, whereas they may not want to start researching their own communicating skills at this point. If they do, so much the better; given that communication is a shared activity, shared research makes a lot of sense. A suggested communications log is shown below: you may wish to adapt or modify it to suit your own situation.

However deeply or superficially you decide to record and analyse your communication activities, the result should be to heighten your awareness of their sheer volume and variety, and the central part they play in your activities.

Why communicate?

If communication is so large a part of our activity as a manager, it is worth pausing to reflect what we are trying to achieve by all this effort: how does communicating contribute to the achievement of our goals and objectives? If it does not do so, directly or indirectly, it

Communications log

Day/time	My role[1]	Activity[2]	Partner(s)	Purpose[3]	Medium[4]	Duration	Quality[5]

Notes:

1. Role is that of transmitter (T), receiver (R), or both (I) (as in any interactive transaction).
2. Activity is speaking, writing, listening/watching, reading or interactive (speaking and listening/watching).
3. Purpose is best described in your own words; be as specific as possible rather than use generalisations like 'get information'.
4. Medium distinguishes formal and informal meetings, phone calls, letters/memos, etc.
5. Your subjective judgement of the effectiveness of your part in the transaction, perhaps on a scale of 1–5 (an optional column).

is superfluous, and can be eliminated (or retained as a form of self-indulgence, not a necessary part of the job).

It follows that communication at work (as opposed to the purely social situation) needs to be oriented to action: in some way, directly or indirectly, it will potentially contribute to someone doing something they would not, or might not, have done without it. There are a lot of loopholes in this requirement, necessarily, because this is not an exact science. Thus 'directly or indirectly', 'potentially' and 'might' all open the door to a variety of interpretations in any particular case. Nevertheless, it establishes an important principle: *at work, we are not communicating for the fun of it, but to help us get something done*.

It is important, because we live in a world of communication overload that threatens to swamp us. We can easily spend a lot of our time in communication activities which do not actually contribute to the job: anything which can help control the situation is valuable.

So a good question to ask of any communication activity (as of any management activity), is 'Why am I doing this?' If the relationship to the job is immediate and obvious, and the communication is directly functional, there is no problem; the difficulty arises when the connection is indirect.

There is a whole nebulous area of 'keeping in touch, keeping informed, maintaining personal relationships' which falls into this category of indirect and potentially useful communicating activity. It is clearly an essential part of the manager's job, but because it is ill-defined and also to some extent a matter of personal predilection and style, it is difficult to control. If not controlled, it can become almost infinitely time-consuming.

Some personal guidelines of my own are listed below. I offer them as benchmarks from which you can evolve your own, because they will depend on both your personality and your situation. These work well for me (I don't claim to observe them without fail!):

— make personal contact (face to face or by phone) with those with whom I have a direct reporting relationship, up or down, every week;

— walk the job, that is, the site area for which I am responsible every day I am there;

— visit remote sites at a regular planned frequency (including customers and suppliers);

— give personal contact priority over paperwork.

The common thread running through these principles is the relationship building/maintaining element, as opposed to the functional, information content. The most significant contact is on the social/emotional level and the content may just as well be social as work related. If the personal relationships are good, the relevant information will tend to flow almost of its own accord: conversely, if the relationship is not good, the information will be suppressed or blocked out.

Because contacts of this kind are predominantly to do with personal relationships, what is being said is much less important than what is being communicated by tone of voice and non-verbal signals. For this reason, face-to-face contact, where possible, is twice as valuable as the phone. Similarly a visit to them provides the opportunity to pick up additional signals from their environment – the demeanour of the other people, the appearance of the site and all the other intangibles which go to make up the atmosphere of a particular workplace.

Equally, there is a high premium on non-verbal communication skills: the ability to see and observe and to pick up the nuances of the tone in which things are said. And the ability to create the impression you want to create through your own appearance, bearing and tone. 'The medium is the message' and in these cases *you* are both medium and message.

All of this makes this kind of communicating difficult to control. When does relationship-building degenerate into mere gossip and chit-chat? At what point do diminishing returns set in for the time invested? I confess I have no satisfactory general answers to these questions. Fairly tight scheduling of the time made available provides control of a sort – provided you can correctly judge in advance the time required, and this is not always possible. Regular social occasions are also valuable in providing a more relaxed, informal exchange to supplement the strictly work-related contact – provided that they are organised to be genuinely enjoyable and not an additional chore on top of the job itself.

Planning your communication

If communication is so large a part of a manager's job, it makes sense to go about it in a planned, systematic way, with clarity about the objectives and the methods to be used in each significant transaction. Clearly not every communication will need to be planned; there are many trivial or routine transactions which can be allowed to go through automatically.

The significant ones are those that recur frequently, or take up a large amount of time, or carry substantial prizes or penalties for success or failure. Your communications log (see page 115) will help you identify which these are. Or you may be able to identify them straight off without detailed analysis.

Either way, your communication planning for individual events will be easier if you have previously thought through a coherent communications strategy for yourself, as a subset of your total job strategy. Assuming you have already defined your job objectives (and if you have not it is high time you did so), what is the communication strategy that will best help you achieve those objectives?

As I wrote the above, I realised I had not done it for myself. So I took a break to do it, and discovered that I was neglecting one important area of activity. The exercise took less than half an hour; the strategy need only consist of a few sentences (say, four to six) setting out your general intentions in the area of communication. I recommend it to you.

You will probably find (as I did) that your strategy has been expressed in 'transmitting' rather than 'receiving' terms. It is natural enough to think in terms of transmitting activities, since these are the ones which are generally easier to initiate than the receiving ones – you can only listen when someone is prepared to talk to you!

However, we have already seen that we all do more 'receiving' than 'transmitting' and the strategy should give at least some consideration to how I will use my communication receiving activities to help achieve my job objectives. (If they are not going to help, why am I doing them?)

When it comes to planning individual communications, it is again the transmitting activities that are most susceptible to planning, because we are initiating them. However, many of the receiving activities are also a conscious decision on your part – like reading, or attending a presentation or lecture.

The only communication events which are necessarily unplanned are the interactive ones initiated by someone else – the incoming phone call, someone stopping by the desk to chat, the chance encounter in the corridor. Many of these will be trivial enough not to need planning, but it is easy for them to slide imperceptibly into deeper water. As they do so they are liable to become unsatisfactory for want of proper planning and appropriate structures or methods. When this is beginning to happen, it's worth calling a halt or time out to reschedule the meeting for another time, allowing for proper planning or preparation. 'Sounds like this is sufficiently important to give some time to sorting it out properly. How about four o'clock this afternoon?' Or, 'I don't have the information to hand – I'll call you back in an hour's time.' There is no need to allow yourself to be caught on the hop over something important.

Planning the communication will cover the two dimensions of subject matter and method, that is, the content (what) and the process (how). It is not uncommon to plan the content, in the sense of collecting the data, getting your thoughts in order, and generally 'doing your homework'. Planning the *process* is much less common, and at least as rewarding.

It involves considering the alternative ways the communication might proceed, and selecting those which seem most likely to achieve your objective. To do this you need to be clear about your objective, the answer to the question 'Why am I doing this?' One way to get to this answer is to imagine that the communication has been completed and you are very pleased with the outcome. What would you have at the end of the communication that you did not have at the beginning? Let this be your objective.

Then decide your method. First, the medium – face-to-face meeting (his place or yours?), phone call or memo/telex. Then the procedure: some of the possible options for different kinds of meeting are described in Chapter 6. But there is no need to restrict yourself to these; draw up whatever plan seems appropriate in the light of your own experience. Having done this, it is worth adding 'criteria for success' – how will you know whether you achieved your objective or not?

I suggest you write all this down, along the lines shown in your meeting plan (see p. 120). It need not be lengthy, but it will focus your thinking and send you into action with a clear idea of what you are going to do. Afterwards you can refer back to it to see how well your plan worked, so that you will be wiser next time.

The next step is to implement the plan, which immediately raises the question of whether you disclose it to the other parties to the communication. Although there may be situations where you may choose not to because the climate is adversarial rather than co-operative, my preference is overwhelmingly for disclosure, with a willingness to modify it to accommodate alternative ideas. Only in this way can you establish a mutually agreed process with the possibility of a genuine meeting of minds.

The alternative, that is, imposing your process plan without disclosing it or getting agreement to it, is potentially manipulative.

Meeting plan

Meeting with	*on*	
objective(s)		
method		
medium		
criteria of success		

You may get the result you want, but in doing so you may damage the relationship through a sense of resentment that in some way they have been out-manoeuvred. Besides, the other parties may also have a different process plan of their own, which they too have not disclosed. You will then be in the ridiculous situation of engaging in a communication exercise with different ground rules, almost as though you are speaking two different languages. It is like two people going on court, one to play tennis and the other badminton, and wondering why they have an unsatisfactory game.

I see this sort of thing happen often enough, and I ascribe it to lack of planning on either side. If either or both have worked out a plan, it surely makes sense to put it on the table and get agreement to it.

Researching your communication process

Modern technology, in the form of tape-recorders and more particularly video-recorders, has provided the means for studying communication processes in a depth that was never previously possible. Much of the material in this book is derived from analysing videotapes of meetings with the people involved in them.

Remarkably little use has been made of the technology for these purposes, probably because its original applications were in quite different fields. Thus the audio tape-recorder was initially used for dictating, as an alternative to the shorthand typist, and subsequently as an entertainment medium instead of the record player. Even when it has been used to record meetings or phone calls, the purpose has been to capture the content, not to research the process.

Television, from the beginning, has been seen as an entertainment and advertising medium, a follow-on from radio. More recently, domestic video cameras and tape-recorders have been taking over the role of home movies, to record baby's first steps, weddings and other family occasions. These uses, mostly in entertainment, have directed attention away from its potential as a serious research and learning medium. (If computers had first been used for video games, would they have been taken seriously as business machines?)

It takes quite a mental effort to reframe the tape-recorder and video tape-recorder as scientific research instruments. That is what they are, or can be, when used in this way: they provide data on the communications process that was never previously available by other means.

In the history of science, whenever a new research instrument comes into use, a new field of knowledge opens up. Thus Louis Pasteur used the microscope to create the science of biology. In our own day the radio telescope opened up new dimensions in astronomy. In the same way, sound and video recording gives us totally new insights into human communication.

Videotape research is 'revolutionary' because it enables us to study at the same time the two parts of the transaction, the transmitting and receiving, and to do so repeatedly if necessary. Hitherto we had to rely on our experience, which covered only half the transaction; the other half we had to guess at. We knew the intent of our transmissions, but not their effect on the recipient; we knew the effect of the recipient's transmissions on us, and not his or her intent.

Now it is possible to see and hear ourselves as others see and hear us. Robbie Burns's prayer – 'Would that God the giftie gie us/ To see ourselves as others see us' – has been answered.

When we do see and hear ourselves for the first time, the result is universally shock, horror and amazement. Is that really my voice, do I really sound like that, do I really look like that? Yes, you do, and that is how the rest of the world experiences you every day.

The degree of shock is a measure of the difference between our self-perception and the reality perceived by the recipients of our transmissions. The gap between the intent and the effect of our communications becomes less surprising when we see what it is like to be on the receiving end of our own transmissions.

The tape also makes it possible to examine the transaction with the other parties involved. As they review an exchange, both parties will probably be able to recall how it was for them at the time, for example, 'When you said that, I felt depressed, because . . .' 'That wasn't my intention at all. What I was trying to do was . . .'

Having established that there was a mismatch, it then becomes possible to explore the reasons why it might have arisen and, more constructively, how it might be handled differently next time to make the communication more effective. Over a period of time it is possible to identify recurring situations that need to be changed, calling for changes in habitual practices, on the part of both transmitter and receiver.

Gradually you can develop a self-awareness of your own communication style, make deliberate changes to it and monitor their impact on your effectiveness. The practicality of doing this will vary according to your individual situation. There should be little difficulty in tape-recording your half of your phone conversations, for example. It needs no permission from anyone else, and you will be astonished to discover how different your way of speaking is according to who is on the other end of the phone.

My colleagues in the United States conducted an experiment on these lines with a group of managers from the same company. They met to listen to each others' tapes. As the first one was played, another member of the group said immediately, 'Bet I know who you're talking to' – and was correct. Surprised, they attempted to do the same with the other tapes. Every time they were successfully able to identify the unheard partner in the phone conversation, solely from the changes in the tone of voice and manner of speaking – authoritative, deferential, friendly, hostile, etc. (I had a parallel experience when talking to the chief executive of a large British company in his office, when a phone call came through from the president of the corporation in the United States. Immediately the strong, confident, rather aggressive man I was talking to was transformed into a deferential, placatory and altogether less impressive figure!)

To record the complete communication either on sound or video requires the co-operation of the other parties – obviously it is undesirable to record people without their permission. Preferably the research should be a shared activity, because the transactions can be examined in the light of the experience of both parties. If that is not possible, it is still worthwhile to listen to it on your own, if only to discover how much is new and surprising – things that you missed when the conversation was actually in progress.

Video-taping is a bigger step, with a bigger pay-off; it is twice as rich in data, because it contains the non-verbals as well as the tone.

With today's equipment it is technically easy, and not particularly expensive, to set up a camera and recorder in any office. However, it is more obtrusive than a simple tape-recorder, and other people may be reluctant to be videotaped (they can find it threatening).

For formal meetings, involving a significant number of people, video-taping is potentially an extremely powerful research tool. It is not too fanciful, in my view, to see a video camera and recorder as a permanent feature of any boardroom or meeting room, switched on as a matter of routine for any meeting (we do this in my company). You do not need an operator for the camera; set up in a fixed position, it will provide a good enough record for research purposes, without the distraction or editing introduced by an operator.

The tape is then available for review and learning. If the meeting was successful, that is, productive, enjoyable, time-efficient, what was it about our way of conducting it, and ourselves, that made it so? If we know, we can repeat it, and make all our meetings equally successful. Conversely, if we are not pleased with the meeting, or part of it, we can use the tape to identify what went wrong and suggest changes in our way of operating that will prevent a recurrence.

I am often asked whether the known presence of the video camera affects the behaviour of the participants so as to make it unrepresentative of their normal behaviours. At the conscious level, it would appear not to; participants say that once they get absorbed in the subject matter, they forget about the presence of the camera.

At an unconscious level, it might be different. When I ask groups how typical of their normal meetings a particular video-taped session was, I sometimes get the answer 'better behaved, more disciplined, possibly due to the fact we knew we were being video-taped'. There is also a curious phenomenon in our own internal meetings – when things go wrong, and we want to examine the tape to find out why, we often find that it has not been recorded, for some accident such as the tape running out, camera has not been switched on, etc. I have an open mind, but the coincidence is suspicious.*

But even if the video does bias behaviour in a positive direction, that does not detract from its value. The improved behaviour is a gain in itself, and there is still plenty to learn from the tape of a better than average meeting – in particular, just how much scope there is for further improvement.

In practice, if you regularly video-tape all your formal meetings, there is no need to review the tape every time. Nor need you spend a

* I suspect there is a similar factor at work in the House of Commons' determined refusal for so many years to have its proceedings televised!

lot of time doing it — ten or fifteen minutes spent revisiting a particularly interesting episode is all that is needed. And the time investment will be amply repaid by the time saved in subsequent meetings!

Even when it is not possible to have a video or audio tape of your communication, it is still valuable to go through a review process after important communication events. If you had a formal plan for the event (see page 120), you can reflect on how well or otherwise the plan worked. To what extent in fact did you follow the plan? What parts of it would you retain if you were doing it again and what parts would you change?

Similarly, at the end of a formal meeting, it is useful to ask all the participants to review their experience and feed back their comments, preferably in writing, anonymously if necessary. Doing so begins to create an awareness of the communications issues and the potential for improving the communication performance, as a result of the feedback.

Any review process, whether from sound or video tape or from memory, needs to be structured as a positive learning experience and not allowed to become negative or critical. Make a point of identifying all the successful aspects of the event, before going on to consider what you would wish to change and how you might change it. This procedure keeps the review balanced; it also avoids the danger of inadvertently losing some good aspects as you seek to change something else (throwing away the baby with the bathwater).

Video in particular needs to be handled in a positive and constructive way, because it is such a powerful feedback tool. The dismay experienced by everyone seeing themselves on video for the first time is a symptom, I believe, of the negative emphasis in our culture and conditioning. People are so shocked by themselves because they are focusing on the aspects they dislike, without giving themselves credit for all the positive aspects of their behaviour. Unless you actively redress this balance by acknowledging all the positive aspects of your communication performance, watching video becomes too painful to be an effective research and learning medium.

The power of video as a research tool has been acknowledged independently in *Our Masters' Voices* by Max Atkinson, who has applied it with fascinating results to the ways politicians 'go about their business of trying to win our hearts and minds and votes'. He says categorically, 'with the aid of audio and video tape-recorders, the workings of various subtle processes can be brought more closely into view, whereupon it becomes possible to begin to answer questions that previously seemed unanswerable'.

My own experience of applying audio and video research to communications at work (and that of colleagues who have been doing it for twenty-five years) exactly parallels Atkinson's. The effect is revolutionary. For the manager it means that a great deal of conventional wisdom, the accumulated experience of successful managers, needs to be re-examined. Many of the assumptions that managers make about their communications are seen to be self-fulfilling mindsets – for example, the belief that it is necessary to manipulate meetings to achieve the results you want.

If you find that some of the views expressed in this book run counter to your own experience, do not immediately reject them on that account. It may be that some new knowledge has become available since you formed your current habits of communication, and that you have something to gain by trying out alternatives.

The communication climate

A major factor in the quality of any communication is the climate in which it takes place. 'Climate' is of course a metaphor to describe the prevailing attitudes and habitual behaviours of the group within which the communication is being attempted. As a metaphor, it is not particularly precise, but the principal characteristic that affects the communication is the degree of friendliness/hostility that exists between transmitters and receivers (particularly in the face-to-face situation). At the extremes, the differences are quite clear; the receivers can be characterised as:

Hostile	*Friendly*
Critical	Sympathetic
Sceptical	Open
Challenging	Supportive
Intolerant	Tolerant

In turn these characteristics affect the speaker (or writer), as follows:

Hostile environment	*Friendly environment*
Cautious	Relaxed
Guarded	Open
Defensive	Honest
Selective	Revealing

It is clear that if the quality of communication is all that mattered, we should try to create a friendly, supportive climate. But the communication is a means to an end, and the end may well be better served by poor-quality communication than good – a communication designed to obscure or mislead rather than illuminate. An answer to a parliamentary question, or almost any party political debate, are cases in point, but they are not limited to the world of party politics – management has its own politics!

The underlying issue is whether the manager's role is essentially adversarial (where one party wins and the other loses), or co-operative (where both parties can win). I believe strongly that it is co-operative: it is about the creation of wealth, through a system of specialisation, which has to be mutually beneficial to all the parties engaged in it, if it is to endure. The concept is nicely captured by the Mars Corporation's 'mutuality' principle: 'A mutual benefit is a shared benefit; a shared benefit is a lasting benefit.'

If 'mutuality of benefit' is the manager's goal, how is it that so much behaviour, together with associated communication practices, is adversarial? Primarily, I believe, because the role models we are presented with in our society are all drawn from the adversarial mould. Party politics I have already mentioned – what a shocking example of non-communication it provides to the country, because of its adversarial character. (If you doubt this, try listening to the broadcast of parliamentary proceedings). The legal system is likewise set up for adversarial conflict between prosecution and defence. So also is the television interviewer who tries to put his guest (often a politician) on the spot, for the purpose of entertainment, as opposed to genuine communication.

The adversarial models extend deep into the education system. Every university has its union society, a training ground for aspiring politicians, and schools have their debating societies – debating again being an adversarial activity. It is hardly surprising that new entrants to management, particularly graduates, arrive with a communication style that is essentially adversarial in its underlying assumptions. These assumptions are so deeply ingrained, and so unconscious, that it comes as a surprise for them to discover that there is an alternative and superior style of communication.

To be fair, the adversarial – critical and challenging – style developed in and practised by the educational system has a worthy purpose: to develop high standards of rigour, clarity and quality of thinking. The assumption, which I do not accept, is that this is the best and most efficient way to develop such standards.

Equally, there are business organisations that seem to thrive on a challenging adversarial style of behaviour. They do so, I believe, by recruiting from that minority of the population that can cope with such an environment. Even so, there is a substantial cost; much of the energy of those talented individuals goes into protecting themselves from attack, and the communication style is guarded and consequently inefficient. My experience of introducing alternative, more co-operative ways of working to such people convinces me that it is possible to achieve much better-quality communication without any loss in the quality and rigour of the thinking.

So far, I have been talking of the communications climate as though it is a given, outside your control. One of the dangers of the 'climate' metaphor is the implication that it has to be accepted, like the weather, as a fact of life that you can adapt to but you cannot change.

The communications 'climate' (or more appropriately 'culture') is not like that. It is itself partly the result of the way in which communication has been carried out in the past. Each new communication reinforces the existing culture or begins to change it. You have it in your power at least to propose the communication protocol or ground rules that you would like to follow. The other parties can accept, reject or propose modifications to your proposal, and you have the opportunity to decide whether you have an acceptable basis on which to proceed with your communication or not.

Two examples come to mind to illustrate what I mean.

Gordon Mandry (then of the Manchester Business School) starting a presentation to a group of senior managers, said, 'I'll take questions as they arise, on the basis that straight questions will get straight answers, and dirty questions will get dirty answers.' There was laughter, but no dissent, and he certainly did not get any dirty questions, from a group I knew to be quite capable of producing them!

In the second case, I was making a sales call on a prospect I had not met before. I said, 'I'd like to give you a general description of what we do, then hear about your activities in the same field, to identify if there are areas of common interest and if so explore them in more depth. If not, we will end the meeting.' He replied, 'I'm happy to hear about what you do, but I'm not sure I want to tell you what we're doing.' 'OK,' I said, 'I'll start with my piece, then you can decide in the light of it whether you want to tell me anything or not.'

In both cases an explicit communication contract was being entered into: establishing the contract can go a long way towards establishing the climate you want, at least temporarily, for the duration of that transaction.

The fundamental contract for any communication to be successful is that both parties, transmitters and receivers, want the communication to take place. If they do not, there is little point in proceeding ('none so deaf as those that will not hear'). This contract is rarely made explicit; it is assumed to exist.

Yet a very large proportion of communications are unsolicited, and the assumption that the receiver wants to receive them may be quite erroneous. A recipient bombarded with communications he or she does not want can be forgiven for reacting in a hostile manner (consider the common attitude to junk mail). In this way the communication itself is influencing the climate for future transmissions of a similar kind from the same source.

Another major way in which you influence the climate is the model you yourself provide, and the effect your way of communicating has on the recipients. You can 'set the tone' in the way you interact with people. If you are perceived to be patronising, to talk down, you will be resented, and the resentment will be manifest in sullen silence or overt hostility. If you are considered dogmatic and close-minded, expect equal dogmatism in return. (Note that it is the perceived effect of your style, not your intention, that matters.)

Conversely, if you are prepared to accept disagreement as an interesting alternative view of the world, worth exploring for what you might learn from it, you set an example of open-mindedness which may well be followed.

In fact, people very often respond to the expectations you communicate to them, either directly or indirectly. To take a common example from my own work, if I want someone to identify the good points of an idea, I say, 'I'd like you to tell us all the things you like about that idea,' and the person does. If I say, 'Does that idea have any good points?', I may very well get the answer, 'No.' In the first case, I have communicated an expectation that the person will be able to find good points; in the second, I have implied that he or she might not be able to.

If you can communicate to your communication partner the expectation that the communication will proceed in a constructive, co-operative way, it probably will. Here, as elsewhere, positive expectations can be self-fulfilling.

So the communications 'climate' is to some degree a matter of choice: you can attempt to establish a style and a contract which create an acceptable climate, or decide not to proceed with the communication in an unacceptable climate. Or reinforce the existing climate by behaving in conventional ways. The choice is yours. Good luck!

3. Communication components and channels

Components of communication

In all this communicating activity, what precisely are we trying to transmit, and what is actually being received? It is worth being precise about this because different types of material call for different modes and styles of communication, and the different types of material are of different value, according to the situation under consideration. Moreover, without a common understanding between transmitter and receiver about what kind of material is being exchanged, the chances of successful communication are poor indeed.

I find it useful to distinguish the following categories:

— factual information;
— opinions (including forecasts, interpretations, value judgements, etc.);
— goals, wishes, objectives, strategies, plans;
— ideas;
— feelings.

Factual information deals essentially with the past and present; not the future.* In principle, a fact is verifiable; the future, by definition, is not, until it ceases to be the future. So 'it is raining' is a factual statement; 'it is going to rain' is an opinion, no matter how strong the probability.

* From the Latin, a fact is 'that which has been done'.

Opinions are by definition subjective; they reflect the different ways in which we see the world. It is possible, indeed normal, for two people to look at the same facts and draw different conclusions from them, interpreting them in the light of their different experience.

Goals, wishes, objectives, strategies, plans fall naturally together, because they are related to the future and imply value judgements about what is desirable. Again they are subjective (and might be considered a subset of opinions). Like-minded people can share common goals and objectives, and indeed must do so for an organisation to have unity of purpose.

Ideas are thoughts about what might be done to achieve certain objectives. They may range from known solutions about what has worked in the past to entirely novel and untried courses of action. Because they relate to the future, there can be no absolute certainty that they will achieve the objective (even the known solutions of the past may not work next time).

Feelings are totally personal and may be communicated either as information ('I am feeling anxious') or more directly and powerfully as emotional outbursts, tears, laughter, blows, etc. The transmission and reception of feelings is much more of a non-verbal than a verbal activity.

Running through these categories is a distinction between what might be called 'subjective truth' and 'objective truth'. Subjective truth is a truth about me: my feelings, my values, my wishes, my judgements about what will happen in the future. Objective truth deals with the external world and can be independently verified.

An objective 'truth' can be mistaken. I may have a view about the external world which can be contradicted by independent evidence, and if it is brought to my attention I will no doubt change my belief.

But most subjective truths are matters of opinions, values and beliefs that are in principle not capable of verification. Consequently it is meaningless to think in terms of 'right' and 'wrong' about such matters: a subjective truth is right for the individual who thinks that way (and others like him) and wrong for those who do not. Any attempt to resolve the issue and decide who is 'right' is likely to be a waste of time.

Yet many of the discussions I observe among people at work are essentially of this kind. In my view they are generally a waste of the time and energy of the people involved, and rarely achieve anything. We live in a very opinionated world where most people seem to have opinions about most things, and an urge to express them. Yet comparatively few of us are interested in the opinions of most other people on most things. As a result there is a great excess of opinions expressed over the demand for them, a communications mismatch that can be avoided, thereby freeing up a good deal of lost time and energy.

Questions

Questions and answers are a sufficiently large component of most interactive communications to warrant separate consideration. Significantly, they do not fit neatly into the categories listed above (facts, opinions, ideas, wishes, feelings), because they can be used to communicate any of those components, but indirectly.

Questions are inherently ambiguous, because they may be asked for many different purposes. If you doubt this, invite colleagues or friends to help you draw up a list of the reasons why people ask questions. They will probably start with reasons such as:

— To obtain information.
— To clarify understanding

and to continue (perhaps after a pause) with other questions such as:

— To draw attention to something someone has overlooked.
— To show that one is on the ball.
— To interrupt the flow.
— To check whether an idea is feasible.
— To change the direction of the discussion.
— To see if a person knows what he or she is talking about.
— To lead that person into a trap.
— To trip the speaker.
— To answer (or avoid answering) another question.

If a question can arise from so many different motives, many of them hostile or otherwise dangerous, it is difficult to know the reason behind an individual question. We guess, make inferences from tone of voice or previous knowledge of the questioner – and stay on our guard! Guarded and defensive, or aggressively counter-attacking, is the typical posture of someone who is being questioned.

What is true of the single question is even more true of a barrage of questions. And questions seldom come singly; one begets another, and they spread round the group like an epidemic. Apply the collective label 'interrogation', with its sinister overtones, and it is easy to see why our response to questions is guarded.

The anxiety comes from the uncertainty about the intent of the questioner; we don't know what his or her purpose is. So the anxiety is just as likely to be triggered by an innocent, constructive request for information or clarification as by a devious destructive question.

George Prince (the chairman of the Synectics Corporation) estimates from his research into thousands of video-taped meetings, that approximately '70 per cent of questions are with an underlying intent to put pressure on the target of the question'; another 15 per cent mask an idea (the question has been asked to check whether the idea is feasible, before voicing the idea).

It follows that the ambiguity of questions can be eliminated by identifying the purpose behind them. As a questioner, you can declare your purpose as you ask the question: 'my reason for asking is . . .' As the recipient of a question, you can legitimately respond with 'If you tell me why you are asking, I can answer the question appropriately.' Or you can make your own guess and check it out: 'I presume you are asking because . . . Is that correct?'

Coming clean about the purpose of questions in this way begins to eliminate that 70 per cent of questions that put pressure on the recipient and begins to change the culture from an adversarial one to a more open and co-operative one.

Most people have difficulty in believing that questions can be destructive; we have all been taught that it is a good way to learn and find out about a problem or a situation. I can only suggest that you observe your own experience of questioning and being questioned and experiment with the idea of identifying the purpose of questions in the way described above. I think you will find that you will reduce your QQ (question quotient) and improve your communications and working relationships with those you interact with.

New and second-hand information

With success rates for face-to-face communication around 25 per cent (or even as high as 50 per cent with improved communication skills), it is clear that the quality of information can deteriorate rapidly as it is passed on through intermediaries. Simple arithmetic shows that with a 25 per cent success rate, at the second transfer the probability of success is 25 per cent of 25 per cent, that is, 6½ per cent – sixteen to one against, in racing terms. Even with 50 per cent success rate, we get down to these odds at the third transfer.

Clearly, passing on information by word of mouth through several stages is likely to result in a garbled message. 'Send reinforcements, we're going to advance' will almost certainly become 'Send three and fourpence, we're going to a dance', or something equally inaccurate. If you doubt this, try the experiment of passing a message round a small group, one person at a time, and observe how it gets changed at each stage.

Whenever a message is to be passed on, written back-up (or something equally permanent like an audio or video tape) is essential. John Garnett, of the Industrial Society, lays down the following rules for his briefing groups systems:

— wherever anything is to be passed on, note-taking is obligatory;

— when something needs to be passed through three or more levels of management, a brief setting out the main points should be provided. (Personally I would say *two* or more levels of management.)

While this danger may be well understood in the context of *transmitting* information, it is much less obvious in the information-receiving process. Yet a great deal of the material we receive is second-hand at best; often it will have passed through many more than two hands. To the extent that it has been passed on in writing, there is a safeguard, so long as the *original* is transferred unchanged. Usually it will have been 'improved' at each stage – condensed, edited, annotated, amplified, etc., to the point where the original piece of first-hand information is unrecognisable.

A manager receives a great deal of second-hand information – his or her in-tray is full of it. Go through your own in-tray one day and sort it out into first-hand and the rest. If there is anything of importance in the second-hand batch (and there may well be), check it out with the prime source – that is, if you can find it; it may require some detective work.

In a hierarchy of the kind that most managers work in, there is a particular danger arising out of the tendency to 'tell them what they want to hear': the material is re-presented to make it acceptable, to 'get it through' the next level of management. When this happens, the person at the top gets a very distorted picture. I have two examples, one from my own experience, the other (dare I say it?) second-hand.

When I worked in a large multi-national corporation, I visited my opposite numbers in the United States to exchange information and experience. I was particularly proud of a simulation model my team had developed. I thought it might be useful to the Americans and mentioned it to the vice-president. 'Oh, yes,' he said, 'we've got one of those. Talk to Joe about it.' I went to see Joe. 'I understand you have a simulation model . . .' 'Yes,' said Joe, 'I'm not sure we've got all the bugs out of it yet; have a word with Harry.' Harry said, 'It isn't actually working yet – Bill will tell you how far he's got with it.' Eventually I found Bill. 'That thing?' he said. 'We gave up on that months ago – far too difficult to do what they wanted.'

And neither Bill, nor Harry, nor Joe, nor the VP were the slightest bit interested in our model – but that's another story, called 'Not Invented Here'.

Here is the second example. A director of another American multi-national was surprised to discover that his corporation owned a small company in one of the smaller European countries, with a 5 per cent share of a static market, outside the mainstream of the corporation's business. He was curious to find out how they came to own such an anomalous business, and decided to trace the steps that led to the acquisition.

What he found out (so he told me) was that the original proposal had in fact stated that the company had a 5 per cent share of a static market. At successive levels of management the proposition had been 'improved' and the proposition was finally sold on a prospective 25 per cent share of a market growing at 20 per cent per annum – a much more glamorous deal. At each management level the 'improvements' might have been justified as changes in presentation; cumulatively they were monstrous.

At the everyday level, a great deal of second-hand information comes by word of mouth. Some of this is essential message-switching. Somebody phones when you are not in and leaves a message. If the message is immediately written down, and what is written is checked back with the sender, the communication will be effective. In my own small company, we keep a central message book for this purpose; it is also useful as a general information source about 'what's going on', through which people can hear about developments that may affect them.

However, if the everyday, verbally transmitted information relates to interpersonal matters, we are on dangerous ground. 'I hear that Mary is having problems with John over his timekeeping' sounds harmless enough as a passing piece of conversation, but in reality is quite insidious. It raises the questions, 'Why is he telling me this?' 'What does it have to do with him, or me?' 'Where did he hear it?' 'Who told him and why?' Unless there are satisfactory answers to these questions, the remark is mere gossip, and dangerous gossip at that. Dangerous not only because of the scope it provides for distortion and malice, but because it intrudes on the working relationship between Mary and John. If there is in fact such a problem, it is for the two of them to sort out, face to face, without the involvement of third parties unless they both feel a third party can help. Only if they are unable to resolve it between themselves should it be referred to a higher level of management.

In my company, we have established the principle of 'direct dealing'; if you have a problem with what someone else is doing, you take it up directly with them. Nine times out of ten it can be resolved without involving anyone else.

Too often in our society and our businesses, people baulk at this approach: they 'don't like to make a fuss', they worry about hurting someone's feelings, or they are afraid of a possible reaction. But the problem has to find expression, so they talk about it to a sympathetic third party. The third party, once in possession of the information, is under irresistible pressure to pass it on, either through an urge to be helpful, or to liven up an otherwise uneventful day. Gossip is a great source of entertainment, but a thoroughly unreliable source of information, particularly about other people.

A story from my own experience illustrates the point. In the late 1950s I did a piece of research about the British export trade, in which I came to a tentative and highly qualified conclusion that about forty companies generated 30 per cent of the total volume. The research was not published, but that particular conclusion was quoted with its qualifications in a letter to *The Times* by my boss, Sir Roger Falk (at the time that the Prime Minister Harold Macmillan declared that 'exporting is fun'). Some years later, I was surprised to read in a speech by Harold Wilson that 'Board of Trade figures show that forty companies generate 30 per cent of export volume'. I questioned the source of the data and discovered that there were still no official figures, but my own highly tentative estimates had acquired apparent authority through the columns of *The Times* and multiple repetition.

Words, tone and non-verbals

The words we use are only one kind of 'symbol' by which we try to convey our meaning to the listener; we also use non-verbal symbols such as gesture and intonation.

An American psychologist, Albert Mehrabian, attempted to

measure the relative importance of the three channels, words, tone of voice and other non-verbals (gestures, facial expressions, posture changes – commonly referred to as 'body language'), when there was inconsistency between messages being conveyed by the different channels. He came to the startling conclusion that the words were relatively unimportant – creating less than 10 per cent of the impact, compared with nearly 40 per cent from the tone of voice and over 50 per cent from the 'body language'.

This ranking comes as a shock to anyone like myself whose formal education has put a heavy emphasis on the skilful use of words. Unless your tone of voice and your body language are reinforcing rather than contradicting the words you are using, the message will not get through. Or as the song says, 'It ain't what you say, it's the way that you say it.'

If you have difficulty in accepting the primacy of tone and non-verbals in the face-to-face encounter, try this experiment. Imagine a husband/wife exchanging the words, 'You're back.' Think of the range of messages those words could convey, from ecstasy to hatred, via relief, anxiety, apathy, etc. – all derived from the tone and the body language. For the first twelve months of our lives all our communicating – transmitting and receiving – is done via tone of voice and non-verbals, because we are not able to talk! Perhaps it is hardly surprising we come to rely heavily, without being aware of it, on our non-verbal listening, particularly to pick up the emotional messages.

A great deal of communication can take place without any words at all. The raised eyebrow, the curled lip, the frown, the glare, all say a great deal; so also can more obvious physical gestures – the arm around the shoulders, the pat on the back, the squeeze of the hand – and posture changes, shifts in position, etc.

Eloquent as they all are, they suffer from two disadvantages in the management context: they are largely out of our control, and they are open to serious misinterpretation. As managers, we are putting out non-verbal signals all the time we are dealing with people face to face, without knowing what those signals are or how they are being interpreted.

Today, we can use video feedback to discover our most typical non-verbal signals, and most of us are pretty shaken by the discovery (see page 121). I believe such self-awareness is valuable in giving us a general sense of what the recipients of our non-verbal signals are likely to be experiencing. It can suggest a general direction for changes in style – for example more relaxed, more assertive, more patient.

But is it fatal to allow self-awareness to spill over into self-

consciousness and try to change specific non-verbal signals. It will be seen as contrived and the impression will be one of dishonesty. A colleague once told me I should smile more. As a general direction, it was good advice – I appeared over-serious, more serious than I felt in fact. But a smile is only genuine when you are feeling relaxed and happy: a conscious deliberate smile will look bogus. (Fortunately I am more relaxed these days and do smile more!)*

How far, and with what success, you can deliberately change your non-verbal signals is clearly illustrated by politicians who have been coached by professionals in the way they come across to the public. The most striking case is Margaret Thatcher, who has used voice tuition to lower the pitch of her voice and slow down her rate of speech, had dental capping treatment to make her smile more attractive, and adopted hair-styles, clothes, jewellery and make-up recommended by TV experts. With what effect, you must judge for yourself.

The interpretation problem arises partly because the gestures are potentially so rich in meaning, and partly because the recipient's interpretation will be affected by his or her own state of mind and attitude towards the transmitter. There was, for example, a most expressive incident towards the end of the 1985 US Masters Golf Tournament. As Seve Ballasteros and Bernhard Langer moved to the final hole, Seve put his arm round Bernhard's shoulder in a gesture which seemed to convey that he was conceding defeat, congratulating Langer on his achievement and offering support over the final hole (where Langer might still have lost ground to other contenders). A rich gesture indeed, which received glowing tributes from the commentators, particularly as the personal relationship between them was generally thought to be cool at best.

What we do not know is how Langer experienced it. Hopefully he felt all the warmth, generosity and support the commentators

* Max Atkinson gives a fascinating account of 'Charisma as Method' (see References).

saw. But he could quite easily have felt embarrassed by such Mediterranean effusiveness, irritated by the disturbance to his concentration, possibly even patronised by condescension. (Apparently not, because he went on to complete his victory.) The potential scope for misunderstanding is enormous.

Our Western management style does not usually run to such grandiloquent gestures, but the scope for misunderstanding is still there. In spite of the books written on the subject, there is no generally accepted code of 'body language'; you cannot learn body language as you learn French or German. In fact you already know it. You have been learning and using it from your earliest moments, when it was the only form of communication you could understand.

What you can do is to increase your awareness and receptivity by improving your observational skills. Many managers do not keep their eyes open. They do not see what is happening around them; they speak and listen without looking at the people they are talking to (I find this more true of graduates than non-graduates, and of men than women). A good check is to close your eyes and mentally picture what the other people in the room are wearing. Write down your description and then check it with the reality.

Secondly, you can check out the message you are receiving from the non-verbals. If you think a person's attention has wandered, you can say, 'You seem to have something else on your mind.' If he is looking at his watch, 'I get the impression you're pushed for time.' It does not matter whether your interpretation is accurate or not; once it is out in the open, it can be confirmed or corrected.

I have a habit of frowning when I am thinking about something complicated. It can give the impression I am angry or upset. My colleague, John Alexander, lets me know when it is happening. 'You're frowning, Vincent. Anything wrong?' Usually it takes me by surprise – I am not aware of what I am doing and the impression it is creating.

Finally, be aware of the cultural differences in non-verbal signals around the world, if you work with multinational groups. I once taught a course in England which included a man from Sri Lanka. His English was not very fluent, so I took special trouble to check that he had understood. He would slowly shake his head and I would explain again. Then somebody told me that in Sri Lanka shaking the head means 'Yes'!

Silence

At first sight, silence would seem to be the essence of non-communication. Yet we know that in some circumstances silence can speak volumes. It is also a potent tool in the communication tool-box, both for speaker and listener.

For the speaker, it adds emphasis to a point, allowing time for its full significance to sink in. Handled skilfully, it can build up anticipation for what is to come – the pregnant pause. It gives the opportunity to make eye contact with the audience and gauge their reactions. It is an essential component of the timing of one's delivery.

For the listener, silence can buy time, either to digest what has been said, or to consider a response, or both. Silence will often lure the speaker into saying more than he or she may have intended (which might be useful in a quasi adversarial situation such as negotiation).

Silence is golden, says the proverb. It is also difficult (*silenzio e duro*, according to an Italian pun). It can be embarrassing, as in those awful dinner parties when the conversation dries up and nobody knows how to get it going. It seems then to signal the breakdown of the dialogue, the end of the communication.

The embarrassment creates a strong urge to fill the vacuum. If you do not want to say anything, resist the urge to say something just to break the silence. You can depend on someone else doing so. If, when working with a group, you make a request for comment or feedback and nothing is forthcoming, there is no need to panic: someone is guaranteed to talk within sixty seconds or so, and if you are ready for it, you can be comfortable with the silence. (Providing, of course, that they have not all read this!)

There is in fact no such thing as 'an uncomfortable silence'; there are only people who are uncomfortable with the silence. It is a matter of choice for you whether you are going to be uncomfortable with any particular silence.

Of course, if you frequently find yourself confronted with silence when you are inviting interaction and dialogue, you need to look at what you are doing to have that effect. There could well be something in your style that is a conversation-stopper – too many *ex cathedra* statements, too many put-downs, too much 'constructive criticism', etc. Listening to or watching a tape of yourself in action will give you the answer; or you could ask the people you are dealing with to tell you what is happening.

4. Communication occasions and their characteristics

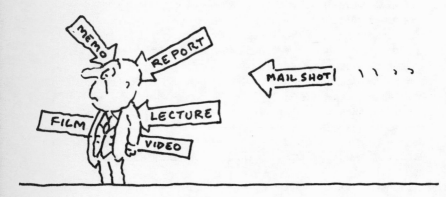

The communications matrix

To get to specific ways of improving communication effectiveness we need to move on from generalisations about communications as a whole and explore the different communication occasions and their characteristics. Meetings, phone calls, letters, books, presentations and so on are all intended to achieve communication objectives, but are qualitatively different in their strengths and limitations for the purpose of communication.

There are several dimensions along which we need to distinguish different types of communication, as follows:

— face-to-face versus remote or indirect;
— the interactive versus one-way;
— mass versus individual/small group;
— verbal versus non-verbal;
— permanent versus transient.

I have mapped out the characteristics of different kinds of communication occasions in the communications matrix chart. Below I want to comment on some of the major differences, from the point of view of both the transmitter and the receiver.

Communication occasion	Characteristics				
	Words	Tone	Non-verbal	Pictures	Person-alised
Interactive					
Meetings, formal	Y	Y	Y	P	Y
Meetings, informal	Y	Y	Y	U	Y
Phone conversation	Y	Y	N	N	Y
Non-interactive					
Lectures, speeches, etc.	Y	Y	Y	N	N
Letters, memos	Y	N	N	P/U	Y
Books, articles	Y	N	N	Y	N
Film and video	Y	Y	Y	Y	N
Posters	Y	N	N	Y	N

Y = yes; N = no; P = possibly; U = unlikely.

Informal face to face

The person-to-person meeting in pairs or small groups is a major part of our daily experience, at work and outside it. It is interactive and potentially progressive: statements can evoke a response, understanding can be checked, ideas information and opinions can be exchanged, and agreement reached. It is potentially the richest and most productive form of communication, since it uses multiple channels – words, tone of voice and non-verbals in an interactive way.

The informal meeting is often spontaneous, and therefore unplanned, for at least one and possibly both parties. A stops by B's desk or drops into his office and says, 'I need to have a word about . . .' Or they happen to meet in the corridor, and one of them says, 'Oh, by the way . . .', and gets into the subject.

The spontaneous interchange is fine for dealing with small items and exchange of uncontroversial information. However, they can very easily slide into more substantial issues, and half an hour can easily slip by before either party quite realises what they have got themselves into. In these cases, some of the principles suggested for formal meetings (see page 120) can be applied to put some structure and order into the discussion, so that the communication is effective and the time is well spent.

Formal meetings

The formal meeting has all the potential advantages of other face-to-face meetings: all the channels of communication (words, tone, non-verbals) are in operation; it is an interactive occasion, an opportunity to reach common understanding, agreement and decisions to act. As a formal occasion it has the additional advantage of being scheduled in advance, providing the opportunity for advance planning so that everybody attending knows what the purpose of the meeting is, what preparation they need to do, what sort of contribution is expected from them, etc.

Given all these favourable conditions, how is it that formal meetings have such a bad name? *Meetings, Bloody Meetings* is the way John Cleese titles his training film, and it aptly captures the widespread frustration with formal meetings, particularly the time they consume in relation to the results they achieve.

Formal meetings are one of the great opportunity areas for improving the effectiveness of communication at work. Later in this book I will be proposing structures and procedures for different kinds of meeting. One of the starting points for better meetings must be clarity about the purpose of the meeting; the purpose will define the structure and procedures that are appropriate.

However, before discussing different kinds of formal meeting, there is one characteristic that they all share: *the predominant activity has to be listening, not speaking*, for reasons of mathematical logic. A meeting can only proceed if one person talks at a time (if two people talk at once it is impossible for either of them to be listening, or for the other participants to *hear* what is being said, let alone listen to it). If only one person can speak, the others present need to be listening — if they are not, what is the point of the speaker speaking? Assuming there are more than two people present, the amount of listening required outweighs the amount of speaking by a factor determined by the size of the meeting.

Thus, in a meeting of eight people, if only one is speaking at a time, each participant will spend on average seven-eighths of the time listening. This, as we shall see when we come to examine listening in more depth, is no easy task. Even to remain silent for seven-eighths of the time (and remaining silent is *not* the same as listening) seems to be the maximum that most people can achieve.

From conducting and observing many thousands of meetings, I and my colleagues have come to the empirical conclusion that eight people is the maximum feasible size for any participative type of meeting (it is different for lectures and presentations, where one person is doing all the talking and everyone else is expected to remain silent virtually all the time). When the numbers are larger than eight, side conversations inevitably start up, with the result that those engaged in the side discussion are no longer part of the mainstream meeting. There are in fact two meetings in progress simultaneously, with each one distracting the other – a recipe for chaos. Yet participative meetings of more than eight people are quite common. They can generally be avoided by clarification of the purpose of the meeting and appropriate design of the meeting structure.

When oversize meetings cannot be avoided, there are some simple techniques available to the chairperson or meeting facilitator to keep the situation under control. To deal with side conversations, you can simply stop the main meeting with a hand signal, to focus attention on the side meeting, which then withers away in embarrassment – a somewhat punitive technique, but effective in discouraging a repetition either by the offenders or by others. Alternatively the chairperson can simply announce, 'We have two meetings going – let's get back to one.'

Another powerful reason for keeping meetings as small as possible is the complexity of communication, defined as the number of 'interfaces' in any situation. *Communication complexity increases geometrically with the size of the meeting:* a meeting of five people has ten 'interfaces'; a meeting of ten people has forty-five. The difficulty of running the meeting efficiently increases with the communications complexity, so that above a certain size (probably four or five) the meeting needs a full-time controller who is not a participant, if it is to function effectively.

Telephone conversations

A great deal of communicating, at work and elsewhere, is done by phone and it's worth pausing to think about the special characteristics of a phone conversation. Like the face-to-face meeting, it is interactive with all the benefits which that can bring. What is missing is the body language, a reduction of over 50 per cent in the channels of communication available. When talking to someone you know well, it is often possible to visualise the body language that goes with the words and tone of voice. The danger is that you visualise inaccurately. With strangers the visualisation is even more likely to be inaccurate: how often does somebody you meet turn out to be very different from your expectation based on phone contact.

Since we use body language to pick up emotional messages, it follows that the phone is a dangerous medium for discussion of anything likely to have a high emotional content.

The second major characteristic of the telephone is that it always interrupts (unless the call is expected owing to prior arrangement). So recipients are being summoned to a 'meeting' they may not want to attend, without any choice in the matter, because they do not know what the meeting is till they pick up the receiver.

One conventional, but expensive, solution is to filter incoming calls through a personal secretary ('Mr Jones for you. Do you want to speak to him?'). As well as being expensive, this ritual runs the risk of alienating Mr Jones. And it can become quite ludicrous if Mr Jones is using *his* secretary to make the call.

Robert Townsend, in *Up the Organization*, advocates having a phone-free period, during which the operator simply takes the name and number of the caller and promises that the person will ring back later that morning – a promise that is always kept.

My own solution is to check, whenever I make a call, that it's a convenient time to talk and, if not, agree an alternative time. With incoming calls, if they are seriously inconvenient to me, I will say so and arrange an alternative time for the call.

Letters, memos and reports

The written word stands on its own, without the help, or hindrance, of intonation or body language. That is both its strength and weakness: it is a limited form of communication, but it is free from the potential ambiguity of the non-verbal channels (although a written communication does have a 'tone' which is presumably an inference about the way it would sound, if it were spoken).

It can be carefully considered by the writer to give very precise expression to what he or she wants to say and to take account of the probable impact on the reader – an advantage compared with the spontaneity of a face-to-face or telephone interaction. I find it useful to distinguish two phases – the first in which I get out of my head what I want to say, and the second in which I try to read it from the recipient's point of view and modify it as necessary in the hope that the message received is the one I am trying to transmit.

Because it is permanent (unlike the transient phone call or face-to-face discussion), the recipient is also free to give it careful consideration. So too can the people to whom that person may decide to send copies – the audience may turn out to be wider than you anticipated when you wrote.

The written word, therefore, is particularly suitable for the permanent communication of precise information, for example, contracts and agreements. As a process for getting to the agreement, they are far less efficient than the interactive, face-to-face communication, or the more limited telephone conversation.

Presentations, lectures, speeches and sermons

I have put all these in the same category because to some degree they have in common the characteristic of addressing a (more or less) captive audience with limited interaction between speaker and audience. There are differences of degree, of course: in the sermon the audience is wholly captive and interaction between audience and speaker is not encouraged. The lecturer's audience is slightly better placed to get up and walk out (though not where attendance is compulsory for degree-getting purposes) and questions may be invited at the end, so that there is some element of interaction. A speech is similar, although if it's a political speech the interaction may come earlier, and less politely, in the form of heckling, and the scope for walking out is considerably greater.

The business presentation warrants particular attention (and gets it in Chapter 9) because it is so much a part of the culture of modern business organisations. Again, the audience is semi-captive: convention and politeness require that you stay to the end (unless, of course, you are very senior, in which case you may come and go as you like, on the understanding that, being very senior, you must have other more important matters to attend to!). Interaction is generally accepted, at least to the extent of questions, ostensibly to clarify understanding.

The presenter, the lecturer, the speech-maker and the preacher all hold the floor: it's their meeting, they are on their feet, they are in control. They have at their disposal all the channels of words, tone of voice and non-verbals, plus the additional power of visual aids – slides, overhead projectors, flip charts, etc. They are in this position of apparent power by virtue of the assumed value of the message they have to deliver.

It is a heavy responsibility, one which can only be discharged successfully by a skilled performer. I use the word 'performer' advisedly, because the skills are essentially those of the entertainer – that rare ability to hold the attention of a group of people for an extended period of time. (It is no accident that in these days of politics by television, the President of the United States is a former film actor: he has the relevant skills, particularly superb timing of the delivery of his lines.)

In my experience, only a very small proportion of the people who undertake this task have the appropriate skills. Consequently the presentation, lecture, speech or sermon tends to be a very ineffective (and often uneconomic) method of communication. It is often an institutionalised ritual, adopted from habit rather than conscious choice (yes, even the business presentation), and it is usually worth considering whether the communication objective might not be better achieved by other methods.

The university lecturer, to take an extreme case, is given no training whatever in how to lecture; the person is appointed on the strength of subject knowledge and/or research ability. His or her ability to perform the difficult communications task of lecturing is assumed. I suspect that the traditions of lecturing – and preaching – go back to pre-Gutenberg days, when it made sense for the person with the knowledge to disseminate it verbally for students to write down. It could be seen as a batch production method for the copying process, which was the only way to produce books at that time. But the printing press changed all that, and today, five hundred years on with computers, word processors, video and all the other wonders of modern technology, it is surely time to rethink the lecture as an instrument of communication. (Professor Wiio, with whom I discussed the limitations of lecturing as a communication process, told me that he still lectured six hours a week. I asked him why. 'It's in my contract,' he told me!)

Managers who have to make presentations may well get some training in doing so. The better courses on presentation techniques will give them the opportunity to review their own presentation from a video recording and develop appropriate skills. As a result, the quality of business presentations tends to be far higher than that of the average lecture, speech or sermon.

Paradoxically, the more skilful the performance of the speakers in all these situations, the greater the danger that their performance will be remembered for, and judged by, its style rather than its content. 'It was a brilliant speech, but I can't remember what he actually said,' is a typical reaction.

So the speaker has a difficult tightrope to walk, if he or she wants to get the message over (rather than simply create warm feelings). The speaker must be skilful enough as a performer to engage and hold the interest of the audience, while at the same time ensuring that the brilliance of the performance does not overshadow the content of the subject. Personally I find this tightrope too difficult, and whenever I can, I convert invitations to give lectures or make presentations into participative occasions. I devise exercises for the audience to carry out, and then review their experience with them. This way, they are actively involved; they gain experience of doing something instead of hearing information about it; the demands on their listening ability and attention span are reduced, and the demands on my ability to hold their attention are similarly reduced. It works well for me, and the approach is worth considering whenever you find yourself in the position of lecturing or presenting.

It may not always be possible to move the goalposts in this way. Some years ago I was addressing a large conference in Finland. I explained my reservations about the lecture process, with the additional complication of the language barrier (for the Finns, English is a third or fourth language, after Finnish, Swedish and possibly German). As it happened, I had distributed some yellow leaflets and I suggested that if they were having difficulty following me, they should display the yellow leaflet. If I saw a significant number of these appearing, I would know that I needed to stop and change tack. As soon as I made this proposal, the chairperson of the meeting intervened and said, 'I'm sure that Finnish people are too polite to tell a guest speaker they do not understand what he is saying,' and thereby destroyed my experiment!

From the receiving end

In classifying the different types of communication occasion, I have almost fallen into the semantic trap I described earlier, in that I have grouped them in terms of the transmitting process. Only in the case of the interactive communications – the meetings, formal and informal, and phone calls – is the occasion the same for transmitter and receiver: both parties play both roles. We need to look at the non-interactive occasions through the eyes of the receiver: for him or her it is a very different occasion, both qualitatively and with regard to timing. The occasions are:

— receiving letters, memos, reports, mailshots;
— reading newspapers, magazines, books, etc.;
— attending lectures, presentations, etc.;
— watching TV, videos, films.

Receiving letters and memos

How efficient the person is as a receiver in these different situations will depend largely on the frame of mind in which he or she approaches them. A letter, memo or report that the person has asked for will engage the attention more easily than one that is unsolicited. If the receiver regards every unsolicited piece of printed material as junk mail, it will need an outstanding level of skill on the part of the designer of the mailshot to arrest its path to the waste-paper basket.

It can safely be assumed that the receiver sees incoming paperwork in total as a burden – overflowing in-trays are a common complaint – so the probability is that initially, at first sight, the communication will be unwelcome – 'More bumf,' he or she will sigh. Anything the transmitter can do to ease that burden will increase the chance of the message being received. And it all has to be done by words and pictures – there is no tone of voice or non-verbals to help. The permanence of the written communication is a potential advantage; it can be held for future reference, re-read, stored in file – once it has overcome the initial hurdle of attention-worthiness.

Reading newspapers, magazines and books

Here the receiver has the great luxury of choice; nobody *has* to read a newspaper, book or magazine, ever, nor does the person have to continue with one that is unrewarding. Again, the words and pictures carry the whole load, without the help of tone and non-verbals and the permanence of it may give it a second or third chance of being read. (Some of the books I most value have taken me months to read, not because of any failing on the part of the author but because of the richness of the material and my inability to assimilate it any quicker.) Equally their permanence is also an invitation to set them aside in order to 'get round to them later', with the odds against ever doing so (my shelves are littered with half-read books, magazines, etc. that I intend to get round to some time).

All of us today live in a constant state of information overload: in addition to all the directly job-related material that flows across our desks there is an apparently inexhaustible supply of trade and professional journals, magazines, books, not to mention the daily newspapers. (I feel momentarily guilty about adding to the flood with another book: hopefully it will help you to raise the quality and reduce the quantity of your communication handling!)

Conscientious executives know they must 'keep up to date', be well informed, widely read and on the ball; if they are not strong-minded and ruthlessly selective about what they read, they will condemn themselves to a lifetime of carrying a bulging briefcase to and fro.

The development of 'speed-reading' techniques is partly a response to the information overload. Clearly it is worthwhile in its own right to increase the efficiency of the reading process both to save time and improve comprehension. But, for me, it is not the answer to the overload problem. The key questions to ask are: 'Why am I reading this? What do I hope to get from it? Am I getting it?' And if not, to have no compunction about tossing it aside. Sure, you might miss something that might be useful; equally you might be doing something more useful with the time and energy you are putting into the reading. If that bit of information really matters to you, you will probably come across it from some other source — there's a lot of redundancy and repetition in the printed word, and of course the people who *have* to read it are always looking for an opportunity to air their knowledge.

So you can stay relaxed about all the publications you have not read, or have chosen not to read. And preserve your sanity.

Attending lectures and presentations

People attend these sorts of occasion from a whole spectrum of motives, from having to be there for one reason or another, to eagerness to hear every pearl of wisdom falling from the speakers' lips, with many intermediate points. The reason for being there will have a direct correlation with attentiveness; broadly speaking, attention is a function of interest.

In any one audience there will probably be a range of motivation and interest levels, which creates a problem for speakers – how can they connect with such varying levels of attentiveness? My own strategy is to go for a common denominator – entertainment. However reluctant people are to be in the audience, they like to be entertained, so if I can make them laugh a few times, I may possibly keep them listening for the next time. (This is the 'entertain before you inform' strategy.)

For the audience member, listening is the problem – he or she has nothing else to do, and to listen with concentration for extended periods of time is extremely difficult (as we shall discuss later). For the listener, the speaker is competing for attention with an alternative meeting, the listener's own thoughts. The alternative meeting has two big advantages over what the speaker is offering: first, the listener's thoughts are usually more interesting, to the listener, than material coming in from outside and, secondly, they are much more numerous – we think at something like 800–1,000 words a minute, against the typical speaker's rate of 150 words a minute. (This point will be discussed later, p. 185.)

As with reading, being in the audience for an occasion of this sort raises the questions: 'Why am I doing this? What do I hope to get out of it? Am I getting it?' However, if the answers are unsatisfactory, it is not so easy to do something about it, because to get up and walk out draws attention to yourself and could be misconstrued. (It may also be unfair to the speaker – as is the alternative of creating a diversion for yourself by heckling, or tripping the speaker up with a loaded question.)

So it is safer to be discriminating about the lectures and presentations you attend, although it is difficult to be certain in advance. And if all else fails, find an inconspicuous way to get out. Last year I found myself spending an entire day at a conference in the United States listening to an elderly and highly respected American guru droning on about his speciality. I was only there because I was due to perform the next day. Early in the afternoon, as I fought to stop myself falling asleep, the thought struck me, 'I don't need to be here' (unlike all the others, who as employees of the company might have been thought to be displaying an unsuitable lack of interest in the subject). So, choosing my moment, I slipped away, with an enormous sense of relief, and to the envy of the few who noticed.

Watching television, videos and films

Of all the communication-receiving activities, these are probably the least demanding (and most widely practised). The transmissions are usually produced by professionals; they can draw upon the whole array of visual effects, in addition to the words, tone of voice and non-verbals of the the people on view. The spectator is watching from choice – it is the easiest thing in the world to switch off – and is generally in a relaxed frame of mind.

The combination of a rich medium operated by skilled professionals and a casual relaxed audience has its dangers; it is open to abuse, in terms of misleading and selective information and biased interpretation. Statutory bodies like the Independent Broadcasting Authority and the Advertising Standards Authority exist to provide safeguards against abuse, but an alert and critical attitude is the viewer's best defence against being misled.

Studies by the Glasgow University Media Group highlight the dangers, by comparing television news broadcasts with information on the same subjects from other sources, demonstrating a partial and often biased version of the subject on TV. 'I saw it on television' is hardly an adequate basis for forming our view of the world; it needs to be checked from other sources.

5. Meetings, splendid meetings

Introduction

I have already referred to the general attitude to meetings captured by the title of John Cleese's training film *Meetings, Bloody Meetings*. Too many, too long, too boring, with too little achieved, a distraction from getting on with the real work of the organisation.

Does it really have to be like that? Suppose all our meetings were productive, time-efficient and enjoyable – what a transformation that would be in the life of the manager. I believe it is entirely possible, given a clear understanding on the part of all concerned of the purpose of each meeting and the appropriate way of achieving that purpose.

What about the wreckers, the people who come deliberately to frustrate the purpose of the meeting? First, in my experience, there are not many of them around in the business environment; most people want to get on with the job. What looks like, and has the effect of, wrecking behaviour is often pure clumsiness, ignorance of the appropriate way to achieve the results. Secondly, the formats and ground rules proposed here should both reduce the clumsiness and limit the damage done by it. Thirdly, they also tend to make negative behaviour visible and transparent, and therefore much more risky than when it is covert and hidden by the confusion. So much so that they are bitterly opposed by the meeting manipulators, those who consider themselves particularly skilful in getting what they want from meetings at the expense of anyone who gets in their way. Their approach is propagated by Winston Fletcher, in an entertaining but scurrilous little book called *Meetings, Meetings* with the sub-title, *How to Manipulate Them and Make Them More Fun*. (Note the artful association of manipulation and fun: my experience is that meetings can be made more fun without manipulation, and it is the attempted manipulation that makes so many meetings so tedious.) He goes on to describe '21 key strategies with which to outplay, outclass and outmanoeuvre your fellow meeting goers'.

Clearly, if anyone should take Mr Fletcher seriously (and Mr Fletcher seems to) the meetings they attend will be disasters. Your fellow meeting goers are not fools (as the manipulator assumes) and they have no intention of being outplayed, outclassed or outmanoeuvred. So the energy of the meeting is dissipated in a senseless contest in which the parties try to outmanoeuvre each other and in all probability end up achieving nothing.

Even if one party should 'win', the loser will not take it lying down; he or she will fight back, subvert, refuse to co-operate or undermine in one way or another. The win–lose contest becomes lose–lose as the loser sets up a return match on his or her own ground which that person is sure to win. If we are to have successful meetings, we must get away from the idea that 'meetings are manipulation'.

There is another reason for looking at formal meetings in some detail. The roles, structures and processes that are appropriate to different kinds of task are at their most visible in the formal meeting, and used flexibly they will be found to map well on to most informal meetings.

The key to good meeting design can be found in the general design principle 'Form follows function'. If we are clear about the function of any particular interaction, we can select an appropriate form from among those described for the formal meetings.

So what is, or are, the function(s) of meetings? What are they for? Why do we have them, especially if they are such a bore and waste of time?

'To discuss things' is the most likely immediate answer, and it's not good enough. We need to know *why* we are discussing things, what we are trying to achieve when we discuss them, if we are to design a form of meeting that fits the function and if we are to know whether we have been successful. The purpose needs to be expressed in specific terms and the following categories seem to cover most of the situations likely to arise in a business organisation:

— To exchange information – particularly about what people in the group are doing, so they will understand the context of their own activities, avoid duplication and ensure that no important activities are being overlooked; also to hear about decisions that affect them.

— To solve problems/exploit opportunities – here the purpose is to devise new courses of action to correct a situation that is unsatisfactory or take advantage of new circumstances.

— To consult, to gather information and opinions prior to making a decision (note that decision-making is an *individual* activity and not normally a function of the meeting – see below).

— To brief – to inform people about decisions taken, usually at a higher level, that affect them directly.

— To resolve conflict – to explore alternatives to the proposals which are giving rise to the conflict and/or find ways of dealing with the consequential problems they are creating: also to negotiate an agreement, where the parties need to find a mutually acceptable basis to work together.

— To build morale and commitment – particularly in a team.

There are some notable (and deliberate) omissions to this list. First and most important is decision-taking. For me decision-taking is an individual activity, with individual accountability for the success or failure of the decision. So meetings do not, or should not, take decisions; where decisions are needed that affect a group they should be taken by the leader of that group, after consultation with its members. John Garnett in *The Work Challenge* provides a trenchant explanation of this view: although he fails to appreciate the potential of groups to achieve a creative consensus which is neither a compromise nor a majority decision – see below. He says, 'Individual accountability for decisions is important, so that a check can be made later to see who was the person who took the better or less good decision.'

Another omission is 'to debate'. Managers often say, 'We need to debate this issue', and often engage in debate, in the literal sense. The assumption is that by arguing the pros and cons, the better case will emerge victorious, reason will prevail and all concerned will, as reasonable people, accept the conclusion.

The assumption is not borne out in practice. The debating model, much loved and promoted though it is in our society (where schools

154

have their debating societies and universities their students' union), is drawn from the adversarial world of party politics and the law courts. It is quite inappropriate to the business of wealth creation, where all parties can be successful through co-operatively creating mutual benefits (see page 173).

Finally, I have not included 'presentations' in the above list of meeting purposes. Ostensibly, they belong to the 'exchange information' category, but they can easily evolve into the problem-solving or conflict categories. Because of this ambiguity, and because of their popularity as a management ritual, we shall examine presentations separately (see page 159) but we need to be clear that they are a means and not an end or purpose in themselves.

We can now begin to relate the meeting purposes defined above to the components of communication identified earlier (see page 129), namely:

— fact
— opinions (including forecasts, etc.)
— goals, objectives, etc.
— ideas
— feelings

and identify the predominant communication component in each category of meeting, as follows.

Purpose of meeting	Predominant communication components
Information exchange	Facts and opinions
Problem solving	Ideas and goal wishes
Briefing	Facts
Consultation	Opinions
Conflict resolution	Ideas and goal wishes
Morale building	Feelings and goal wishes

Clearly the communication components are not limited to the predominant ones, but they do govern the meeting format that is most appropriate to the type of meeting. Nor are the meeting categories totally discrete; they overlap to some degree, and the purpose may change in the light of developments in the meeting itself. There is no harm in that, provided the change is spotted and acknowledged, and the meeting format is modified accordingly.

In subsequent sections, we describe meeting models that fit the different meeting purposes. Before going into them we need to address the question of who decides which model is appropriate and ensures that it is applied. Traditionally, this is the responsibility of the chairperson, a role we now need to look at critically.

To chair or not to chair

Traditionally, meetings are 'run' by a chairperson. Usually he or she will be the most senior person present, with the principal authority for decision-making. He or she will also be responsible for managing the traffic flow of communications, ensuring that all participants have a reasonable share of the air time, that there is only one person speaking at a time, that destructive behaviour is policed and that time is used efficiently.

Usually the chairperson fails to run the meeting to the satisfaction of the people present (although it may well be run to his or her own satisfaction). Some years ago I was invited to observe the meetings in a large research and development division of a big corporation, which was organised on a project basis. Each project manager chaired the regular review meeting on his own project; all project managers attended all the review meetings. When I interviewed the project managers privately, they were unanimously of the opinion that the meetings in the organisation were awful, except for the meetings they chaired themselves. I had the pleasure of feeding back this opinion to them as a group, prompting some sheepish smiles, but no denials. Clearly each one was using his power as chairman to satisfy his own objectives, to the frustration and dissatisfaction of the other members of the meeting.

It is hardly surprising that a chairperson fails to run what is regarded as a good meeting by those who attend it. To begin with, he or she has far too much to do: the chairperson is trying to manage the traffic flow while also taking principal responsibility for the output of the meeting. More seriously, he or she is combining two functions which need to be kept separate – a sort of combined poacher and gamekeeper who cannot do both jobs well.

The two functions are the management of 'process' and the direction of 'content'. By 'process' I mean the communications methods and ground rules that are being followed; the 'content' is the subject matter under discussion. In short, process is the 'how' of the meeting, content is the 'what'. Content will change from meeting to meeting; process will be common to many meetings.

There are two requirements for the process: first, that it should be appropriate to the task, the purpose of the meeting, and, second, that it should be explicit and clearly communicated to the members of the meeting, so that each one knows what sort of contribution is required from him or her at each stage of the meeting.

The content responsibility is quite different: it is to specify what is the subject under discussion, why it is being discussed, what is required from the meeting and when that objective has been achieved.

The two functions of process management and content direction are not only distinct – they need to be kept separate, to prevent the power and authority that rightly belongs to the control of process being misapplied to achieve the content objectives of one individual. We do not give the job of referee to one of the players in the football match, or air traffic control to one of the pilots in the air. The risk of bias would be too great; it would be suspected even if it did not exist; the necessary perspective and detachment would be lost. Neither job would be done well, because each one demands full-time attention and does not get it.

So it is with the conventional meeting chairperson who is both referee and player, traffic controller and pilot. Such a person cannot exercise the objectivity, detachment and skill to be a good process leader, because there are content objectives to achieve. The chairperson will be tempted consciously or unconsciously to use the process authority to further his or her content objectives, by giving more time to those whose views support his or her own, or cutting short the discussion when it is not going the way he or she wants. Even if the chairperson does none of these things, he or she may be suspected of doing so, and the other members of the meeting will temper their own behaviour according to their suspicions.

It is widely believed that it is the right – indeed the responsibility – of the chairperson to 'steer' the meeting, that is, to use his or

157

her authority over the process to get the required content results. The belief is most strongly held among those most responsible for behaving that way – the successful senior managers of organisations. It arises, I believe, from ignorance – ignorance of the cost of this type of manipulation in terms of demotivation, frustration and loss of commitment on the part of those affected by it, and also ignorance of any alternative way of getting the job done.

Until quite recently very few managers had any training in the management of the process of meetings and its separation from content. They learned their style from observing what their predecessors did, and followed suit. Unfortunately, it is the most senior people who are least likely to expose themselves to the possibility of learning new skills: we may have to wait for a new generation of 'process-aware' managers to rise to the top before beliefs and practices change on a large scale.

The key to better management of meetings is to split the chairperson's role into its two functions – process management and content direction – *and give them to separate people*. The process manager (or facilitator) will concentrate on the communications traffic control, and while he or she is doing so, take no part in the content of the meeting. The content responsibility will be handled by the individual or individuals whose job responsibility is most directly affected by the item under discussion. Some of the time that person will be the senior manager present; at other times he or she will not be, depending on the extent to which the senior manager delegates responsibility to subordinates.

For meetings that are large in numbers (five or six upwards), complex in content, or likely to be contentious, the process manager will probably be another person. In addition to traffic control reponsibilities, he or she can also look after the recording of the output of the meeting, and can therefore replace the conventional secretary of the meeting – in which case the numbers are not necessarily increased.

For smaller meetings, it is feasible to double up the role of process manager with that of one of the participants, provided it is not the participant who is responsible for content direction (to do that would be to reinvent the conventional chairperson!) The role of the process manager can be rotated during the course of the meeting, to share the load and maintain the separation of powers.

An alternative is to break down the process responsibility into component parts and share these around the meeting, so that one person acts as scribe, another keeps control of time and a third person ensures that the appropriate meeting structure is being followed. Again, process responsibility should not be given to the person responsible for directing the content of the meeting. (Just as an orchestra requires a conductor, and a string quartet can play without one, the need for a separate process manager varies with the size of the meeting, bearing in mind that the communication complexity increases geometrically according to the size of the meeting.)

How the content directing responsibility is exercised will vary according to the different types of meeting, as discussed in the following sections. As far as possible, the 'one at a time' principle should be followed, since the meeting can only go in one direction at a time. The remaining participants in the meeting then become resources, whose function is to help the content director achieve his or her objectives from the item under discussion, by contributing their ideas, information and (possibly) opinions, as required.

The basic roles and responsibilities in meetings can be summarised as follows:

— *Process manager* – controls communications traffic, manages time, records results, specifies meeting structure and techniques to be used;

— *Content director* – specifies what is to be discussed, what is required from the meeting and when it has been achieved;

— *Resource* – contributes ideas or information or opinions as specified by the process manager to enable the content director to achieve his or her objectives.

This basic division of labour becomes more complex when (as often happens) several members of the meeting have an interest in 'content direction', but the underlying principles still apply. The ways they are used are described below in the different meeting models that are appropriate to different meeting purposes.

Ordeal by presentation

The formal presentation, in which the presenter, armed with flip charts, acetates or slides, makes a presentation to an audience of typically six to twenty, is ostensibly an exercise in information-giving. In practice, it is not so straightforward and, because the presentation has become so strongly entrenched in the rituals of large corporations, it is worth looking at more closely.

The purpose of a presentation is usually to gain acceptance, for a proposal, an idea, or the conclusions of a study. So it is as much an exercise in persuasion as in communication: the aim is not only to communicate the information but to influence attitudes towards acceptance of the proposition. It is often made by a junior manager to a more senior group, so it is seen by the presenter as an opportunity to show his or her mettle to people who have a say in his or her future career. Equally the audience will be making its own judgements of the presenter's talents, for future reference.

Moreover, the presentation has developed into such an art form in its own right in many corporations that it is likely to be judged as much on the quality of the performance as on the quality of the proposition. 'He made a good presentation' can mean 'He had a confident delivery, handled his visual aids well, kept the interest of the audience, dealt with questions competently' – all judgements that make no reference to the *content* of the presentation.

The presentation can easily turn into an adversarial occasion (indeed they seem to be most prized in organisations with an adversarial culture). The audience knows that they are there to be sold something, and are therefore on their guard, their critical antennae switched on. They know it is a test for the presenter, and they intend to make sure he or she gets a thorough test. They have nothing else to do but sit and listen critically. They see themselves as skilled presenters ('I wouldn't have got where I am today if I wasn't') and are on the alert for technical flaws. (Once I told a board of directors that I was not going to allow a meeting at which a task force I had been working with was reporting its results to turn into this kind of presentation. 'Why not?' grumbled one of the directors. 'We all had to go through it when we were at their level' – rather like public school sixth-formers arguing for the continuation of the fagging system.)

So there is a lot going on in the presentation, both above and below the surface, and the first issue to address, before considering ways of improving your presentation skills, is: is your presentation really necessary? Is it the only, or the most appropriate way to achieve your communication objectives? Often in my view it is not, though you may be locked into it by the culture of the organisation. As an outside consultant, I am in a stronger position to lay down my own ground rules.

There are some situations where the formal presentation is the most appropriate medium. When the same information needs to be repeated many times to many different groups, it is worth investing in devising a high-quality format with suitable graphics and visual aids, not only to save 'reinventing the wheel' each time, but also to ensure consistency in the message delivered by different speakers at different times. Thus an advertising agency may have its standard 'credentials' presentation and a software house a standard presentation of its software products.

Equally there are many occasions when managers automatically decide that 'making a presentation' is the most appropriate format, without considering the implications or the alternatives. In choosing the presentation format the manager is implicitly saying, 'I have studied this matter and have reached a final and indisputable conclusion.' There may be times when such an arrogant position is justifiable, and it will certainly need to be justified, because the audience will be out to prove you wrong. They are after all being presented only with the two alternatives: accept or reject.

The alternative is to convert the presentation into a participative problem-solving type of meeting, where your conclusions represent your 'best current thinking' which is open to improvement and modification from the assembled wisdom of the group. This approach shifts the occasion from the potentially adversarial to the explicitly co-operative; it recognises that the audience has something of value to contribute; it gives them something interesting and constructive to do; it positions you as open-minded and flexible. And there is no better way to gain support and commitment to a proposal than to involve the people whose support you need in its design, even if it is only in applying the finishing touches.

As you will have gathered, I have a strong preference for this approach against the formal presentation. Visual aids can still be used, if they assist in the communication of the ideas, but their role is to communicate and clarify, not to sell. Contrary to the received wisdom, I do not believe ideas should be 'sold'; they need to be 'marketed', that is, adapted and modified to suit the taste of the consumer, the person you want to buy the idea. The format described here is geared to marketing in this sense; the formal presentation is geared to selling.

If you decide to use this approach, the mechanics are quite simple (and surprisingly similar to those described with regard to the consultation meeting). They are discussed in more detail on page 205.

I believe that both you, the presenter, and the audience will find this alternative more satisfying and more productive than the conventional presentation. It will no longer be the ordeal which making a presentation is for many managers, whether they admit it or not.

However, if you are still making formal presentations, you will find some tips on pages 200–204.

6. Meeting models

Information exchange: the agenda meeting

Where the purpose of the meeting is predominantly information exchange, the Synectics agenda meeting provides a suitable basic model, which can be adapted to the needs of a particular organisation or particular meeting.

The key principle is that each member of the meeting has the right to raise any topic for inclusion on the agenda, both before and during the meeting. In doing so, they take responsibility for the content direction of that item: they must specify why they have raised it, what they want from the meeting, and when it has been dealt with to their satisfaction. They also take responsibility for the time taken by the item, and for what, if anything, needs to be recorded in the minutes.

The purpose in raising the item will usually be to give or to get some information, but the format also accommodates opinion-gathering (a particular form of information) and quick problem-solving, when someone wants new ideas for dealing with a problem.

The meeting is run by a process manager, who gives each member of the meeting the opportunity to deal with one of their items in turn. Naturally each individual will choose the most important item first, providing a natural priority-setting mechanism. Taking one item per person in turn creates a sense of fairness in sharing of the time available, which is usually a scarce resource.

Efficiency (and fairness) in the use of time can be strengthened by fixing a time limit per item of perhaps ten minutes. Most information items can be dealt with in this amount of time; if more time is needed, another format such as a presentation or briefing group may be more appropriate. It is also worth questioning whether a meeting is the best medium for exchanging the information: if it needs more than ten minutes, it must be relatively complex or detailed, in which case a written document may be more appropriate. Providing the document has been circulated in advance of the meeting, the time in the meeting can be used to clarify understanding of any points that are not clear (for which ten minutes ought to be enough).

What threatens the ten-minute limit is the 'discussion' that may arise from a piece of new information. The process manager needs to be alert to the nature of this discussion and decide how it should be handled. It may be that the information has generated problems or conflicts: if so, these need to be dealt with under the appropriate problem-solving or conflict-resolution format, probably in a separate meeting, attended only by those directly concerned.

Alternatively the discussion may arise from ideas and opinions stimulated by the information: here the process manager needs to check whether these are of interest to the person who put the item on the agenda and, if not, stop the discussion. Unsolicited ideas and opinions are great time-wasters in meetings (formal and informal) and, because they tend to be heard as criticisms, they can damage the atmosphere of the meeting.

Another device for using the time of the meeting efficiently is to record the time taken for each item against the name of the individual who has raised it. At the end of the meeting it is possible to see who has taken up the time of the meeting: it makes people time-conscious and disciplined in their use of it.

With suitable planning by the process manager, and a little experience, it becomes possible to estimate the time required for the meeting and thus specify its finishing time as well as the starting time. The fixed duration of the meeting becomes a contract between those attending: 'The meeting will start at 2 p.m. and finish at 3.30.' It is vital to keep the contract: the meeting must start and finish on time.

What happens if items are still left over on the agenda when the finishing time is reached? Because this type of meeting is most commonly used for regular management meetings or committee meetings, left-over items can be raised at the next meeting.

Interestingly, in practice the left-over items seem to disappear between the meetings! Each individual has dealt with his or her priority items first, so by definition those left over are relatively unimportant and people seem to find other ways of dealing with them. So perhaps they should not have been on the agenda in the first place!

In addition to its time efficiency, the agenda meeting format also brings efficiency into minute-taking. At the conclusion of each item, the process manager asks the person who raised the item what, if anything, he or she wants recorded in the minutes about that item, and writes up on the flip chart the words used by the owner of the item. In this way the minutes are written publicly and openly, in the words of the person most concerned with each item. At the end of the meeting, the sheets can be torn off and the minutes typed.* This way there is no argument at the next meeting as to whether the minutes are a 'true and correct record' of what took place at the last meeting – they were there for everyone to see at the time. And there is no way an unscrupulous secretary can write minutes of the meeting he or she thought should have taken place – either before or after the meeting!

This method of writing the minutes is suitable when the minutes are for the benefit of the people attending the meeting (or who normally attend it, and may miss a particular meeting). In some organisations it is the practice to use the minutes of the meeting as a communication medium for other parties – for example, head office, higher levels of management, or other functions. The practice is superficially efficient, making one document serve two purposes, but in my view it is undesirable for that very reason – it does neither of the two very different functions well. It does not provide the clear concise record of decisions needed by those present, and it does not provide the background and context needed by remote parties to understand why they were taken. The minutes become a messy compromise, time-consuming to produce and unsatisfactory for either purpose. It is much better to produce a separate report for those who need it, written to meet their needs, and leave the minutes to do their job of providing a true and correct record of what was decided at the meeting.

The agenda meeting format as outlined here does not need to be adopted as a total package. Many of my colleagues and clients have developed their own variations to suit their own personal style and situation. The underlying principles can be used individually or in

* If you use a device called a copyboard, you can get instant A4 size copies of the manuscript minutes, which may make the typing unnecessary.

combination in a wide variety of meetings, formal and informal.

The underlying principles may be summarised as follows:

— separation of process management from content direction (there is no chairperson: the meeting is run by a process manager/ secretary. This role can be rotated among the members of the meeting);

— individual responsibility for content direction for each item, with each member of the meeting able to raise items for the agenda;

— clear specification, by the individual who has raised it, of the purpose of each item (information giving or getting, problem-solving, etc.);

— time discipline – the time limit per item, recording of time spent against each item, and a fixed duration of the meeting;

— visible recording of the minutes, on flip charts in the words of the person who raised the item.

Like any other tool, the agenda meeting format can be used appropriately or inappropriately. One senior manager used the time limit per item to cut off discussion of matters that were important to the group, without revealing that each member of the meeting could raise the same item under his own name at each stage of the meeting. The tool will be used most effectively by those who have been trained to do so, but common-sense application of the underlying principles will provide a quantum leap in the quality of most meetings of this kind.

Problem-solving meetings

The term 'problem-solving' is commonly used to describe two quite different kinds of activity, which require different kinds of meeting format. The two are:

— analytical problem-solving, where the objective is to diagnose the cause of the problem and, having done so, apply the appropriate known solution and;

— creative problem-solving, where the objective is to find a new course of action to achieve a desired objective, probably for the first time ever.

In the first case, a problem is defined (by Kepner and Tregoe) as 'a deviation from the norm', for example a machine breakdown, an interruption in the power supply, a car that will not start. By identifying the cause, the appropriate 'solution' – replace the fuse, put petrol in the car – can be called up and implemented. (Professor Revans suggests that such problems, where the solution is already known, are better called 'puzzles'. I agree; it would prevent the semantic confusion between the two kinds of problem-solving.)

In the second case, a problem is defined as 'the gap between where you are and where you want to be', without any known way of getting from one to the other satisfactorily. The objective is to invent or discover such a way. The solution will be new, at least to the person who has the problem, and there will be no certainty that it will work till it is tried out.

Techniques for both kinds of problem solving are discussed in depth in the Problem Solving section of this book. Here it is only necessary to identify the principal characteristics of each in so far as they determine the appropriate meeting formats, as follows:

Analytic	*Creative*
Logical: identifies cause and effect relationships	*Non-logical:* random
Linear: one item of knowledge leads logically to another	*Lateral:* goes beyond or outside the 'obvious' line of thought
Scientific: tests hypothesis against the data	*Imaginative* not constrained by known and what exists; considers what might be
Convergent: separates essentials from mass of information; screens out irrelevant data	*Divergent:* expands the problem and areas for solution
Deductive: making inferences from the available data	*Intuitive:* jumps to conclusions without 'proof'

The analytical problem solving meeting will be primarily concerned with factual information, its collection and examination, and the deductions to be made from it. In principle it is (or ought to be) a rational, objective and unemotional exercise, though there may be occasions when the group need to be inventive about ways to obtain data that is not immediately available and trade off decisions about the cost and trouble of collecting data compared with its potential value. There will need to be clarity about who is the principal decision-taker on the project, otherwise the meeting can get bogged down in arguments over preferred interpretations and explanations of the data. In process terms it ought to be a fairly easy meeting to run, the main requirement being to maintain the discipline of the group working on the same stage of the procedure at the same time.

The creative problem-solving meeting calls for a higher level of process skills and some special ground rules. Because it is dealing with the unknown and the aim is to invent new solutions, there will be a high level of uncertainty and ambiguity. New ideas need to be encouraged and stimulated; apparently irrelevant material may lead the discussion into new and productive ground.

For the participants, all this is a high-risk activity; they fear that they may make a fool of themselves by voicing thoughts that may be naive, impracticable or irrelevant. The main task of the process manager is to create an emotionally safe environment where the participants are protected from criticism and attack of any kind.

The simplest way to do this is through the brainstorming principle of 'suspending judgement', whereby evaluative comment is ruled out of order. There are no such things as 'good' or 'bad', 'relevant' or 'irrelevant', 'useful' or 'useless' ideas – there are only ideas, all of them acceptable, on the basis that 'quantity breeds quality'.

The process manager needs to be aware that even under conditions of suspended judgement a good deal of internal censoring of thoughts still goes on. There are many techniques* available to the process manager to encourage the participants to voice whatever is in their minds, without fear of rejection.

Having used the suspended judgement principle, and associated techniques for stimulating ideas to generate a wide range of options, the process manager must *prevent* the group from going into a screening process to sort out the 'good' from the 'bad' ideas. The ideas are still at an embryonic stage, and new interesting ideas are liable to be screened out because they are not yet feasible. The short list of 'good' ideas is likely to contain only old ideas – otherwise they would not be known to be 'good'.

Instead, the process manager must introduce a phase of 'developmental thinking' in which new and interesting ideas are

* Described in *Problem Solving*.

given a friendly 'benefit of the doubt' kind of evaluation. The evaluation is made by the 'problem owner' (the person with responsibility for solving the problem). Having first checked his or her understanding of the idea (and at least 50 per cent of ideas are misunderstood on first hearing), the person then identifies all its positive and potentially useful features and goes on to specify how it needs to be improved to bring it closer to a solution, and invites further ideas to do so.

This technique, known as itemised response,* maintains the emotionally safe environment of the suspended judgement rule, while permitting the gradual development of a new idea into a feasible and attractive solution. Because judgements of an idea will vary between individuals, it is important to leave this process in the hands of a single problem owner, until he or she has reached a conclusion. Thereafter a similar process can be used to collect group opinions about it if they are required.

Briefing meetings

Briefing meetings are regular short meetings in which a manager informs the team, as a group, of decisions and other matters that affect them. Typically they will be held once a month, with the timing planned so that decisions from higher levels of the organisation can be passed down to lower levels in sequence. The meetings are short – twenty to thirty minutes – with the bulk of the time devoted to information-giving by the manager and the remainder available for questions.

The process is a straightforward one-way process of information-giving, with provision to clarify understanding by questions from the recipients of the information. As such it does not require any elaborate format, and the responsible manager can handle both the content and the process without the need for a specialist process manager.

The briefing group system is intended to ensure that people in the organisation know what is happening and understand the reasons for the decisions. It has the potential for replacing rumour with fact and filling the vacuum that would otherwise be filled by assumptions and guesswork. As such it is potentially valuable for large organisations with many levels of hierarchy.

* First described by George Prince in *The Practice of Creativity* under the name spectrum policy.

There are clearly dangers of distortion arising in the multiple re-transmission of messages; one safeguard is the rule that a written brief should be provided when something has to be passed on through three levels of management.

Despite its obvious virtues, I find it difficult to summon up much enthusiasm for the briefing group system. The emphasis on one-way, top-down communication diverts attention from the need for genuine dialogue between manager and managed, with the manager doing more listening than talking. (To be fair, the briefing system is intended to co-exist with other procedures for consultation and participation to satisfy the requirement for upward communication.)

There is also an implicit assumption that if subordinates know and understand the reasons for management's decisions, they will be motivated to support and implement them with enthusiasm. Certainly such understanding is an aid to motivation, because its absence creates a vacuum that will be filled by speculation. But motivation is as much a matter of winning hearts as well as minds, and the success of briefing groups will depend as much on how they are conducted and perceived – matters of style – as on the content of the information which is passed on.

If this system is run in the somewhat paternalistic, quasi-military manner of 'management knows best, because it is management', it is as likely to be negative as positive in its effects on motivation. Too often that is the flavour that its advocates* convey however unintentionally.

Consultation meetings

A consultation meeting is one in which a manager collects opinions and ideas prior to making a decision. A decision is more likely to be successful if it takes into account the views and knowledge of those involved in implementing it. Because such people are closer to the action, they have knowledge and experience in depth which is not available to the manager. The fact of being consulted, of having their ideas listened to and considered, is in itself positively motivating.

If the process of consultation is to be valuable, it must, above all, be genuine: the manager must come to it with an open mind, ready to change his or her thinking in response to what is said. This does not mean the manager has to accept the view put to him or her; but

* For a full description of Briefing see John Garnett, *The Work Challenge*, Chapter 9.

if his or her thinking is markedly different from the consensus of opinion, he or she will need to spell out reasons for this very clearly, without disparaging alternative views.

For the process of consultation to be genuine, it must *not* be used when a manager has already reached a decision. His or her mind will then be closed to alternatives, the meeting will sense that that is the case, and instead of getting genuine ideas and opinions the manager will have set up a game of 'guess what's in my mind'. The meeting will endeavour to produce the solution the manager has already thought of, to bring the insulting charade to an end, but the damage will go well beyond the meeting.

Instead of gaining commitment to the decision, an exercise in pseudo-consultation will alienate. There will be resentment, understandably, at the attempt to deceive, at being treated like children. The resentment will find expression in non-cooperation and lack of commitment to the decision.

To avoid these dangers, it is essential that the manager declares his or her position. He or she is unlikely to come to the meeting without any pre-conceived ideas and must put these on the table before inviting contributions from the group. The manager must also make it clear which parts of his or her position are fixed, either for reasons of company policy or personal conviction, and which are open to change.

Given these preconditions, the format of the problem-solving meeting adapts very well to the purposes of consultation. There is the same need for a climate in which people feel able to express what they think and feel without fear of criticism or personal rejection. A process manager can create that environment, by spelling out the ground rules (for example, no judgement of ideas) and enforcing them. The decision-taking manager is the 'problem owner', responsible for directing the content of the meeting. He or she may want to use the meeting only for the collection of ideas and opinions, and arrive at a decision privately, outside the meeting; or he or she may feel able to reach a conclusion in the meeting.

One difference from the problem-solving meeting is that there may be a greater emphasis on opinions than ideas. These can be collected efficiently and openly by adapting the itemised response mechanism for evaluating ideas, to collecting opinions on a group basis. It works as follows:

— The process manager asks members of the meeting to make their own private evaluation of the subject under discussion by writing down

171

(a) what they like about it – all the good features, useful aspects, benefits, etc.;
(b) what they do not like about it – their concerns, anxieties, the needs for change and improvement.

— When everyone has finished writing, the process manager asks for sharing of the views, on the basis that each will be accepted and written up as true for that individual, without argument or discussion. Anyone who disagrees with a point can express that disagreement in his or her own list of positives and negatives.

— The process leader then asks for one positive point from each individual in turn (to prevent one person's views pre-empting the rest) and continues until all the positives have been collected.

— He then does the same with the negatives, at the same time encouraging the contributors to convert their negatives into directions for improvement, for example, if the negative is that the system is too slow, the direction for improvement may be that 'we need to find ways to speed it up'.

— The directions for improvement can then be used to stimulate ideas (if they are wanted by the problem owner), for example, 'How might we speed the system up?' *Ideas:* 'Use telex instead of the mail'; 'Install electronic mail'.

This structured method of collecting opinions acknowledges that an opinion is a truth about the individual who holds it, and it is quite normal for different people to see situations differently. There is little point about arguing who is right or who is wrong (unless there is relevant factual evidence which might change a view). It provides a format for people to say what they really think without fear of being criticised for their opinions.

It is also a valuable format for a manager who wants to test the effect of a decision he or she is currently considering or has indeed already made. The manager must make it clear what he or she proposes to do with the feedback – is the decision open to modification in the light of the feedback, or is he or she only seeking to identify consequential problems arising from the decision, so that they can be dealt with? Either is a legitimate purpose, but the group need to know why their opinion is being sought, and what is to be done with it.

Conflict resolution

The traditional model for resolving conflict is the debate. As I have argued earlier, it does not work. You may 'win' the debate, but in doing so you will probably have lost the support and commitment of the other side. And you have stored up trouble for yourself in the future: next time they will see you coming, dig the elephant traps deeper and wider and camouflage them more skilfully.

Is there an alternative? Not always, but in many cases there is, assuming some common ground and common objectives between the parties and enough open-mindedness to explore alternatives. In Ulster, to take an extreme example, these assumptions would probably not hold, any more than they did between Arthur Scargill and Ian MacGregor in the coal industry dispute of 1984–5.

But in the normal business organisation it is reasonable to assume that common ground and common objectives do generally exist. If they do not, the organisation is indeed in serious trouble, and only radical surgery – removal of one of the contending parties – is likely to resolve it.

Given the necessary preconditions, the conflict can be shifted into the problem-solving mode and tackled in two ways (either or both of which may be appropriate in any individual situation). The first is to view the two opposing views as *only two of many* possible ways of dealing with the situation. It is then necessary to identify the problem that these solutions are addressing and invent alternatives. With both parties involved in the invention process, there is a reasonable chance that together they can develop an alternative solution that is acceptable to both of them.

The second way is to subject each of the existing proposals to a constructive evaluation, using group itemised response as described in the section on consultation meetings and seek ideas for improving each of them by overcoming the concerns and dealing with the consequential problems they generate. Sometimes it will be found that one of the proposals can be developed to the point at which it becomes acceptable to the other party; sometimes a hybrid proposal will emerge that satisfies both sides.

There is no guarantee that this process will necessarily resolve the conflict, but it will at least increase the understanding and mutual respect, where an argument would deepen the division. What is being described is emphatically *not* a compromise, but a 'creative consensus' – the final solution is likely to be of better quality than either of the two original propositions.

Team meetings

Under this category I include all meetings and get-togethers (even conferences) which have as a primary objective the building of morale, commitment, team spirit, etc. It is this emotional dimension which makes them different from other types of meeting, and also make them particularly tricky to handle.

Of course the emotional dimension is present in all meetings to some extent, and the way people feel about the meeting itself will have an effect on their morale and commitment. As a rule, if the everyday meetings are functionally efficient and constructive (following the procedures suggested in the previous sections), the emotional dimension will take care of itself – people feel good about participating in good-quality meetings. Conversely, if the general quality of meetings is bad, there will be widespread frustration and a debilitating effect on the general morale of the organisation.

Equally, I believe that team meetings intended to build morale in a positive way also need a functional focus or task. Thus a sales team will get together to report back their experience in the field and to hear about new promotions, new products, etc., even though the most important purpose of the meeting may be to regenerate their confidence, morale and sense of belonging which may have been drained during their weeks on the road. Similarly a team in manufacturing or some other function will meet to discuss its objectives and the problems involved in achieving them, while at the same time seeking to strengthen teamwork and mutual understanding.

It is of course feasible to set up meetings to deal directly with the way the team is working, but in my experience they are fraught with difficulty. Because of the often deep-seated emotional issues that may arise between individual team members, such meetings can easily develop into something akin to a group therapy session, needing a skilled and qualified group therapist to handle them.

My colleagues and I have experimented with the use of psychotherapists to run team meetings of this kind, with mixed success. While they may have some powerful benefits to offer to small, informal organisations, I do not think they are appropriate in the typical corporation. And they are certainly beyond the scope of the typical manager to run himself. Without specialist control, they can do more harm than good through opening up issues that are beyond the ability of the group to resolve.

Assuming, then, that the team meeting is being held in the context of some functional purpose, we need to identify meeting processes that will ensure that the emotional objectives are also achieved – that the members of the team will leave feeling better about themselves, the team and the organisation of which it is part, than they felt when they arrived. To do this, the meeting must be experienced as having the following characteristics:

— appreciative rather than punishing;
— forward-looking rather than oriented to the past;
— co-operative rather than divisive;
— open and honest rather than guarded or devious.

These characteristics are easy to specify and much more difficult to achieve in practice. Fortunately, the techniques developed for creative problem-solving go a long way in this direction. In order to encourage people to voice ideas in the embryonic, formative stage, it is necessary to create an emotionally safe climate. The same methods of creating an emotionally safe environment can be used to provide the positive characteristics needed for the team meeting.

In particular, the way in which judgements are handled is critical. Criticism, however 'constructive' it is intended to be, will always be experienced negatively, and in my view it has no place in a team meeting. I prefer to take the view that each member of the team is his or her own severest critic anyway, and will be only too painfully aware of shortcomings and failures. What that person needs from the leader and colleagues is appreciation of his or her achievements and for efforts made even when he or she has not been successful (most people are weak at self-appreciation).

Of course the failures and the shortcomings need to be addressed, but in the form of future-oriented problems, goals and wishes – what do we need to do differently in the future to achieve the results we want? Emotionally this is a very different ball game from criticism of past performance. It is also a much more rational use of energy: we cannot change the past, but we can manage the future differently with the help of what we learn from past experience.

Another set of techniques common to creative problem-solving and to team meetings is the use of metaphor and imaging. In problem-solving they are used to stimulate new ideas by getting some distance from the problem and tapping into the mind's subconscious connection-making processes. In the team meeting, they enable people to articulate indirectly emotional attitudes that would be too difficult to express directly.

For example, at a recent management conference, I asked the participants, 'If the company were a motor car, what make and model would it be – and why?' – a simple use of the car as a metaphor for the company. One participant responded, 'It's one of those old Messerschmidt bubble cars – only the driver knows where it's going', provoking a roar of laughter and applause that delivered a very clear and powerful message to the newly appointed general manager.

Similar effects can be achieved by visioning techniques, in which the group are asked to describe a highly desirable future state of the team – 'What will it be like in five years' time, assuming things have gone extraordinarily well?' Again, the method gives licence to express feelings and aspirations that might not otherwise be articulated. Projecting the task into the future, and making it explicitly wishful, creates a situation that is beyond criticism.

If you want to be more ambitious, you can consider borrowing techniques from the world of drama or even party games. In the right circumstances, it can be fun to have the team compose, and perform, a company song. Such exercises can help to mobilise the emotional energies of the team. It is no accident that the All Blacks rugby teams prepare themselves for the game with a Maori war chant and some Japanese businesses start the day with the company song.

However far you choose to go down this road, the key factor in running the team meeting is sensitivity to the emotional factors involved and dealing with them positively and constructively – if necessary giving them priority over the functional objectives. A team with high morale will achieve its objectives anyway.

7. Improving your personal communication skills

Introduction

In the preceding discussions of different aspects of communications I have suggested a variety of ways in which communication generally can be made more effective. I now want to focus on what you, as an individual manager, can do to improve your own communication skills.

Once again, the starting point has to be the distinction between the transmitting and receiving activities. Consistent with the emphasis throughout, I propose to put more stress on the receiving activities – listening, looking and reading – than on the transmitting ones – speaking, presenting and writing – for several reasons.

— Quantitatively, they are bound to be the greater part of your activity – simply because so many transmissions have multiple recipients.

— Qualitatively, they provide the most scope for improvement, because they are generally the most neglected.

— Synergistically, the greater your awareness and understanding of the receiving processes, the greater the opportunity to design your own transmissions to be 'user-friendly', and so have maximum impact on the recipients.

In other words, understanding of the receiving process is the key to being an effective transmitter. An important part of this under-standing comes from working to improve your own receiving skills.

Putting the emphasis on receiving rather than transmitting is probably going to require a much bigger shift of attitude than you may anticipate: almost certainly you think of your work in terms of its communication-initiating activities, rather than communication-receiving. The bulging in-tray, the incoming phone call, the meeting you have to attend – all these feel like diversions from getting on with the real job, the things you want to achieve. And when you are free from such distractions, what do you do to get on with the 'real' job? Very probably you generate letters and memos, make phone calls, set up meetings – communication-initiating activities, which increase the communication-receiving burden of the recipients!

There is a serious mismatch in the supply and demand for 'communications', a great excess of transmissions over willing recipients. In part, this may be an inevitable part of the screening process by which sellers locate the serious prospects for their offerings. Thus a mailshot which has a small percentage response can be very effective in marketing terms, even though, for the great majority of recipients, it represents more 'junk mail'. But it applies equally in management communications generally, and presents a very serious problem of 'communication overload' for the individual manager.

If you are not careful, it is all too easy to be overwhelmed by the incoming tide of communications, much of it redundant and some of it provoked by your own ill-considered transmissions. So discrimination is a key skill: is your communication really necessary? Do I really need to read this document, go to this meeting, send this memo (and to all those people), engage in this phone conversation? Quality, not quantity, is the objective in communication.

One tactic for protecting yourself against one part of the overload, the incoming phone call, is the Townsend technique mentioned earlier: he refuses to take any calls before 11 a.m. and instructs his switchboard to take the name and number of the caller. After 11 a.m. he returns *all* the calls, at the time of his choice and with the advantage of being the caller, not the called. I sometimes wonder what would happen if *all* managers adopted the same tactic!

The major defence against overload, however, is a whole new perspective on information. Modern technology, with the convergence of computers, satellites, word processing, video, copiers and phone systems, is the source of the overload but can also free us from it if we change our attitudes to information.

Coping with information overload

Almost certainly, at some stage or other in your career, you will have heard someone pronounce, with an air of great wisdom, 'Information is power.' (You might even have said it yourself – I suspect I have!) It is put forward as a self-evident truth, with the implied corollary that to be 'well informed' is a high priority.

I believe it is rubbish, and dangerous rubbish at that. Winston Fletcher (in his book *Meetings, Meetings*) points out that 'Knowledge is power' is a seventeenth-century proverb, not a dazzling twentieth-century discovery. Note that the proverb says knowledge, not information, and although information is one kind of knowledge, it is not, nowadays, the powerful kind. It is 'know-how', that is, skills and ability to do things, that is truly powerful, not 'know that', that is, information.

No doubt in the seventeenth century – and indeed, until quite recently – to have exclusive information, to know something no one else knew, put you in a position of power. Thus the Rothschilds are reputed to have made a killing on the stock market through having advance information brought to them by carrier pigeon of Napoleon's defeat at Waterloo.

But developments in telecommunications have 'collapsed the information float', as John Naisbitt puts it (in *Megatrends*). The interval of time in which information was exclusive property to a few privileged individuals before it became generally known has been eliminated by an increasingly sophisticated worldwide telephone and satellite network. (And if you happen to have exclusive information which you use to your financial advantage on the Stock Exchange you are liable to be charged with 'insider trading', a criminal offence.)

The same technology has vastly increased the sheer volume of information that is generated. Naisbitt quotes estimates that scientific and technical information, already doubling every five and a half years, will soon be doubling every twenty months, with the dangers of 'information pollution' and 'drowning in information while being starved of knowledge'. (Note Naisbitt's sharp differentiation between information and knowledge.)

The developments call for a new perspective on information and a new strategy for dealing with it. Information is a resource to be drawn upon as and when we need it, not a commodity to be accumulated and stored in the individual's memory. The skills of

179

knowing how to find the information you need, and how to handle it when you have found it, become much more important than the information itself.

The implications for your own communication strategy are striking. No longer is it necessary to keep informed and up to date by voluminous reading; indeed it is no longer possible. Not only does the volume of information grow at an unmanageable rate, but the diversity of sources of relevant, or potentially relevant information is multiplying at the same time.

Nor is it necessary to be able to retain information in the memory in the same way as has been necessary in the past. Many of the books written about improving thinking skills and mental abilities put great stress on techniques for memorising, assuming that an improved memory is intrinsically valuable. I am not so sure; I suspect that the writers are coming from an academic orientation, where the ability to succeed in examinations is a prime value and depends heavily on the ability to regurgitate information from memory.

In the real world, if you want information you can get it when you need it by looking at the file, the reference book, the computer database, or by asking the person who knows. Providing you know where and how to look, you don't need to carry the information in your own head.

Fortunately the same technology that creates the problem of too much data has provided the means to deal with it, through the technique of networking. Networking is simply the process of talking to the people with whom you want to share information, ideas and resources. If you do not know where to go for a particular piece of information, start by asking someone else who might know; if they do not know themselves, they can put you in touch with others who might, enabling you to reach your goal by a series of successive approximations. It is claimed that six or seven interactions is the maximum that is needed to reach the person who knows. 'With networks to help,' says Naisbitt, 'we can select and acquire only the information we need as quickly as possible.'

I am not of course suggesting that you give up reading, but that your reading takes on an orientation that is geared to this new situation. I suggest you read widely, to increase your general awareness and stimulate your own thinking, rather than narrowly, to accumulate information in your own specialist field. And again it is the quality not the quantity that counts. Read whatever you find stimulating, at a pace you find comfortable, and do not worry about remembering it all, or indeed about the material you 'should' read and have not got round to. (Apart from anything else, it will make your reading a pleasure rather than a chore.)

Finally a word of warning about the quality of much of the so-called information generated by the information explosion. Much of it is second-hand (or third-, fourth- and fifth-hand) and every time it is passed on it is likely to be changed – sometimes enhanced, more often distorted. If you are concerned about the quality of the information, you need to know how it was generated in the first place, and what qualifications attach to it. So you must get as close as possible to the prime source, the individual who first produced it.

The networking approach provides the opportunity to seek out the prime source: as Naisbitt puts it, 'Networks cut diagonally across the institutions that house information and put people directly in touch with the person or resource they seek.' The process of networking gives a new meaning to the saying 'It's not what you know but who you know that counts.' Originally it meant that knowing influential people was the key to advancement. Now it means knowing whom to go to for help and information when you need it. In this sense, 'who you know' is now under your own control; you can build your own network by seeking out the people who can be helpful to you, and whom you can help (since networking is essentially a reciprocal process between like-minded people).

So in today's world it is not so much 'knowledge' that is power, as knowing how to create your own network of friends and resources – a different matter altogether. And the ability to create your own networks depends in turn on your communication skills, particularly the art of quickly establishing a cooperative relationship with a stranger, usually over the telephone.

8. Listening

Barriers to listening

The problem with listening is that we do not see it as a problem. We assume that it is easy, because we do it all the time, and we rarely know that we have not listened successfully. Earlier I quoted success rates for communication of only 25 per cent (under average conditions) to 50 per cent (under the most favourable conditions I know how to create). A little thought about how many factors are at work in the communication transaction begins to explain why the figures are so low and, more importantly, what you can do to raise them.

My colleague John Alexander has invited groups of participants on training courses to list the 'barriers to listening' that they are aware of from their own experience, and has published the following consolidated list.

— Listener has preconceived ideas.
— Listener thinks he knows more than the speaker.
— Listener is worried about something else (for example, time, personal things).
— Listener is tired or physically uncomfortable.
— Listener is afraid of the speaker, or envious, or prejudiced about him, or just not interested.
— Listener is anxious to input his own ideas.
— Speaker mumbles, coughs, etc., or has heavy accent.

— Speaker uses confusing technical jargon or inflammatory words.
— Speaker uses words open to many interpretations.
— There is some external noise (traffic, pneumatic drills, etc.).
— There are interruptions (the telephone, etc.)

Some of these barriers have to do with the speaker, some with the environment, but the most important ones, in my experience, are those concerning the listener. Probably the fastest way to increase the success rate of your communicating is to listen better.

To do so, you need to be convinced that there is a need, or an opportunity. It is quite difficult to discover how good (or bad) a listener you are, particularly if you believe yourself to be a good listener. One way is ask people who know you well – spouse, friends, colleagues – to rate your listening on a scale of one to five (where five is excellent and one is very bad), but you are dependent on both their honesty and their standards. If the general level of listening is poor, they may rate you highly when you have plenty of scope for improvement.

Or you can try a self-administered test. Try listening to the news, on radio or TV, and see how much of it you can recall an hour or two later – not the detail, but the topics covered. (I have to admit that the first time I tried this I scored two out of ten!)

Perhaps the best way is to develop the practice of using paraphrase – playing back to the speaker your understanding of what he or she is saying. If the speaker accepts your paraphrase as accurate as often as not (that is, 50 per cent of the time), you are doing well. (Though the very act of paraphrasing will itself raise your listening level, for reasons I will go into later, and therefore it will bias the test – but it is a good practice anyway.)

Assuming you have decided you would like to improve your listening skills, how should you go about it? I suggest the following five approaches:

— Listen appropriately.
— Manage the meeting in your head.
— Check understanding when necessary.
— Listen with an open mind.
— Develop your non-verbal listening.

Appropriate listening

Listening is not all of one piece; there are different kinds of listening that are appropriate to different situations. It depends on what you are listening for. It could be

— to be polite;
— to get some precise information (such as directions to an unfamiliar place);
— to understand a problem or a proposition;
— to sympathise;
— to find fault;
— to screen out irrelevant material;
— to be stimulated into thinking of new ideas.

You can probably add to the list. Clearly, *how* you should listen depends on *why* you are listening, on what you are listening *for*. If you are listening for directions on how to get to an unfamiliar place, you need to be listening very precisely. If you are listening only out of politeness, you may only need to listen with sufficient attention to make the appropriate noises at the right intervals. If you are listening to be sympathetic, your attention will be turned to the feelings that are being expressed, rather than to the information content. If you are listening to find fault, you will have your critical faculties on full alert – although this is a dangerous practice, as we shall see below, because the critical judgement can get in the way of the understanding which needs to precede it. Listening for ideas needs awareness of the connections being thrown up in your own mind as the speaker talks, with less emphasis on precise understanding of what is being said.

In each situation you need to be aware of why you are listening, and switch your listening into the appropriate mode – almost like tuning your receiver on to the correct wavelength.

Managing the meeting in your head

Listening is difficult, because it does not occur in isolation. There is a continuous stream of consciousness in the listener's head, made up partly of understanding and interpretation of what he or she is hearing, partly of the associations and connections, and partly of other preoccupations and interests that may have nothing whatever to do with the external dialogue.

There is a considerable risk that what the speaker is saying has to compete for attention with what is going on independently in the listener's head. If there is a competition, the meeting in the head is odds-on favourite to win. It is probably more interesting (to the listener), because it consists of the listener's thoughts rather than the speaker's. It is certainly much richer and fuller, because we think so much faster than we speak. Typical speaking speeds are about 150 words a minute, compared with thinking speeds estimated in the range of 800–1000 words a minute, or a stream of mental pictures, each one 'worth a thousand words'.

It is not surprising, therefore, that typical listening patterns, over short periods of time like two to three minutes, have been shown to be as in the diagram on page 186.

Typically, attention starts at a high level, drops to a much lower level as something the speaker says triggers a line of thought in the listener's mind, and comes up to a somewhat higher level when the listener has sorted out the thought to his or her own satisfaction. Often he or she will have been preparing a response to what the speaker is saying, and at the end is listening for an opportunity to speak. (For this reason the curve is known as the rehearsal curve.)

In a meeting of several people, it may be a little while before you can get your rehearsed point into the discussion. The tendency then is to concentrate on getting into the discussion, during which time you are not listening very attentively. 'Waiting to speak,' says John Alexander, 'is not the same thing as listening.'

Note that the listener is preparing a response on the basis of about one-third of what the speaker is saying. It is quite common,

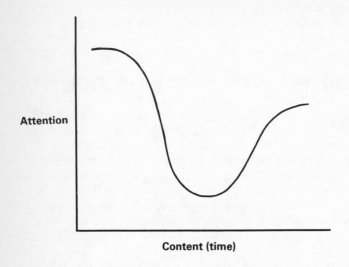

especially with people we know well, to assume we know how they are going to complete what they are saying – we are tempted, indeed, to finish the sentence for them if they hesitate.

The assumption that we know what the speaker is going to say is only one of many 'mindsets' that can affect the way we listen. If we have a poor opinion of the speaker, we will tend to discount what he or she is saying; if we are hostile, we will focus on flaws or points of disagreement. If we think the speaker is a genius, we will tend to hear pearls of wisdom. Different listeners with these different mindsets could hear correspondingly different messages from the same speaker at the same time, because each has unconsciously selected those aspects of the message that support a particular preconception.

To listen successfully, we need to ensure that the 'meeting in the head' complements rather than competes with what the speaker is saying. The connections we make between what he or she is saying and our own databank of experience enable us to make sense of what we are hearing. They are at the heart of communication – the meeting of minds at some point of common experience or understanding. It is hardly surprising that we value the connection so highly that we want to explore it more fully and so drop out of listening into the meeting in the head – thereby missing the rest of the message.

The best solution I know to this problem is not to fight the connection making but to encourage it with a system of note taking that captures the connections but does not explore them immediately. It consists of making a quick key-word note of whatever has occurred to me and an immediate return to high-level listening until the next connection, and so on. With practice the speed of connection making and noting becomes so fast that it is almost instantaneous and can be done without interrupting the high-level listening. The technique is known, unsurprisingly, as 'in–out listening'.

Making key-word notes of the connections can be combined with key-word notes of what the speaker is saying, that is, conventional lecture notes, but in the form of key words rather than phrases or sentences. Tony Buzan (in *Use Your Head*) points out that key words are much more efficient; they save 90% of the time taken in writing and reading longer notes, and the time wasted in searching for the critical points.

Buzan (and others e.g. Mark Brown in *Memory Matters*, Peter Russell in the *Brain Book*) advocates making notes in the form of patterns – 'mind maps' – rather than serially, in linear form. When the main object of listening is to be able to recall what was said, such 'mind maps' are highly efficient. I once gave a forty-five minute lecture on the Synectics problem-solving method. Immediately afterwards a member of the audience, Robert Fleming, showed me his notes in the form of a mind map. On a single page he had captured the gist of everything that I had said.

Buzan also distinguishes between key words for recall and key words for creative thinking, which takes us back to the previous point about the purpose of listening. If the purpose is to be able to reproduce the information, or refer back to it, a suitable key word is one which 'funnels into itself a wide range of special images and which, when it is triggered, funnels back the same images'.

If the purpose of listening is to be triggered into ideas (as it is in creative problem-solving) then the key words in my view should be those which capture the image or association triggered by the speaker's words. Those connections are clues to new ideas; as though they are thrown up by the brain as a file reference to some experience or knowledge that may have a bearing on the problem. Buzan talks of key creative words as those 'which are particularly evocative and image forming'; these would be valuable if the purpose of the listening was to trigger some creative writing, for example.

Noting key words and making mind maps are relatively simple skills which can be developed by practice whenever you are in a position to take notes, which should be the case in most serious working conversations. Occasionally you may find people who are worried by your note-taking (possibly for fear the notes may be used 'in evidence against them'), and if you sense this might be the case it is worth asking permission ('Do you mind if I take a few notes?)'. I do not think that anyone has ever refused me permission; I am after all paying that person the compliment of taking what he or she says seriously.

Checking understanding

Given that one of the great dangers in communication is 'the assumption that it has taken place', it makes sense to check that the assumption is correct. The mechanism for doing this is deceptively simple: play back to the speaker your understanding of what was meant, and ask him or her to confirm that it is accurate, or amend it as necessary. In short, paraphrase and check.

Simple it may be in concept, but its power and effectiveness depends on the skill with which you use it. Appropriate use is a matter of knowing both when and how to paraphrase. Clearly we do not need to paraphrase everything that is said to us – that would make for a very laboured and slow-moving conversation indeed. And it could be self-defeating, because the speaker might well abandon an attempt to communicate out of sheer boredom and frustration.

So, when to paraphrase? The principal occasions, in my experience, are the following:

— when precise understanding is vital – for example, when receiving directions for getting to an unfamiliar place, or instructions to carry out a complex operation;

— when you are not sure you have understood (or you are sure you have *not* understood). Playing back to the speaker what you have received makes it easier for the person to fill in the missing pieces and correct the misperceptions. Simply saying 'I don't understand' or 'would you repeat that?' puts the whole burden of correct communication on the speaker, without giving any clue as to where the difficulty lies. The paraphrase is a way of sharing the responsibility;

— when you disagree with what the speaker is saying. Misunderstanding is a common source of disagreement, and before expressing your disagreement it is worth checking that what you disagree with is actually what was meant. The odds are that it is not. The emotional reaction of disagreeing clouds the ability to listen, so the paraphrase is particularly necessary in these circumstances. It also has the great virtue of slowing down the exchange and gives the speaker the opportunity to restate his or her position more accurately than he or she may have done the first time. The paraphrase and check provides some common ground of agreement between the parties, if only about what is being said, and thus creates a more positive relationship than total disagreement;

— before you express a judgement about what is being put forward – for example, an idea or proposition. The habit of instant judgement is so deeply ingrained in our culture (it is part of a successful manager's image of 'decisiveness') that it very often *precedes* understanding. You will hear many people express opinions about things they have not experienced (a practice that Guinness nicely parodied in the advertisement which said, 'I don't like it so I've never tried it'). Paraphrasing the idea compels you to understand before you judge, a common-sense principle that is widely flouted in practice. The need to make the paraphrase forces you to defer judgement at least long enough to hear what is actually being said, rather than assuming you know already. And it helps you to discover that very often you did not correctly understand the idea, so that your instant judgement was inevitably flawed;

— when responding to a question. We have seen elsewhere that questions can be asked for a great variety of reasons, some straightforward, many devious. If you suspect that the question is anything other than straight, you can use a paraphrase to express your best guess at the reason it is being asked;

— more generally, whenever you suspect that there is more to what is being said than is actually being voiced, you can use a paraphrase to check out the suspicion. Here you are playing back to the speaker the total effect that the communication is having on you, and giving him or her the chance to change that effect, if it is not what was intended.

I do not claim that this listing of occasions for paraphrasing is complete. As you experiment with the technique you will discover for yourself when it is most valuable to you. It is worth observing other people's use of paraphrase too. You will find that those who have the reputation of being good listeners use it a great deal, and with some subtlety.

Which brings us to the question of how to paraphrase, and how not to. Kathryn Thomas of McKinsey and Co., Management Consultants, distinguishes three levels of paraphrase, each appropriate to different situations:

Level one is a fairly literal playing back of what has been said. It is appropriate to such things as directions for finding an address, or steps in carrying out a series of operations.

Level two is an expression of what the statement has meant to the listener, from the listener's frame of reference. So the paraphrase contains an element of interpretation; it is a description of the 'second transformation' (from Schumacher's four stages of communication quoted at the beginning of this book). It is my understanding of what you meant, not what you actually said in so many words. Level Two paraphrase is appropriate to the communication of ideas and opinions, where Level One is limited to information.

Level three goes beyond what has actually been said to what the listener believes is behind the statement, including the feelings or viewpoint from which the statement (or question) is being made. In a sense it is a guess, or intuition, on the part of the listener, but instead of keeping the guess private, he or she checks it out openly with the speaker. The listener is probably playing back impressions picked up from the tone of voice and non-verbal behaviour of the speaker. As we have seen earlier, these are much the most important parts of the message, when there is conflict between them and the words themselves. A Level Three paraphrase, therefore, is particularly valuable as a way of acknowledging (and checking out) an unspoken emotional message. It is also useful as a way of handling both questions and negative reactions. It is essential, when responding to a question, to know why it is being asked: a Level Three paraphrase is a best guess at where the question is coming from. Even if the guess is not accurate, it will probably elicit from the speaker the real reason for asking the question, and the listener is then in a position to respond appropriately.

When someone is disagreeing with you, either overtly or non-verbally, a paraphrase along the lines, 'I have the impression you see it differently; if so I'd like to hear about it', brings the reaction out into the open and acknowledges its legitimacy. It also starts the discussion of the disagreement on a positive note: 'Yes, I do see it differently.'

Similarly, you can use a Level Three paraphrase when you suspect that someone is inviting you to play 'guess what's in my mind', that is, inviting ideas and opinions when the person has already made a decision. 'I have a sense that you've already made your decision. Is that correct?' If the answer is yes, then you may legitimately ask what the decision is, and why it is still being discussed.

A Level Three paraphrase can also be a valuable tool for anyone in a teaching or coaching role (and this includes managers, one of whose roles, whether they realise it or not, is to act as a coach or trainer for the people who work for them). By paraphrasing the difficulty that the teacher believes the student is having, he or she can help the student articulate the problem, and make the initial connection with the student's existing knowledge (which is essential if the new material is to make any sense).

Given the many varieties of paraphrase and uses for it, and the potential benefits which make it such a powerful tool, it is worth taking some trouble to learn to use it appropriately and skilfully. The simplest place to start is with Level One, where the need is most obvious. 'I'd like to check that I've got that' provides a straightforward explanation of why you are paraphrasing. It also takes responsibility for the need for paraphrase: it arises from my shortcomings as a listener, not from your garbled ways of speaking.

Similarly a Level Two paraphrase can be expressed as 'I'd like to check that I've properly understood what you are saying before we discuss it', again taking responsibility for the need to paraphrase. A Level Three paraphrase might be expressed, 'I have the impression that . . .', again a truth about me, rather than a statement (or an accusation) about the speaker. I am quite happy to have my impression corrected, if I have got it wrong.

Note that all these formulations attempt to introduce the paraphrase in natural, everyday language, as a natural, everyday practice (which it will become, over time). There is a danger at first in using it in a heavy-handed, mechanical way, with phrases like 'What I am hearing you say is . . .', which quickly grate on the recipient. They also sound as though you are putting words in his or her mouth, whereas the intention is to play back your experience, not the speaker's. As with any powerful tool, handle it with care.

It will be clear that the benefit of checking understanding goes far beyond the prevention of accidental misunderstandings and crossed lines (though this in itself would be sufficient reason for doing it). Essentially it is a process of sharing responsibility for the success of the communication, and in so doing creating a bond between speaker and listener.

In addition, knowing that you are likely to want to paraphrase is a strong incentive to listening at a high level of attention. It is disappointing to discover that what you heard is not what he meant. The practice of paraphrase gives you feedback on how well you are listening, and this awareness will encourage more attentive listening.

You may be left with the feeling that this is all very well, but hardly practical in the busy everyday world. A former colleague of mine was trying to explain it to the person sitting next to her at a dinner-party. He said: 'That's impossible – people would never stand for you repeating back to them what they've just said.'

She replied, 'You think people would object if you tried to check your understanding of what they were saying?'

'Yes I do.'

'Well, I've just done it to you, and you don't seem to be objecting.'

The man conceded the point gracefully and spent the rest of the dinner-party chuckling over it.

Listening with an open mind

I referred earlier to the tendency to make instant judgements on what is being said, at the expense of accurate listening, and advocated paraphrase as a mechanism to help you defer judgement at least until you have understood. But the problem of listening in a judgemental frame of mind goes deeper than that – it can cut you off from much of the value that the speaker has to offer you. A judgemental mind tends to be a closed mind. It pays to stay open-minded when you are listening, because then you are more likely to learn something new, either directly from what the speaker is saying, or from the connections and thoughts triggered in your own mind.

What is needed is change of mindset, from listening to agree or disagree, to listening to find out what new discoveries are to be made. The new mindset starts from an acceptance that everyone is likely to have a different view of the world, based on their different personalities and experiences. I do not have to adopt the other person's point of view, but accept that it is valid for him or her, and I may have something to learn from it.

I may not need to make any judgement as to whether that person is 'right' or 'wrong' (that is, whether I agree with his or her view or not): I may simply absorb the opinion into my databank as his or her view, which might (or might not) turn out to be interesting or useful. Certainly I need to defer any judgement until all the returns are in, that is, until the person has finished speaking and I have checked my understanding.

Assuming you do need to make a judgement, it is possible to do it in a reasonably open-minded way, by getting yourself off the binary agree/disagree, right/wrong hook. Instead of judging the message as a whole in this way, look at it in detail. You will probably find that there are parts you agree with and others where you differ. It is worth acknowledging the areas of agreement: to do so establishes the common ground between yourself and the speaker and puts the differences of view into a truer perspective than if you simply focus on the differences. The differences are worth exploring in some depth; it is arrogant to assume that because you differ you are necessarily right and he or she is wrong. It may be that the speaker knows something you do not know, and that you have something to learn from him or her.

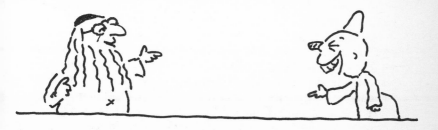

A Finnish proverb asks, 'When a fool talks to a wise man, who benefits the most?' The answer is the wise man, because he is good at learning; that is why he is a wise man. The fool is a fool because he does not know how to learn, so he does not learn even from the wise man. The wise man listens with an open mind.

There are of course times when you cannot afford the luxury of listening with an open mind – generally when you are fighting for your life in some kind of adversarial win/lose situation, like a debate or legal case. Even here, you do well to acknowledge, mentally, the strong points of your opponent's case, so that you steer the argument away from those areas to the areas of weakness.

It is even better to avoid the adversarial situation altogether if you can. Once you find yourself in an argument, the communication channels are already breaking down. When a topic is 'hammered out on the anvil of debate', the noise of the hammering tends to drown the communication.

Non-verbal listening

Given that the tone of voice and non-verbals (gestures, facial expressions and other 'body language') convey a much larger proportion of the message than the words themselves, when there is any inconsistency between them, it follows that we need to listen to the tone of voice, as well as the words, and also watch as we listen. In fact these are skills we all had as babies, when for the first year of our lives we responded only to tone and non-verbals.

Many of us, however, need to rediscover the skills we had as children. The processes of education, particularly higher education, put a premium on words and the development of verbal skills. The non-verbal skills tend to atrophy as a result of intellectualisation, one symptom of which can be excessive preoccupation with words.

It is noticeable that people with relatively little formal education seem to be better listeners than 'intellectuals', partly because they have never lost the skills of non-verbal listening. It is, I believe, an important factor in being 'streetwise', that is, sharp and perceptive about what is actually happening around you, as opposed to the naivety and absent-mindedness of the proverbial professor.

If, like me, you suspect that your non-verbal listening is not all it could be, it is worth deliberately cultivating your imaging/visualising skills. Look carefully at the mental pictures you have; deliberately conjure up mental pictures; look closely at the world around you and mentally photograph it so you can retrieve the pictures at will; try your hand at sketching. Experiments by George Prince with a group of old people (who are notoriously bad listeners) demonstrated that, as their imaging skills improved, there was an enormous improvement in their listening ability.

On the other hand, I would be wary about getting too involved in the study of so-called 'body language'. I am not convinced that any such common code necessarily exists. I suspect that we intuitively know the 'language' already, all that is needed is to heighten our awareness to make sure we pick up the signals.

Non-verbal listening is far from being an exact science and

it is often useful to check your impressions with a Level Three paraphrase. That pained expression could be indigestion rather than a negative reaction to what you have just said!

9. Speaking

Speaking for easy listening

From our consideration of the problems of listening, one key requirement stands out for the speaker: if you want to get your message across, make the listener's job as easy as possible – *speak for easy listening*. (There are of course occasions when the speaker's objective is not to get a message across, but rather to obscure or confuse. I once asked my boss how I should handle a lunch meeting with a staff man from head office. 'Speak him fair and tell him nothing,' said my boss cheerfully, assuming I knew how to achieve this feat. Such situations belong to the adversarial cultures with which I am not concerned here.)

There are some relatively simple ways to make the listener's task as easy as possible: a list of guidelines is given below. They apply both in informal conversation and the more formal presentation, speech or lecture, although in the informal situation there is less need to use all of them all of the time. The formal speech or presentation has some special characteristics which are dealt with separately.

Some guidelines:

— Establish a contract that the listener wants to hear what you have to say – do not just assume it. 'I want to tell you about . . . Are you interested?' If the answer is yes, you can reasonably expect his or her full attention and co-operation in trying to make the communication a success.

— Tell the listener what to listen for. He or she needs to know, 'Why are you telling me this? What sort of response do you want, if any?' As we have seen, there are many different modes of listening, from listening to obtain precise information to listening to give support or sympathy, or to provide ideas. The speaker who makes it clear what his or her purpose is enables the listener to tune in to the appropriate listening wavelength. For example, the speaker describing a problem may be looking for ideas on how to deal with it; equally they may only want sympathetic understanding. The listener who starts coming up with ideas when the speaker is looking for sympathy is likely to end up in a game of 'Why don't you ... Yes, but ...' (to his or her great frustration). The listener has been invited to play a different game: 'ain't it awful'.

— Connect with existing knowledge. This is best illustrated by the way people give directions. They start by establishing a common reference point. 'Do you know Trafalgar Square? Well, from there ...' In the unlikely event that the listener does not know Trafalgar Square, it is necessary to find another common point. In deciding on a starting point for the information he or she is giving, a speaker is implicitly making an assumption of a common reference point with the listener. There is a lot to be gained by making the assumption explicitly: 'I'm assuming that you are familiar with ... Is that assumption correct?' If it is not, some further explanation is needed if the new information is to make sense. It is particularly important for experts to check out their assumptions with non-experts, to avoid 'talking over their heads'.

— Headline the main point of the message. We saw from the listening curve (p. 186), that the listener's attention is at its highest point at the beginning of the message. Strike while the iron is hot: get your main point over then, in the form of an attention-catching headline (the same technique the newspapers use to catch attention). If you observe a lot of discussions (as I do), you will find that people commonly do just the opposite. They start their contribution with a preamble, often a rationale for what they are going to say, which does not make sense because they have not yet said it. By the time they get to the point, the listener may well have dropped out into the meeting in his head. I believe the practice of 'building up' to the point is so widespread because people are accustomed to an adversarial environment and have learned to build a defensive wall around their contribution before revealing it. Unfortunately, the defensive wall gets in the way of the communication process, and the contribution is likely to be rejected because it has not been heard or understood. There are dangers in headlining your contribution in an adversarial culture, but the solution lies in changing the culture rather than in wrapping up the ideas in armour-plating!

— Keep it simple, because the simplest messages are most likely to be understood; as John Garnett says, 'It is what people receive that matters, not what is transmitted.' Keeping it simple is partly a matter of language, and partly a matter of structure. The language needs to be that with which the listener is familiar. Jargon is fine as a shorthand between specialists who are used to it, but a great turn-off for the uninitiated. The listener generally does not like to display ignorance by asking for explanations of unfamiliar terms. Avoid ambiguous words, which are open to multiple interpretations. As regards structure, short sentences and short paragraphs are much easier to listen to than long ones. You must finish the sentence once you have started on it; many people go off at a tangent, when a fresh thought strikes them, leaving the original sentence unfinished and the listener confused.

— Talk in specifics rather than in generalities. Specifics are concrete and easy to grasp, whereas generalities leave the listener guessing what, if anything, the speaker has in mind. (He or she may of course be using the generalisation to conceal the fact that he has nothing in mind!) People commonly use generalities because they are safer, less likely to be attacked, than specifics. Hence the popularity of motherhood statements, which take the discussion no further forward but at least command general agreement. Saying 'We must develop products that suit consumers' changing life-styles' is a safe generalisation, and not very helpful. 'Let's develop a frozen product for use in microwave ovens' gives us something more concrete to understand and work on. In many organisations, I find people talk in code. One part of the code is to use generalisations that the initiated can interpret in ways the speaker intends, leaving the uninitiated in the dark and the speaker safe from attack. Talking in code is a characteristic of an adversarial culture.

— Make statements rather than ask questions, or at least say why you are asking. The reason for this rather surprising dictum lies in the multifarious uses of questions. Some of these uses are straightforward and legitimate – to obtain information or to clarify understanding. Many of them are devious or hostile. Unless the listener knows why you are asking, he or she will respond cautiously, because your question could well be of the devious, hostile variety. Explaining why you are asking will reassure the listener, and also enable him or her to respond most appropriately. It will also prevent you from asking devious questions – once the purpose is disclosed, the question is no longer devious! It follows from this that the best way to respond to a question with an undisclosed purpose is not to answer it but to find out what is behind it. 'Tell me why you are asking' will flush out the purpose, if it is straightforward. If it is not, you have avoided the trap, and presented your questioner with a problem. (If the questioner is the boss, this could be risky, but if you have a boss who asks questions without being prepared to say why, you are in trouble anyway!)

Making presentations

I have already declared my reservations about the formal presentation as an efficient means of communication (see p. 159). I accept, however, that the presentation is here to stay, and there will be occasions when you have decided that your presentation is really necessary, either from choice or because you have no option. In these situations, you can either follow the conventional wisdom of the experts in presentation skills, or you can try my preferred route of what I call a participative presentation.

Planning

For the conventional presentation, Reg Hamilton of Communication Results, who regularly runs courses on presentation skills, recommends the following five-vowel mnemonic as a basis for a presentation plan.*

A for ATTENTION, ACTIVE LISTENING
Grab the attention of your listeners by talking about a subject important to them.

E for EXCITEMENT, EMPATHY,
  for EXPERIENCE, EVIDENCE
Use ideas and concepts that you can enthuse over so that your listeners become excited too. Acknowledge and use their experience to support your proposals. Use evidence that is relevant and credible to them.

* From *Effective Communicating Course Workbook*, © Communication Results.

I for INVOLVEMENT

Involve your listeners by checking for understanding, acknowledging their non-verbal responses and initiating questions.

O for OUTLINING LISTENER BENEFITS

Outline and agree the benefits your listeners will gain from your proposal (or have gained from your update, etc.). If trying to sell, persuade or convince, these are the small affirmations that lead to 'Yes'.

U for UNDERSTANDING, UNITY

Ensure that your listeners understand what your idea or proposal means to them; what action or decision is necessary. Achieve unity of purpose between yourself and your listeners by stating the action step in terms of the benefits your listener will receive. For example, in order to ensure that you receive (BENEFITS) all you have to do is (ACTION).

You will notice that the word 'listeners' appears under each heading; the approach is entirely listener-oriented. Unfortunately, it assumes that you know what is important to your listeners, what will make them excited, what is their experience, etc. Often you will have to make assumptions and guesses about the answers to these important questions. Even so, the discipline of thinking through and making explicit your assumptions about the listeners' interests is essential to get you thinking about your presentation through the eyes and ears of the recipients.

Reg Hamilton recommends that you define the aim of your presentation in language that incorporates the listener's purpose in coming to the presentation. Your aim will probably not be the same as the listener's, but it needs to encompass his or hers. He also suggests that you practise your answer to the question 'Why?', if the listener should challenge your aim or objective. Until you have a satisfactory answer to this challenge, you have not defined the aim of the presentation successfully.

Organising the content

Obviously you have to think through the content of what you want to present and organise it in a coherent structure. 'Coherent' needs to be interpreted from the listener's point of view, not the speaker's. You are approaching the subject from a position of close familiarity and a high level of motivation – the subject is important to you. For the listeners, it may be relatively unfamiliar and less important. Your structure needs to follow the logic of their interests, attitudes and experience (as far as you know them).

Your criteria for choice of material, degree of detail, etc., are again determined by the listener's viewpoint rather than your own. The John Garnett dictum applies again: what is received is more important than what is transmitted. However, your own attitude to your material is an important element of the chemistry of a presentation. Enthusiasm and confidence are infectious; boredom, indifference, anxiety and (to some extent) nervousness will turn the audience off.

Your material will need a structure or format, both for your own benefit and that of the listeners. It helps to keep you on track and, if you share it with the audience in advance, it gives them a map of the course which enables them to know where they are. You will find a number of formats advocated in the literature. They range from the simple military one of 'Tell them what you are going to tell them, tell them, then tell them what you have told them' (suitable for a hierarchical structure where you are issuing orders), to more sophisticated multi-stage and two-tier goal approaches.

You may find it useful to use the mind map method (described on page 187) for organising the content of your presentation. The central idea or theme of the presentation is shown in the centre of the map with various sub-themes branching out from it, with further sub-branches as appropriate. As new ideas and thoughts occur to you, they can be slotted in wherever they seem to fit. Important links can be made with arrows; geometrical shapes like triangles, circles, squares, cubes, etc., can be used to code or group items, and colour can be used to highlight and distinguish different areas. 'Each idea is left as a totally open possibility, so that the pattern grows organically . . . Once the pattern has been completed . . . all that is necessary is to decide the final order in which to present the information' (Tony Buzan, *Use Your Head*).

Whether it is feasible or desirable to deliver your presentation direct from the mind map, without translating into linear notes, I am not sure – so far, I have not attempted it myself. In principle, it ought to be possible. My own (heretical) view is that it does not matter greatly which format you adopt so long as you have chosen it consciously for this particular presentation (not out of habit). And you need to be flexible enough to depart from it if you find it is not working.

Visual aids

The main purpose of visual aids (apart from showing how sophisticated and up to date you are) is to add a visual reinforcement to the spoken word. It follows that visual aids should be *pictures*, not words (pictures include charts and diagrams). Ideally the picture should not use words at all, and never more words than can be taken in at a glance. The words on the visual aid should never be read out to the audience – to do so is insulting, suggesting they cannot read for themselves.

It is astonishing how frequently these rules are broken by presenters who display visuals of dense text (or figures) and then read through them. If you need to refer to such material, it is preferable to circulate documents or a report containing it.

A secondary function of the visual aid is to provide a focal point for attention. To the extent that they do that, they take attention *away* from the speaker. It is desirable to provide diversions up to a point, but at the end of the day what you are really presenting is yourself. Make sure your visuals, and your equipment (overheads, slides, flip charts, videos), are your servant, not your master.

Audience contact

The success of your presentation depends more than anything else on the relationship you create with your audience. If you have set yourself up (or have been set up) to make a presentation, you have joined the entertainment business, however temporarily. Your audience will be with you so long as they are enjoying themselves.

Reframing your presentation as an entertainment for the audience will compel you to look at it in a fresh light. What are the exciting, surprising and amusing elements in what you have to offer? How can you dramatise them? What can you (fairly) play for laughs. 'Make 'em laugh' is as relevant an objective for the presenter as it is for the comic or the after-dinner speaker. While they are laughing they are relaxed, well disposed towards the speaker and alert for the next trigger. The fact that your subject matter is deadly serious does not mean that you have to be solemn about its presentation. Serious points can be made in amusing ways, as the great cartoonists constantly demonstrate. Laughter, moreover, is one of the most tangible forms of audience response you can get. You need that response to judge how well or badly you are doing. You also need to be aware of the other non-verbal signals, such as nods of approval, yawns, fidgeting, etc.

As you speak, therefore, your eyes need to be on your audience, not on your material, most of the time (hence the importance of mastering your material in advance, and keeping your prompts or notes to a minimum). Reg Hamilton suggests working to one simple rule: 'Every word you say must be addressed to an individual in the audience, and you must, before you finish, have said something to everyone.'

The participative presentation

Having dealt as fairly (and I hope as helpfully) as I can with the conventional presentation, which I generally dislike, I now want to describe my preferred alternative. A participative presentation is a continuing dialogue between the speaker and audience; it actively involves all members of the audience as much as possible. For them to be actively involved they need to have something to do other than just sit and listen.

The feasibility of a participative presentation depends on the numbers in the audience, the nature of the subject matter and the degree of risk the presenter is prepared to take (the first time you do it, it feels very risky; you need to be thoroughly *au fait* with your subject, because you will need to improvise a good deal).

If you are going to use this approach, you need to explain what you are doing, and why, to the audience at the outset and get their agreement to try it out. If they have come expecting a conventional presentation, they may feel cheated if an alternative is imposed on them without their consent. They will be listening in order to challenge, when you want them to listen to contribute. I usually explain my rationale by using the listening curve (see p. 186) to highlight the difficulty of sustaining attention over a long period; most people can identify with this problem and are usually willing to experiment with an alternative.

I use two principal methods to obtain audience participation. The first is to give a brief five- to ten-minute statement of my case, without any detailed substantiation of the argument. I then ask for feedback from the group, in terms of the parts they agreed with, found useful and interesting on the one hand, and then the points with which they disagreed, found confusing or wanted to explore in more depth. I record the feedback (or sometimes the second half of it only) on flip charts, with the name of the individual who raised the point. I then work through the list of points as an agenda for the rest of my presentation, checking that I have dealt with each point with the person who raised it. I give priority to items raised by several people.

I find that this method is feasible with small groups, up to about a dozen. It enables me to tailor my presentation to the interests of the audience, and treats them as individuals rather than a homogeneous mass. It seems generally to go down well.

I believe the same approach can be applied to presenting proposals and recommendations, provided you are prepared to invite the audience to get involved in the final shaping of them. In other words, you are presenting your conclusions as your 'best current thinking', which is open to improvement and refinement from the experience and ideas of the audience.

Conventionally, the presenter is expected to have the complete answer, which is tested by challenge from the audience. If it does not withstand the challenge, the proposition (and the presentation) 'fails'. This is the norm of an adversarial culture, and in my view it is wasteful. It fails to make use of the knowledge of the audience in a constructive way, and it misses the opportunity to engage their commitment by involving them in the final shape of the proposition.

The participative presentation requires a less arrogant, less macho ('I know all the answers') posture on the part of the presenter. It is a more modest and open-minded approach, which acknowledges that others may have something to contribute. It is not, of course, a substitute for adequate preparation; if the audience feels the presenter has not done enough homework and is asking them to do the work for him or her, it will fail.

The mechanics of the participative presentation of a proposal are as follows:

— Position what you are doing as presenting your best current thinking for constructive feedback and improvement.

— Present the proposal with as much (or as little) detail as is necessary for understanding by the audience.

— Provide an opportunity for clarification of any points that were not clear.

— Collect feedback in the form of a group itemised response (that is, positive aspects and areas for improvement).

— Obtain ideas to achieve the required improvements and develop them to the point where they can be built into the original proposal – it is your choice whether you accept them or not.

— Check that the revised proposal is now acceptable.

You will find it helpful to use an independent process manager to 'chair' this type of meeting: it will leave you free to concentrate on the subject matter. He or she will look after the positioning, ensure that questions are limited to genuine clarification, not hidden criticisms, ensure that the feedback is balanced and constructive and generally keep the structure of the meeting under control.

The participative approach can also be applied to lectures and speeches, by involving the audience in experiments and exercises which illustrate the point I am making. If I were lecturing on communication, I might set up exercises on in—out listening or paraphrase to be done in groups of two or three. During this period I wander round the audience, listening in to some of the exercises and lending a hand to anyone who asks for help. Subsequently I can review their experience with them.

My colleagues and I have used this method with audiences of up to sixty or eighty. The energy (and noise) level during the exercises is tremendous, and the feedback we get is very positive. It enables the audience to *experience* what the speaker is talking about, instead of relying on the information he or she is giving them. And it shares the responsibility for the success of the occasion between speaker and audience, thereby relieving the speaker of the total burden. In my experience, it allows me to approach the lecture in a more relaxed frame of mind, and I probably do a better job for that reason.

There is no guarantee that the participative lecture will always work. I tried it one Friday afternoon with a class of third-year engineering students in a polytechnic. They were accustomed to the normal classroom type of lecture, and I suspect they had their own strategies for dealing with it – like chatting among themselves, reading or dozing off! Some of them seemed to resent being asked to do something active. Maybe the participative lecture only works with a voluntary audience!

Using the telephone

The telephone is so much a part of our everyday life you may feel insulted by the suggestion you may have something to learn about using it more skilfully. Yet few of us are given tuition in making best use of the phone, and a little conscious thought can make it a more useful tool, and less of a time-waster.

Incoming and outgoing calls are different in kind (at least initially) and need to be considered separately, the incoming call (i.e. the receiver's viewpoint) first.

The incoming call is almost always an interruption – managers are not generally sitting around waiting for the phone to ring. The interruption may be welcome, or necessary; equally it may not be. There is no reason to allow the phone to take priority over your other activities. Once you know who the caller is and what they want, you have every right to say, 'This is not a convenient moment for me', and either give the caller an alternative time, or undertake to call them back. Calling the person back gives you the advantage of initiating the call and enables you to be mentally prepared to deal with the topic (which you may not have been when the call came in).

It is much better to handle the calls yourself than to use a secretary to filter them. Secretaries tend to have their own opinions about what is good for their boss, who should talk to him or her and who should not. These are judgements for the manager; when you do not want to be interrupted, cut off all calls and tell the switchboard to take the name and number of each caller, so you can return the call. And be sure to do so.

With the outgoing call, you become the interrupter and I believe it is both courteous and efficient to check whether the timing is convenient for the respondent. To enable the person to decide, he or she needs to know who you are and what you want to talk about. If it is not convenient, you can reasonably ask for an alternative time that will be.

A telephone call, like any interaction between two or more people, is a meeting, and as such it will have a process (that is, the way it is conducted) as well as a content or subject matter. The process may be informal and implicit, but unless it is appropriate to the purpose of the call, the 'meeting' will not be a success. If you are initiating the call, you have the responsibility to make it clear why you have called and what you want from your respondent, so that he or she will know what sort of 'meeting' he or she has been called to and you can both be on the same wavelength.

To do this you will need to think before you phone and draw up some sort of plan, however rudimentary, for the call. It is all too easy to pick up the phone and make a call without having thought through what you want to achieve and how you are going to achieve it. A simple note of 'objective', 'method' and 'criteria of success' is all that is needed; the investment of a few minutes to think it through will save time in the call itself.

I have a preference to stand up when I am talking on the phone. Subsequently I discovered that some sales training organisations teach that it is a way to communicate energy and urgency. They could well be right, and it is certainly worth trying if you do not already do it. With new cordless phones you can walk around too!

Finally, be aware that your tone of voice varies according to whom you are talking to on the phone, as was shown in the experiment described earlier, when a group of managers were able to guess correctly who the other party to the conversation was, from a tape recording of one party.

Communicating by film and video

If you want to communicate by making video tapes for viewing around the organisation or by prospective customers, get professional help. Viewers are used to professional standards of video production from years of watching TV at home. If you have used a video camera for researching meetings or for making home videos of baby's first steps, you will be aware how far they fall short of professional quality.

You also need to be conscious of the limitations of video. Theoretically all three channels of words, tone of voice and non-verbals are working for you, but it is not the same as being there in the flesh. The video is only two-dimensional; you miss the 'feel' of actually being present. (I notice this difference when I use video for training purposes: I go from one room where I have been watching a meeting on TV into the room where the meeting is actually taking place. The difference is palpable; the real world has an 'atmosphere' that the video flattens out and fails to capture.) And the video, unlike a live presentation, is not interactive; you cannot get feedback from the audience, or adjust your presentation according to their reaction.

In spite of these limitations, video is a tool that needs to be considered in relation to the alternatives available. I suspect it is underused because relatively few managers (myself included) have training or experience in the use of it.

If you are likely to be interviewed on broadcast radio or TV as a representative of your company or industry, be sure to get professional training well in advance. The TV interviewer's objective is to produce interesting and entertaining programmes, not to present you in a sympathetic and attractive light. That's your responsibility.

Much TV interviewing is adversarial in its approach; the interviewer or producer may have a case to make or a point to prove, and will be looking for grist to that mill. He or she may not scruple to cut your interview into small pieces and show them out of sequence and in an unfavourable context. He or she is in control of what is transmitted and what effect it creates. Even the most competent and articulate manager can be made to look an idiot in the process.

With professional training you will be better equipped to decide whether to accept the invitation to be interviewed or not, and handle it with credit to yourself and your company if you decide to go ahead.

10. Reading and writing

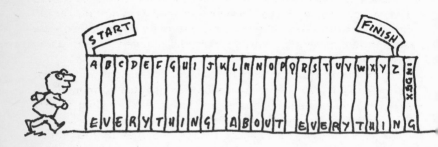

Reading: quantity versus quality

The idea that we are all poor readers probably comes as a shock (just like the idea that we are all poor listeners). Yet compared with the standards that can be achieved, the generally accepted level of reading competence, even among well-educated people, is poor indeed. Peter Russell in the *Brain Book* suggests that most people still 'hear' the sound of the words as they read, as though they were being spoken aloud, and this limits the speed of reading to between 200 and 300 words a minute.

If we can learn to read visually, the speed of reading can be multiplied several times, without loss of comprehension. Russell quotes results achieved by Florence Schale who found that most people were able to read at 2,000 words a minute or more, with comprehension at least as high as that of 'normal' readers reading at one-tenth of the speed.

Does it follow, then, that we should all rush off to a speed-reading course? I have to confess that I have never done so, for the same sort of reason that I do not fly to the United States by Concorde – for me it addresses the wrong part of the problem. The hassle with air travel lies in getting to and from the airport, parking the car, checking in, going through security, immigration and customs; the flying time itself can be used to read, write, relax, listen to music, etc., and it is no great advantage to shave two or three hours off that.

Similarly, for the typical manager the amount of time he or she should *properly* spend reading, in relation to the other activities he should be engaged in, is probably quite small. Ability to read more quickly, even several times more quickly, would probably not save that much time.

It would of course enable you to read a lot more in the same time (and maybe enable you to get your essential reading done in the office instead of taking it home). I would not want to let my own reluctance to develop my reading skills discourage you from doing so.

Yet the conditions of 'information overload' described earlier, and the potential of the networking approach to get the information you want when you want it, suggest to me that speed of reading is likely to be a relatively minor consideration in a manager's success.

For academics, it is a different matter; they live by the printed word, their success is measured by the amount they publish, and each publication must list the source of their material, in the same way as every Ph.D. thesis is based on a literature search. Reading must be a major activity for the academic, and training in speed-reading would be a marvellous investment for them (I wonder how many learn).

An alternative and distinctly iconoclastic approach was described to me many years ago by Alistair McKay when managing director of Standard Telephones and Cables. 'Each day,' he said, 'I go through as much of my in-tray as I have time for. At the end of the day my secretary puts the rest on the shelf. At the end of the week she takes the piles and puts them in a single pile on the top shelf. At the end of the month she throws the papers on the top shelf away. If anything important was among the shelved papers, somebody would be sure to chase me for it.'

I am not recommending Alistair's approach, you understand; in fact I'm not sure I ever believed him, and have certainly never had the courage to try it myself. Yet the spirit of it is appealing – the firm refusal to get bogged down in the paper, the self-regulating element of letting people chase him for what was important (and he was the boss, of course).

For me, reading is not a problem. I have long since pruned to a minimum the things I feel I must read, and spend my reading time on the things I want to read. But if reading were a problem, I would like to try the McKay method (if I dared) before taking a speed-reading course!

Writing for easy reading

It is giving a hostage to fortune to write about writing – the way I write either speaks for itself, or I have no credibility. If you have stayed with me this far, I must assume my writing style is at least acceptable enough for me to put forward a few ideas about ways to improve your writing skills in a management context.

If the key to success in speaking is to make the listener's job as easy as possible, the same principle applies to writing – write for easy reading. The reader almost certainly believes he or she has too much to read (everyone seems to believe they have an intolerably bulging in-tray). The reader will only welcome your addition to that burden if it is inviting, interesting and helpful. For the uninvited communication (for example, the mailshot or brochure), it is estimated that you have on average thirty seconds to capture the reader's attention long enough to interrupt the progress of your communication from hand to waste-paper basket! Brevity is a major virtue, because it avoids the reaction 'I can't be bothered to plough through all that.'

The written communication at work is a functional object, not a literary one. The criterion of success is whether it delivers the required information, provokes the appropriate action or elicits the desired attitude. So you need first to be clear what it is you are trying to achieve, and that a written communication is the most appropriate and effective medium available to you. Maybe one or more phone calls, a meeting or presentation might do the job better – they all have the advantage of being interactive, and using more channels of communication than the words alone. On the other hand, the written communication is more considered – you can revise it before sending it. And it is permanent: it can be re-read and referred to many times. Are these advantages, or disadvantages, for the particular task in hand?

Nowadays I find myself using written communication principally to confirm arrangements made face to face or by phone, or to create interest which might lead to such a meeting. With more distant contacts, in Australia and New Zealand for example, the letter still has to take a bigger load, although even here improved telecommunications are reducing the role of the written communication.

Different criteria apply in those businesses in which written material like reports is the tangible end product of their work – for example, market research agencies, management consultants, technical agencies. Although the report will almost certainly be an adjunct to other forms of communication such as presentations and meetings, it is also a physical manifestation of the business. Its literary and presentation standards reflect the values of the company and influence its image. So it needs to be of high literary and visual quality, as well as functionally efficient. At McKinsey's, I understand, all reports go through a professional editorial department before they are finally issued.

I find it helpful to view writing as a three-stage process:

— Get the material out of my head on to paper (or tape or TV monitor).

— Read it through to check that what I have written is what I actually meant to say (Schumacher's first transformation).

— Read it again as though I were the recipient. What is it likely to mean to him or her?

The last step is an exercise in imagination: I do not know what it is like to be the recipient, but I can make an intelligent guess. In any event this step is a constant reminder that what I am engaged in is an exercise in communication, not literary self-expression. (Much of our initial training in writing is in self-expression, rather than functional communication. The academic models, like the school and university essay, are not particularly relevant to written communications at work in most cases — the Civil Service is a possible exception.)

If your 'written' communications are in fact dictated, it may be more difficult to follow these three steps. If you dictate to a shorthand typist (does anybody still do that these days?), you will have to wait for a typed draft, which is a bit wasteful, though less so if a word processor is being used. If you dictate on to tape, you can play it back and amend it, but listening to it is not the same as reading.

Personally, I do not find I can dictate efficiently anything but the briefest of communications. When dictating I tend to become verbose: my brain is more in tune with the pace of my pen rather than my tongue. Eventually, I suppose, all managers will type their own documents on computerised work stations, and the revision can be done from the screen or from a printed draft that can be modified easily. Dictations for transcription will then become a thing of the past. A dictated tape sent through the post will remain an option, but not one that the recipient is geared to use.

Paradoxically, one of the effects of modern technology has been to increase the scope for manuscript communications. We no longer type internal memos, but simply keep a copy of the manuscript from the copying machine. The practice can also extend to external communications to friends. It has the advantage of being more personal; unfortunately, you really need to have more legible handwriting than mine!

When it comes to 'writing for easy reading', the principles have much in common with 'speaking for easy listening' (see page 197). They include:

— telling the respondent 'what to read for' — why you are writing and what sort of response you want;
— connecting, as far as possible, with existing knowledge, to establish a common reference point (but when writing you have to guess rather than do it interactively);
— headlining the main point of the message, in such a way as to gain the reader's interest (while retaining credibility and originality — 'double your profits in a year' fails on both counts);
— keeping it simple — simple words, short, simply constructed sentences, short paragraphs. When writing, there is a particular temptation to dot all i's and cross all t's, because there is time to do so and because additional thoughts and qualifications keep occurring to you as you write, so you end up with a messy sentence like this one.

Sir Ernest Gowers, in his classic *The Complete Plain Words*, sums up the elements of good writing with elegant simplicity.

— You must know your subject
> your reason for writing
> your reader.

— You must be clear
> simple and brief
> accurate and complete
> polite and human
> prompt.

He was writing initially for civil servants, but his principles are widely applicable, and his book is a gold mine of sensible guidance. If you follow his precepts, your writing will be easy to read, and effective for that reason.

11. Conclusion

The principal message of this exercise in communication has been that communication is far too important a part of every management job (and of everyday life) to be taken for granted. Technology is increasing drastically both the quantity and speed of communication, and cutting its cost, but the big opportunity lies in improving the *quality*. I believe there is tremendous scope for improving the quality and effectiveness of our communication, if we choose to do so, and that improvement can be one of the most important innovations in management in our time.

The ways of improving the quality of communication are essentially simple. They start from an awareness of the richness and variety of the communication process, and its essentially two-sided (transmitting and receiving) nature. Feedback from tape recordings (audio and visual) helps to develop this awareness by providing opportunities to examine both sides of the transaction at the same time. The receiving end of the process (listening, looking, reading) provides the greatest scope for potential improvement, partly because it is the most neglected, and partly because it is quantitatively the largest part of the communication activity (because many transmissions have multiple receivers). Moreover, sensitivity to the receiving process makes for more effective transmission, because the most effective transmissions are those that are easy to receive – hence 'speak for easy listening', 'write for easy reading'.

Given that 'the greatest danger in communication is the assumption that it has taken place', it pays to check whether it has or not. The skill of paraphrasing, to check the understanding of what has been said (and perhaps more important, what has not been said, that is, the unspoken assumptions), can ensure that the communication does not go by default. Like any other technique, paraphrase can be used (or abused) at varying levels of skill and subtlety. Knowing that you are going to attempt a paraphrase at some point is in itself a powerful incentive to listen attentively. You can feel foolish if your paraphrase is wide of the mark, but it will have served a valuable purpose in signalling the failure of the communication.

Awareness of your own thought processes can make you a more efficient recipient of external communications. Your attitudes to the transmitter and your habitual mind sets will colour the way you listen and what you hear. It is necessary to manage the 'meeting in your head' as well as the public meeting, and to integrate the two; the techniques of in–out listening and mind-maps can help with this integration.

When it comes to the more formal communication occasions, especially business meetings, an agreed structure and some simple ground rules for behaviour will raise the quality of communication substantially, and save a great deal of time (and energy) as well. What the structure of the meeting should be depends on its purpose, specifically defined: 'to discuss' is too vague a definition – we need to know 'with what object in mind'. We can then select the appropriate meeting structure, which will make clear what kinds of contribution – information ideas or opinions/judgements – are required, and from whom.

The perfect meeting is one in which each participant knows what kind of contribution he or she can most usefully make at each stage of the meeting, to achieve both his or her own objectives and those of the other participants in the meeting. It is a win/win objective, not the adversarial objective of getting what I want at the expense of the other participants.

Like any other skills and techniques, communication skills can be misused, to mislead or manipulate. Many senior managers, who have learned their job in generally adversarial environments, have survived and prospered by their manipulative abilities. Not surprisingly, they are reluctant to let go of these methods, which have served them well as individuals. Yet such practices are costly to their organisations because they create a guarded, cautious environment, in which no one is prepared to say what he or she really thinks and feels, and no one is prepared to take the risk of getting involved in innovation and change.

What's more, the manipulative devious practices are unnecessary; in most cases it is possible to achieve the objectives of all parties once they are openly stated, given sufficient skill in problem solving.* In the cases where it is not possible (or necessarily desirable) to satisfy all parties, it is entirely legitimate for the person with authority to decide 'this is what we are going to do', with or without consultation – provided the person's communication is open and direct.

Given that communication – both receiving and transmitting – is such an integral part of management (it permeates almost all management activity), it is clearly a major responsibility of every manager to ensure that his or her own communication skills are of

* See the companion volume, *Problem Solving*.

the highest order. I trust that the approaches described in this book will enable you to make your own decisions about ways to improve your own performance as a receiver and transmitter of 'communications'.

In a world where the speed, volume and sophistication of communication activity are increasing so rapidly, a parallel increase in quality and skill is sorely needed!

References

Max Atkinson, *Our Master's Voices*, Methuen, 1984.

Tony Buzan, *Use Your Head*, BBC Publications, 1984.

Peter Drucker, foreword to Parkinson and Rowe, *Communicate* (see below).

Winston Fletcher, *Meetings, Meetings*, Hodder, 1985.

John Garnett, 'The Work Challenge', *Industrial Society*, 1974.

Glasgow University Media Group, *Bad News*, Routledge, 1976.
— *More Bad Bews*, Routledge, 1980.
— *Really Bad News*, Writers and Readers, 1982.

Ernest Gowers, *The Complete Plain Words*, Penguin, 1973.

Reg Hamilton, 'Presentations Workbook', *Communications Results*, 1985.

Charles H. Kepner and Benjamin B. Tregoe, *The Rational Manager*, McGraw, 1965.

Albert Mehrabian, 'Communication without Words', *Psychology Today*, December 1969.

John Naisbitt, *Megatrends*, Macdonald, 1984.

C. Northcote Parkinson and Nigel Rowe, *Communicate: Parkinson's Formula for Business Survival*, Pan, 1979.

George Prince, *The Practice of Creativity*, Harper and Row, 1975.

Professor Revans, quoted in Bill Critchley and David Casey, 'Second Thoughts about Team Building', *Management Education and Development*, vol. 15, part 2, 1984, pp. 163–75.

Peter Russell, *Brain Book*, Routledge, 1979.

E. F. Schumacher, *A Guide for the Perplexed*, Sphere, 1978.

Robert Townsend, *Up the Organization*, Coronet, 1971.

Teamwork

Contents

1. Teams and teamwork

Introduction

If you look back over your working career, you will probably be able to identify some periods, two or three perhaps, that were outstandingly enjoyable and satisfying. Your colleagues were a pleasure to work with, the boss was a good guy (maybe *you* were the boss), there was excitement in the air, laughter too, and you were successful or on the way to a big success. The job, the people and the circumstances all seemed to come together in a mysterious, positive chemistry. Those were the days, that was a good time . . .

It would be nice always to have such good times. I cannot guarantee that you will ever do so, but I do believe that by working at the issues loosely labelled Teamwork, you can greatly increase your chances. My own experience, especially of the fifteen years I have spent building the business I started, has convinced me that success in business depends critically on the elusive teamwork factor. Trying to understand that chemistry, formulating explicit teamwork objectives and working continuously to achieve them, are probably the most important tasks in management.

The correlation between the quality of teamwork and business success is simply explained in the following model (introduced to me by John Philipp of Synectics Inc.):

— The individuals in the team have a fixed amount of potential energy.

— Each individual uses as much of his energy as is necessary to ensure his emotional 'survival', i.e. to avoid getting hurt and to lick his wounds or get revenge if he is hurt.

— The balance of his energy is available to devote to the task.

— The diagram shows how the energy available for the task increases dramatically as the improving team climate reduces the amount of energy the team members need to put into safeguarding their emotional well-being.

Success and the team climate

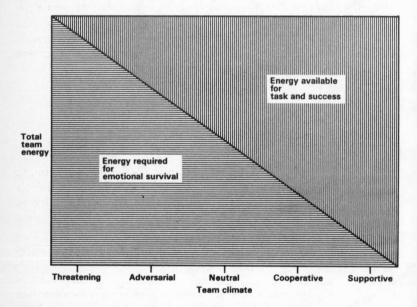

Although the model illustrates neatly how much the success of the operation depends on the quality of the teamwork, it tells us nothing about how to arrive at quality. That is the topic of this book, with the caveat that I do not have any sure-fire, cast-iron solutions. In fact, I do not believe there are any in this area; the appropriate level and style of teamwork depends on the situation in question, both the nature of the operation and the people involved.

Nor does the model say anything about the quantity of teambuilding activity required. This again depends on the people and the type of task they are engaged in. There is a strong temptation, especially among professional teambuilders, to assume that 'more is better'; an assumption which has been exposed and demolished very effectively by two of their members, Bill Critchley and David Casey.

In a perceptive paper called 'Second Thoughts on Teambuilding',* they argue that 'there is a very large proportion of most managers' work where teamwork is not needed (and to attempt to inculcate teamwork is dysfunctional). There is, at the same time, a very small proportion of their work where teamwork is absolutely vital (and to ignore teamworking skills is to invite disaster).' It is a salutary warning, and I return later (Chapter 2) to their method of distinguishing the two areas of work from each other and their proposals for handling them. The key issue at this stage is the need to be clear about the range of meanings involved in the apparently simple concepts of 'team' and 'teamwork' and the kinds of situations for which each of them is, or may be, appropriate.

The concept of 'team'

So, what is a team? I find myself wanting to resist this question, to brush it aside with a remark like, 'We all know what a team is; there's no need to be pedantic about it.' And I know myself well enough to be aware that that is a tactic for ducking the issue because it is a tricky one.

There is no choice but to attempt a definition and then see how it stands up. Here we go, then. For me:

A team is a group of people working together to achieve common objectives and willing to forgo individual autonomy to the extent necessary to achieve those objectives.

This is a pretty minimalist definition. It says nothing about the size of the group – the smallest team consists of two people only (as in the case of a husband and wife or a two-man bobsleigh team). There are even pyschologists who talk about teamwork between the sub-personalities within an individual person!

What about the upper limit? From sport, where much of the team metaphor comes from, we tend to think of a number like fifteen, from rugby union, as a maximum. American football, of course, takes us up to forty, albeit organized into specialized sub-teams and

*In *Management Education and Development*, vol. 15, pt 2, 1984.

substitutes. English football operates a 'squad' of perhaps sixteen to twenty, from which teams of eleven are drawn.

In the context of management, the old theories of span of control, which suggest that a manager cannot deal effectively with more than five to seven people reporting directly to him, tend to limit the typical management team to around seven or eight people. From my own experience of conducting participative meetings I know empirically that members of a group must not number more than eight if effective working is to be guaranteed.

Such conclusions point to a group needing to be fairly small in size to be considered a single team. Even a rugby team splits into a pack of eight and seven backs!

Does it, then, make sense to talk of a whole organization working as a team? (The Taylor Woodrow company has a logo of a tug-of-war team pulling on a rope and the slogan 'Teamwork builds'. The figures holding the rope always look to me as though they are about to collapse on their backsides for want of anything to pull against!)

I believe that a whole organization can work as a team if its members develop a common style of working that is constructive and co-operative and enables them readily and naturally to form temporary teams whenever they need to interact with each other. Perhaps this should be described as 'teamwork', and an organization viewed as a network of teams, temporary and permanent, following a common teamworking style, rather than a single large team.

'Working together to achieve common objectives' was the second component of my definition. In the sporting environment, the objectives are usually obvious; in the business they need to be articulated and made explicit. The functional objectives of a team are usually specific enough; for operational units they are determined by the organization's planning and budgeting processes, and for the staff departments by 'management by objectives' techniques or zero-based budgeting.

But a team may well have additional, less tangible objectives set for it either from above or from within. It may, for example, be expected to be a training ground which grooms people for jobs elsewhere in the organization, or to keep the organization at the leading edge of its particular field. On the other hand, a team itself may decide that one of its objectives is to create a high quality of working life for its members.

Whatever they are, objectives need to be not only explicit but also commonly understood. It is all too easy to state objectives and assume that everyone, inside the team and outside it, has the same understanding of them. I have argued elsewhere* that this is unlikely to be the case: the odds are not better than evens, and probably worse, that objectives will be understood the same way by all those concerned. Explicit paraphrasing and checking out is essential for something as fundamental as a team's objectives.

I also referred in my definition to 'common' objectives, implying that each member of a team shares its objectives and identifies wholeheartedly with them. In a sense, by joining a team, the individual member 'signs on' to that team's objectives; he enters into a contract as a condition of becoming a member of the team.

The degree of *commitment* with which he signs on, however, can vary enormously according to the circumstances. At the lowest level, he may be in the team because he needs a job, and this team was willing to take him on. He may have been compelled to join this particular team by the organization, as the price for continuing his career in it. He may have signed on with enthusiasm when he joined, but has now become disillusioned, or no longer accepts the way the objectives have changed over time.

In fact, the individual team member is in a team in order to satisfy his own personal needs, which are not identical with those of the team; in order to do this he is prepared to make a contribution to the achievement of the team's objectives. The better the balance between the individuals' contributions and the satisfaction of their needs, the more harmonious the team is likely to be. (I return to the question of the individual and the team later, in Chapter 2.)

The final component of my definition was 'willing to forgo personal autonomy to the extent necessary to achieve the common objectives'. By joining a team you limit your freedom to do as you like, but only, in my view, to the minimum degree needed for the team to succeed in what it is trying to do. If the constraints put on personal autonomy are perceived to be unnecessary, they are resented and commitment is reduced.

But the phrase 'to the extent necessary to achieve the common objectives' begs a lot of questions. What is the necessary extent, and can it be reduced in creative ways that allow the individual to maintain his autonomy without jeopardizing the common objectives? If not, should the objectives be changed? And at the end of the day, who decides?

Some companies explicitly demand that, as a condition of membership, the individual subordinates his own interests to those of the business. The philosophy of McKinsey and Co., the

*See *Communication*.

229

management consultants, can be summed up a follows: 'Client first, the firm [McKinsey] next, the individual last.'*

While it is possible to admire the quasi-religious fervour of such self-abnegation (and acknowledge McKinsey's undeniable commercial success), my personal ideal is rather different. I believe that the individual is in business for himself and responsible for his own decisions about his personal priorities in life.

I also believe that by using our creative abilities it is often possible to find a way to satisfy the requirements of both the individual and the team. There is usually more than one way of skinning any particular cat; if a proposed solution demands a trade-off between the interests of the individual and those of the team, it is not a particularly good one. Maybe, even probably, a better solution can be found if it is sought.

Not every situation can be resolved in this way, and how to deal with the trade-off is a matter of judgement. Ultimately that judgement is the responsibility of the team leader. (If a team is part of a larger organization, some of the constraints will be imposed by the rules and conventions of the organization. The team leader is then simply the channel through which the constraints are exercised).

Although the team leader has the ultimate responsibility for deciding the degree to which the autonomy of the team members is to be constrained, he has to exercise his responsibility in a way that does not erode the commitment of the team members. He needs to establish the constraints through a consultative process of problem-solving and negotiation, thereby producing an explicit set of general rules to be observed by all team members and individual 'contracts' covering each member's area of responsibility. I shall be returning to these issues, both from the point of view of the individual team member and that of the leader, in later chapters.

Team metaphors

Part of the difficulty in defining 'team' in the business context stems from the fact that it is a word drawn from the parlance of other worlds, particularly, although not exclusively, that of sport. In one respect, sport is a peculiarly inappropriate source of metaphor for business, because sport is ostensibly a win–lose activity, whereas business in the main, is a win–win activity.

This distinction is so crucial that it is worth some elaboration.

*Davis Maister, 'The One Firm Firm', *Sloan Management Review*.

Every sporting contest is designed to have one winner and one or more losers. In the language of game theory, sport is a zero-sum (or negative-sum) game in terms of the result of the contest.

Business, on the other hand, is about the creation of wealth. Although there is competition in business, it is possible for all competitors to be successful, in the sense of generating sufficient wealth to reward team members (employees and shareholders) adequately. Business is therefore a positive-sum game, in which it is possible for all players to be 'winners'. Competition may result in some being *relatively* more successful than others, but only in a minority of cases are there out and out losers, i.e. businesses which fail.

Sport becomes a positive-sum game if you take the Olympic or Corinthian view of it, according to which participation is what matters, the result being incidental. Timothy Gallwey expresses this eloquently:

> Winning is overcoming obstacles to reach a goal, but the value in winning is only as great as the value of the goal reached. Reaching the goal itself may not be as valuable as the experience that can come in making a supreme effort to overcome the obstacles involved.
>
> Competition then becomes an interesting device in which each player, by making his maximum effort to win, gives the other the opportunity he desires to reach new levels of self awareness.*

When using the team metaphor, therefore, it is important to be clear that, in principle, all business teams can be winning teams. Unlike a sporting team, a business team does not have to defeat its opposition to succeed. Its criteria of success are positive – the satisfaction of the needs of its 'customers' (in the widest sense of the term), who are the recipients of its output.

I think it is useful to get away from the sporting metaphor for a moment and look at some other types of team. They illustrate the wide variety of situations from which the team concept is drawn and may suggest diverse ways of thinking about the concept in the context of a business environment. (I am indebted to Terry Simons for much of the material that follows.)

Horses/mules/dogs

These non-human teams share a harness and pull together; the harness belongs to someone else – the driver! The team members just pull; all that is wanted from them is their muscle – no

*The Inner Game of Tennis, Random House, 1974.

intelligence, no individuality. The 'teamness' of a group like this is a measure of individual non-existence.

There have not been many direct human equivalents of this type of team since the time of the pyramids or the First World War – perhaps a Boat Race crew! In the business environment, I can think of the old card-punching rooms or groups of comptometer operators bashing away at purely mechanical tasks under the eagle eye of a dragon-like supervisor.

In today's business world, automation, computers and robotics should have made this type of team redundant, at least generally speaking. Of course, situations may well continue to arise that call temporarily for working in this highly disciplined and unquestioning manner – when it's 'All hands to the pumps!' to deal with a crisis, for example.

It's as well to acknowledge the validity of this mode of working in such situations, and to be prepared to switch into it when occasion demands.

The orchestra

An orchestra is made up of skilled professionals performing under the direction of a conductor. *What* they produce is laid down in the composer's score; *how* they produce it – with what nuances of interpretation (variations in light and shade, dynamics and the balance of forces) – is decided by the conductor. (As an amateur cellist who has recently joined a local orchestra, I find this team analogy particularly intriguing.)

I can think of many business equivalents, where the functional specialists are experts in their own field and the chief executive's role is to co-ordinate, balance and control (i.e. to be the conductor). In place of the composer's score is the business plan, its individual parts directed at separate functions and adding up, hopefully, to a harmonious whole.

Where the conductor and orchestra have an advantage over their business counterparts is in the instant feedback the one gives the other on the results of its efforts. Yet my conductor's repeated exhortations to the orchestra members to listen to each other would be equally apt addressed to members of a business team!

The conductor's ability to control is based on the respect of the players for his understanding of the music, his ability to communicate what he wants from them and his respect for their professionalism. Mutual respect is the basis of the relationship, with clear recognition from both parties as to the other's area of specialized expertise – not a bad model for a chief executive.

I am reminded of a BBC Master Class in which the conductor, Zubin Mehta, taught a cruel lesson to a group of aspirant conductors. He turned to the Israel Philharmonic Orchestra and asked them to start playing Stravinsky's *Rite of Spring* on their own, without his guidance; which they did quite adequately. 'That's what they can do without a conductor,' he said to his trainees. 'Anything you do has to be an improvement on that.' I sometimes wish I could set up a similar demonstration for chief executives!

The circus

A circus thrives on the range of talents that are exhibited, yet at the same time must have a degree of integration and coherence that makes it a single business unit that moves smoothly from one location to the next. You expect to see a lion-tamer, a clown, a trapeze artist, a juggler, a strong man, a horse-rider, etc., etc. (the more etceteras the better). Yet you expect to pay a reasonable amount for your ticket. You also expect the whole lot to appear and disappear overnight. In order for these expectations to be fulfilled, all the talents must be contained in comparatively few people, who must also play their part moving the big top.

This sort of team requires people who are not only specialists in skills that are unique to them, but who are also prepared to take on roles within the working unit in order to maintain the firm.

Most business teams have elements in common with a circus. Quite apart from individual skills to be exercised –

— juggling figures;
— taming customers;
— swinging deals;
— wrestling with unions;
— looking sexy;
— keeping everyone happy

– there are common tasks to be attended to:

— getting the best out of everyone;
— making things happen;
— seeing opportunities;
— maintaining standards;
— preserving external relations;
— obtaining resources;
— getting the product out.

Missionaries

In a team of missionaries, the members work alone. They go into the alien field to do their work, with very little interaction with other members of the team. They cannot rely upon the sort of support in their everyday work that members of other teams have. Yet they must support and be supported by the movement, by the cause. The 'teamness' of what they do is a sort of invisible net of confidence – confidence in each other and in the faith that they preach; knowing that, however difficult the opposition, they are contributing towards a whole.

This sort of team, typical of sales representatives for new products, speciality salesmen and political conspirators, needs a quite different sort of person from that required by a circus or Boat Race. Its members must share a bond of expectation. They must *expect* their colleagues to be playing an equal part. They must take it for granted that the rest of the team is preaching to the unenlightened – and preaching the same faith. This is why sophisticated bands of salesmen get together annually for simplistic acts of mutual worship of 'our product', 'our founder' and 'ourselves'. It is a means of reinforcing their expectations.

The lesson that emerges from this exploration of team metaphors is very simple; before building your team, you must be sure what sort of team you need! What you do to strengthen one could be anathema to another. There's no point in improving the autonomy of horses, going away for a religious thrash with a circus, or improving the working-together talents of people who hardly see each other for most of the year!

Before leaving the team metaphors that I think have relevance to business teams, I would like to examine a few others that in my view are not relevant and can be positively misleading. As well as looking at what a team is, we need to consider what it is not.

A business team is not a family. A family is linked by ties of blood, not common purpose. Membership of a family is involuntary – you are born into it; you do not choose to join it. The obligations of family members to one another go far beyond those of a working team and are based on emotion rather than function. There is a hierarchy in both the family and the business team, but the family hierarchy relies on parent–child relationships, not adult–adult relationships as does the business hierarchy. (For more about hierarchical relationships in a business team, see Chapter 2.)

Similarly, a business team is not a social club. A social club, like a business team, is motivated by a common purpose, but here it is the personal enjoyment of individual members, rather than the achievement of a common external objective. In a social club you can opt in or out to the extent that suits you individually, and still retain your membership as long as you pay your dues. A business would not survive very long run on that basis!

Finally, a business team is not a therapy group! A therapy group exists to provide an environment in which the participants can explore their emotional problems and discover new ways to relate to themselves and to the world at large. The bond between them comes from the mutual support they provide each other as they undergo similar experiences. Of course, a business team can benefit from an understanding of, and tolerance for, the emotional needs of its members, and a team of emotionally well-balanced people will probably perform better, over the long term, than a team of neurotics. (Although as I write this, I realize that it is more a statement of my own values than an observed fact. I can think of some successful business teams that could be described as pretty neurotic!)

It is also true that team members can and do derive satisfaction of some of their emotional needs from their membership of a business team – a sense of belonging and of shared achievement, for example. However, it is *not*, in my view, the responsibility of the team to satisfy the individual's emotional needs, rather the responsibility of the individual. He may well get help from fellow team members, but here they are acting out of friendship – albeit friendship that developed within the team – not out of responsibility as team members. I do not accept that the individual can reasonably complain if a team fails to satsify his emotional needs. That is not what teams are for.

Nobody, of course, explicitly claims that a team is a family, a social club or a therapy group – some people simply behave as though they think it should be! They impose unreasonable expectations on it, expectations that could only be imposed with propriety on a family, club or therapy group! Their disappointment when these unreasonable expectations are not met can be manifested in complaints about the poor quality of the teamwork. A sympathetic team leader can easily be seduced into trying to solve teamwork problems that do not actually exist – a dangerous diversion of energy.

McKinsey & Co. have an answer to this problem, too. They refuse to recruit people, however capable, whose ego needs are too great to be accommodated by their style of working!*

*Maister, op. cit.

Teamwork is . . .

Another way to try to capture what is meant by teamwork was suggested by my colleague, Lucy McCaffrey. Using the famous 'Love is . . .' cartoon as a model, she suggested we collected a list of 'Teamwork is . . .' sayings which might illustrate the variety of ways in which good teamwork manifests itself.

My own list was as follows:

— everyone pulling in the same direction;
— everyone pulling their weight;
— always having support available when you want it;
— being accepted for what you are, warts and all;
— going to do something you've overlooked, and finding it done for you;
— getting help when you need it and no interference when you don't;
— feeling it a pleasure to see your colleagues – at work and socially;
— everyone mucking in to retrieve a disaster;
— everyone pitching in without complaint when there's a crisis;
— enjoying each other's successes, commiserating with each other's setbacks;
— sharing success and failure;
— sharing an exciting vision of the future;
— being pleased to get together with your colleagues;
— depending on your colleagues to deliver what they promise;
— dancing to the same rhythm.

Various colleagues* contributed the following additions (exercising an editor's privilege I have selected the ones I like!):

— having people who understand to talk to;
— having people to help you build and grow;
— being able to sleep at night;
— not knowing who scored the goals;
— closing ranks against external, negative forces;
— enjoying working with others;
— being able to share when you want to (and not if you don't);

*My thanks to John Alexander, Jasmine Dale and Alison Cozens.

— a feeling of belonging;
— knowing what was said will be done (and if it isn't, hearing about it in time to do something about it);
— feeling of equal value;
— missing someone when he/she leaves;
— being able to enjoy everyone's good points, and live with their bad ones;
— not having to hold anything back – whatever is said is meant and taken constructively;
— a tree swaying in the wind – individual branches may break off, but the tree stays strong;
— knowing what your colleagues would think;
— sharing the load;
— the sum of the individuals' capabilities multiplied by the number of individuals;
— sometimes carrying, sometimes being carried;
— all working towards the same objective;
— a level of trust and openness which allows for total communication;
— knowing clearly who is doing what when;
— not having to be asked;
— knowing what you have to do and what you don't because someone else will;
— taking care of each other;
— looking out for each other.

No doubt you will find some of these resonating with you and others not; some may indeed conflict with your idea of teamwork. Maybe you can extend the list with some suggestions of your own.

Whatever else it shows, the list demonstrates that teamwork is a rich and complex concept, capable of many interpretations and meaning different things to different people. Later in this book (Chapters 2 and 3) I explore ways of giving effect to these diverse interpretations through the concept of 'autonomous teamwork' and interpersonal relationships of high quality.

2. Autonomous teamwork

The individual and the team

Teamwork, like motherhood and apple pie, tends to be regarded automatically as 'a good thing'. As with all good things, more tends to be seen as better (particularly by the 'experts' in the field!). To describe someone as 'a good teamworker' is a clearly positive endorsement. Describe someone as 'a loner', or even 'a bit of a loner', and there is unavoidably a negative implication to the message (unless you are proposing to parachute the person in question behind enemy lines!).

This pro-teamwork bias is, I believe, dangerous, because it tends to discount the importance of personal autonomy for the individual. People work with maximum commitment and energy when they are doing what they have chosen to do, and are doing it in the way they believe is best for them. If they have no emotional ownership of the task, if they are doing it only because they have been told to, or because it is merely a means of earning a living, they cannot bring their full energy and enthusiasm to it.

Clearly a business organization or team cannot consist of individuals all doing their own thing in their own way and in their own time. (Neither can a hippy commune – the experiments of the sixties revealed that here, too, people required some rules and shared commitments in order to survive at all.) Ideally methods of working are developed which integrate the cohesion and consistency of a good team with the personal autonomy the individual needs to work with full commitment.

I consider this to be an entirely practicable ideal and one which can be realized most of the time (though not 100 per cent of the time). As well as valuing their personal autonomy, people also like to work with others; they like to be helpful, to be supported and to identify with a whole (preferably successful) that is larger than themselves. It is natural, therefore, for people to work in a team, especially if it operates in a way that values and encourages individual autonomy.

The Synectics concept of 'autonomous teamwork' provides the mechanisms for reconciling these apparently contradictory forces. It starts from a recognition that each individual is in business for himself, i.e. to achieve his own personal goals and fulfil his own ambitions while continuing to live his life as he wishes, and that it is entirely right and proper that he should be so.

The individual has to achieve most of his objectives through inter-action with other people, who are also in business for themselves. In their interaction, they become a temporary team, with both parties committed to securing outcomes that are successful for both of them. It is a win–win concept of teamwork, just the opposite of the concept inherent in the sporting metaphors so often applied to business teamwork, according to which, for one team to win another must lose. It is a concept of 'mutuality of benefit', that is so well expressed by Mars Inc. as one of the five principles on which it operates:

A mutual benefit is a shared benefit; a shared benefit is a lasting benefit.

To secure win–win outcomes requires the belief that it is indeed possible to do so, and a degree of skill and imagination in problem-solving sufficient for the invention of numerous alternative methods of achieving the same objective. They are most easily secured when all parties possess these qualities, but they are still attainable when only one possesses them.

The underlying belief is that there is nearly always more than one way of skinning the cat; if the method I first think of conflicts in some way with your interests, we can invent an alternative method that does not, and/or invent other ways to look after your interests. The problem-solving skills required to do this are described in detail in the companion volume to this book, *Problem Solving*.

Synectics brings a whole new dimension to the concept of 'team'. My team now becomes 'anyone with whom I am currently interacting', including my colleagues in the unit, department or project group to which I belong (my permanent team), as well as outsiders – customers, suppliers, public authorities, etc. I am a member of one permanent team and many temporary teams, and the same win–win style of working extends to all of them.

It can even extend to my business competitor as well. We have common interests in expanding our shared market, maintaining high quality standards and finding specialized segments for ourselves where we do not come into head-on collision. In principle, I believe it should extend to the VAT inspector and the Inland Revenue, but I have some difficulty stretching it quite that far!

Clearly there have to be some exceptions to the win–win generality. Some situations are designed for only one winner – election to Parliament, for example, or a law court, where either prosecution or defence has to win. Some business situations are of this kind – airlines competing for a licence to fly a particular route, for instance. But business in general is about the creation of wealth, and if we are ingenious enough, we should be able to devise solutions that satisfy all the parties involved.

I am not talking here about compromise. In sporting terms, a compromise is a drawn game or a dead heat. Both parties gain something, but both also give up something and have to settle for second best. A win–win outcome entails both parties being positively pleased with the result, because enough additional value has been created to satisfy both their requirements.

Within the permanent team, the win–win style of working makes for maximum autonomy and mutual co-operation, and should harness the full commitment and involvement of all the team members. Again, there are inevitably occasions when no win–win solution can be invented and it is necessary to accept a compromise. If there is only one cake and no time or materials to bake any more, we can decide to split it or toss for it.

If a team member finds that he is *frequently* failing to satisfy his needs and resorting to compromise, it calls into question whether he actually belongs within the particular team. Every permanent team operates within its own norms and according to its own values, implicit or explicit; in joining a team, the individual enters into a contract (usually implicit) to operate accordingly himself. Difficulty in 'fitting-in' is usually a symptom that the contract has not been accepted or understood – not surprisingly, because it is rarely made explicit.

Because such problems occur quite frequently, there is a strong case for trying to make the norms and values explicit. In my experience, it is a difficult, time-consuming task to draft a concise set of principles which convey fundamental beliefs and act as guidelines for the way team members are expected to operate. It is also an extremely rewarding exercise, because it raises important issues and forces a team to think through where it stands in relation to them. As General Eisenhower said, 'Plans are useless, planning is essential.' i.e. the process of getting there is more important than the end result.

For the top management team of any organization, the articulation of the organization's values is an important part of its responsibility for strategic planning. Just as a mission statement summarizes in a sentence the unique purpose of a particular business, so a statement of values (or principles or beliefs) defines the character of the organization it is seeking to create.

To be of value, such a statement has to be genuine; the top management must themselves believe in it, and be seen to operate in accordance with it. (I know of one company where the statement is known as the Hypocritic Oath! Clearly, if it generates such a cynical response, it is doing more harm than good.) The values stated must also be promulgated actively throughout the organization and communicated in such a way that everyone knows what they mean in practice. Booklets, videos, training sessions and so on have to be used to ensure the necessary level of understanding and commitment.

From experience of working with two American companies that have put a great deal of effort into the formulation and communication of their values statements, I am convinced that they make an important contribution to the quality of management and teamwork (which is exceptionally high in both cases). I was curious to know how widespread the practice was in UK industry, so I wrote to the chairman of the hundred largest companies to ask for their company's equivalent statement.

The response was illuminating. Not more than a dozen companies replied, and only one or two had anything of the kind I was looking for. Interestingly, two of the largest, which were both going through a period of major change, said they were currently working on it. Another chairman said robustly that he wanted nothing to do with such new-fangled American nonsense. All in all, an interesting dog that did not bark, and an interesting reflection of the quality of top management in the UK.

In the absence of any such guidance from the corporate level, it is unrealistic to expect individual departmental or unit teams to fill the vacuum themselves. They have to operate within the corporate culture, which exists even though its values may not be made explicit. But team members are well advised to discuss among themselves periodically what kinds of behaviour they wish to promote in their team (and also what to discourage!). A team functions better if all its members work to the same ground rules.

The existence of such understanding makes it easier to cope with the problems of the dissident team member. It helps to reveal whether he has specific difficulties which are susceptible to win–win problem-solving, or whether he is fundamentally out of sympathy with the team and its values and has never genuinely 'signed-on' and entered into the team contract.

If he is out of sympathy with the rest of the team, the sooner he and the team part company the better for everyone concerned. Trying to accommodate the dissident member can be an enormous drain on the team's emotional energy. In two cases in my own experience, both the dissident individual and the team prospered markedly after the former's departure (in one case the reduced team doubled its productivity).

There is a psychological theory that every team has to have a scapegoat. The dissident member is merely the focus of unresolved conflicts and dissatisfaction in the team as a whole. It is an intellectually intriguing theory (and one that seems to appeal to intriguing intellectuals!). I do not know what empirical evidence there is for it; my own experience is that we have problem members at some times and not at others, but I am not sure whether we are more successful with or without them. Certainly the quality of my work life is much better without them!

The concept of action responsibility

For 'autonomous teamwork' to be effective, there has to be clarity in the team about each individual's roles and responsibilities. If the individual is 'in business for himself', we need to know *what* business he is in. And the sum of the individual businesses must add up to the total task of the team.

The concept of action responsibility is of each person being uniquely responsible for what he himself does, and not responsible in the same way for what other people do. Of course a manager is accountable for the performance of the whole organization he manages, but he exercises that responsibility only through the things he does personally.

It is a salutary, difficult and worthwhile exercise to describe your own action responsibility. It requires honest and accurate answers to the question, 'What do you do at work?' The answers must be specific and expressed using action verbs which describe what you actually *do* (preferably in language that makes sense to a ten-year-old child). The fudging verbs of the conventional job description – to ensure this, to control that, to manage the other – simply will not do. You need to explain *how*, to say what you *do* in order to ensure, control and manage these things.

For a senior manager especially, the exercise can have some alarming implications. First, not much that he does has any direct bearing on the success of the enterprise – he does not make anything, design anything or sell anything. Second, in doing the kinds of things that he does – specifying tasks, allocating resources, monitoring performance – he does not seem to exercise much power.

True, he has the power to award brownie points, recommend (or not) for promotion, hire and maybe ultimately fire. But this kind of power is pretty indiscriminate, rather like a nuclear deterrent – most effective when it is not actually used but kept in the background as a potential bribe or threat. The power to do the things that actually make the organization prosper (or not) – to design, make, buy and sell – exists lower down the organization (like the knives and handguns of guerillas in the jungle).

Your action responsibility defines your true power, the extent to which you can actually make things happen. It defines the space within which you exercise your autonomy; it must not be encroached upon by other team members, any more than you can encroach on theirs without risk of eroding their autonomy.

To ensure that each individual's autonomy is respected, the team can adopt what I call the 'mind your own business' principle, i.e. team members are left to carry out their own job in their own way, without advice, help, ideas, criticism or opinions from their colleagues, unless they ask for such, except when what they are doing or proposing to do impacts on another team member's area of responsibility.

Given the nature of most teams' operations, such interactions are likely to be quite frequent; they call for consultation and, if the impact is negative, some creative problem-solving between the two parties. The purpose of the problem-solving is to find an alternative way to achieve the objective of the proposed course of action, and/or to find ways to eliminate or deal with the negative effects of the proposed action.

In the course of this problem-solving, each party makes his own judgements about ideas that he would have to implement and does not attempt to interfere with his colleagues' right to do the same. So

243

selling, persuading, advising and giving second opinions (If I were you, I would . . .') are out of order. For difficult problems, it is useful to enlist the help of a third team member, both as a source of independent ideas and to ensure that the disciplines are adhered to.

Solving problems together is a bonding experience that strengthens the links within a team through the sharing of the experience of success, and through the appreciation of colleagues' contributions. In a healthy team, it is not restricted to those situations in which one member's proposed action causes problems for a colleague. It is normal for any individual to ask for help whenever he is stuck or wants a better way to handle a situation than he can think of on his own. The initiative for problem-solving, however, must come from the problem-owner for it to be genuinely helpful.

Too often, enthusiastic team members, in their eagerness to be helpful and supportive, insist on imposing their ideas and opinions on colleagues who are perfectly satisfied with the way things are already. This not only wastes a lot of time (particularly if the recipient feels a need to respond politely); it is also destructive – the recipient experiences interference rather than help. Unsolicited ideas are easily taken as criticism. The 'mind your own business' rule is:

Offer ideas and opinions only when they are wanted.

This self-denying ordinance is not easy to follow. When we have what we think is a good idea, we feel it important to share it with the beneficiary at the earliest opportunity, regardless of whether he is interested or not. My colleague, Jason Snelling, solved this problem by instituting the unsolicited idea contract: when an unsolicited idea is offered, the recipient is under no obligation to acknowledge or comment upon it. (In a problem-solving meeting, he has strict obligations to check his understanding of the idea and to evaluate it constructively.)

Another difficulty is the urge to advise or help a colleague when he is not looking for advice or help. Clearly there are occasions when a colleague has a better judgement of the outcome of what I am proposing to do than I have (and vice versa), either from superior information, past experience or just a different perspective. In these cases I am foolish not to listen to what he has to say and to reconsider my decision in the light of it.

The way in which advice is offered is all important. If a colleague tells me that what I am doing is wrong and that I ought to do it differently, I am likely to resent his interference and to defend my actions. The exchange achieves nothing and damages our relationship to some degree. An offer of help needs to be extended in such a manner that it is clear my autonomy is respected. If a colleague says, 'I can see some problems that you may not have anticipated. Do you want to hear about them?', he alerts me to the dangers he perceives while acknowledging that I may already have thought about them. The choice of whether to discuss them or not is left to me. I cannot possibly object, and I perceive the offer as a genuinely helpful one.

The teamwork of the autonomous

The concept of action responsibility and the 'mind your own business', rule might seem at first sight like a denial of teamwork and a recipe for individualism. They are not, but I have given them emphasis to counteract a widespread tendency to subordinate the interests of the individual to the presumed interests of the team. Having stressed the autonomy, I now need to underline the teamwork dimensions of 'autonomous teamwork'.

There are at least four:

— the individual seeking help with a problem;
— interactive problem-solving to resolve conflicts;
— discussion of general team objectives, strategies and values;
— day-to-day supportive behaviour at the emotional level.

For the individual team member to seek help with a problem is not as easy as it sounds. The ethos of many organizations states, implicitly if not explicitly, 'You are paid to solve your own problems.' Consequently, 'to seek assistance is considered a confession of inadequacy'.* In such an environment, any problems an individual has are attributed by that person to the shortcomings of someone else – 'I am certainly not going to confess my own inadequacy!'.

Team members who behave like this spend a lot of time and energy offering unsolicited ideas and advice to each other, criticizing each other (or worse still complaining about each other to other team members or to outsiders) and endlessly debating the rights and wrongs of their opinions. Needless to say, they never actually get round to *doing* anything to improve the situation.

I remember running a five-day training course for one group of

*Dr R. C. Parker, 'Creativity: a case history', *Engineering*, February 1975.

this kind in a major British company some years ago – and a difficult course it was. Towards the end of the fourth day my most vigorous critic said, 'Of course, we all do each other's job here', and immediately became my most vigorous supporter! He had put his finger on a key weakness not just of the team but of the whole company. Interestingly, he left the company not long afterwards, and it continued to progress towards its inevitable extinction a few years later.

Adopting the principles inherent in the concepts of action responsibility and minding your own business is a valuable first step in changing a situation of this kind: at least it cuts down the amount of 'noise' – purposeless and fruitless discussion. It needs to be reinforced by positive encouragement, so that seeking assistance is seen as a demonstration of open-mindedness and willingness to learn, rather than a confession of inadequacy. Someone seeking assistance will still feel he is running a risk by doing so, because he may indeed expose his ignorance of solutions that are known to other people. It is far better that he should learn of these, however, in a supportive environment, rather than feel the need to cover up his ignorance.

The problem-solving orientation of a team is reinforced by the interactive problem-solving employed to resolve conflicts (described earlier). Opportunities are signalled by any kind of argument or debate. (As a generalization, I would risk saying that if an argument cannot be converted into problem-solving it is not worth continuing!) A key question is, 'In what way is it [the issue you are raising] a problem for you, in your area of action responsibility?' If there is no satisfactory answer to this question, the issue is probably not worth discussing.

The one exception I would concede is when the issue is of critical importance to the success of the team as a whole, which brings in the third dimension of teamwork mentioned – discussion of team objectives, strategies and values.

Depending on the nature of its operation, a team needs to meet periodically – monthly, quarterly or at least annually – to clarify what it is trying to achieve and what kind of team it wants to be, and also to review its progress. These meetings are of critical importance to the success of a team (particularly if they are infrequent – frequent meetings provide more opportunity to recover from any that might be unsuccessful).

At their best, team meetings provide an opportunity to renew the cohesion of a team, to clarify the direction it is taking, to recharge emotional batteries, to sort out internal problems and generally to put the team on a sound footing for the forthcoming period of time. Conscious of this potential, team members come to meetings with high expectations and are disappointed if reality does not live up to these expectations.

At their worst, team meetings provide an opportunity for frustrations to be unloaded, smouldering resentments to erupt, unexpected problems to surface and sharp divisions to emerge. Team members rightly expect to be able to let their hair down and speak freely. The team leader has to be able to let this happen without it becoming destructive, a responsibility shared by the team members.

For all these reasons, team meetings present, in my experience, one of the most difficult areas of team management, and call for particular care and skill in their planning and conduct. It helps to start by acknowledging their importance and their complexity and by demanding that all team members share the responsibility for their success (though the ultimate responsibility in this as in all aspects of a team's operations rests with the team leadership).

Given their importance, dates should be fixed well in advance and in an ideal world are regarded as sacrosanct, with all team members making them a top priority in their calendars. The realities of the external world make this a difficult ideal to achieve — business pressures, the demands of higher management in the large organization and personal and family responsibilities of team members all conspire against its realization. If at all possible, meetings should go ahead as planned, with individual absences being accepted in exceptional circumstances.

Furthermore, these meetings (perhaps more than any others) require careful planning on the part of the individual who is going to be responsible for conducting them. This may be the team leader, but it does not have to be; he may delegate the task to a team member or bring in an external specialist as a facilitator. Using an outsider means that all team members, including the leader, can concentrate on the substance of the issues being discussed, leaving the process decisions to the specialist facilitator. If he knows his job, he runs the meeting in a way that maximizes the probability of each team member achieving his objectives, and the team as a whole leaves in better shape than that in which it arrived.

To do this, the facilitator needs to know in advance what each team member wants to achieve from the meeting, and they of course need to be clear themselves. When I am running a meeting of this kind (as an external specialist), I hold planning meetings with each individual, to explore the frame of mind in which they are coming to the meeting and the topics they wish to raise. In particular, I ask them to imagine themselves leaving the meeting extremely pleased with the event, and ask them, 'What would have to have happened for you to depart in that frame of mind?'

From these discussions, I obtain the information necessary to assess what might be achieved at the meeting and the chances of meeting the expectations of the participants in the time available. I have a sense of whether everyone is in fact coming to the same meeting, or whether it looks more like being a series of separate meetings. I also hope to have a feel for the emotional temperature of the group and any storms that are likely to blow up. (It is not, of course, an exact science – more like weather forecasting, in fact.)

It is now possible, in consultation with the team leader, to draw up an outline plan for the meeting, with the approximate time to be devoted to the various topics. I also have my own ideas as to the most appropriate techniques to be employed for different parts of the meeting. All of this, however, is a provisional plan only; events may well demand some instant changes of direction!

For most team meetings, an external facilitator is a luxury which cannot be afforded, but the same kind of planning as he would carry out needs to be undertaken by whoever assumes responsibility for running a meeting. If meetings are held fairly frequently, a standard format probably evolves to take care of routine matters, but meetings must not be allowed to become so routine that they turn into a mere formality.

What needs to be discussed is determined by the issues raised by team members, including the team leader. It is part of a team leader's action responsibility (which I cover in Chapter 4) to focus his team's attention on strategic issues – the team's mission or purpose (why it exists as a team at all); its strategies for fulfilling its mission; its values and means of operation.

This is a most important point, for it is the shared objectives and values which distinguish the permanent, or core, team from the temporary teams which each individual forms with the external people he interacts with on a win–win basis. It is these shared objectives and values, articulated as an exciting vision of the future, that mobilize the emotional energy and commitment of team members.

For the formulation of strategy to have this emotional impact, it must obviously be a participative process, even though initiated and ultimately controlled by the team leader. In participating, every member of the team has the opportunity, and the responsibility, to contribute his thoughts, wishes, ideas and opinions about the future of the team. It does *not* mean that every member has the right to *decide* about the future.

A business team (or any other team which exists in order to achieve anything in the real world) is *not* a democracy, in the sense of one man, one vote. Nor can it operate on the basis of everyone agreeing to everything. Teams that try to work in that way remind me of wartime convoys, proceeding at the speed of the slowest ships, their members huddled together for mutual protection!

On the contrary, the ultimate decisions on strategic matters fall within the action responsibility of the team leader. A leader is most unwise to go ahead without the broad support of team members for the direction he is taking, but he does not need (nor should he seek) the endorsement of each team member for each step of the way.

A team member who finds himself fundamentally out of sympathy with where his team is going, after offering his divergent views unsuccessfully to his colleagues and leader, has to decide whether it is still a team he wants to belong to. If this is so, he must sign on wholeheartedly to the strategy in spite of his reservations.

Equally, a leader who cannot get support for a strategy he wants to pursue has to develop an alternative strategy – or find another team or another job! A team can only work if all members know where they are going and are committed to getting there.

The fourth way in which autonomous individuals act together as an effective permanent team is through their caring for one another, particularly on a day-to-day basis. The whole question of interpersonal relationships within a team is so crucial to its success that it is examined in depth in Chapter 3. Here I want to draw attention to some of the kinds of behaviour that differentiate relationships between colleagues in a permanent team from those between members of a temporary team (however win–win those latter relationships may be).

Between close colleagues there is sharing at the emotional level as well as the functional. They rejoice in each other's successes and commiserate with each other's setbacks. There is a logic in doing so, because individuals' success contributes to a team's success, provided objectives are properly aligned. But there is more than logic: to provide emotional support when it is most needed is an important *raison d'être* for a team. It is one of the dimensions that make a team more than a collection of individuals.

Such emotional support can be forthcoming only when relationships within the team are based on the win–win principle. It cannot co-exist with internal competition of the win–lose variety. There is a place for healthy competition, of the kind that sets new and higher standards and stimulates emulation. (As I write, my own position as principal business-getter for my team is under severe threat from two younger members who are achieving previously unheard of levels of success. For me, it is a source of delight, while at the same time I strive to raise my game to meet the new standards they have set.)

Finally, autonomous members of a team work on a basis of mutual trust – or the assumption that each is working to the best of his abilities, knowledge and emotional condition to achieve his own and the team's objectives (the two being mutually compatible). Trust is a delicate plant which grows from shared positive experience of each other's behaviour, particularly under difficult circumstances. It can quickly be destroyed by a single let-down, real or perceived. A valuable guideline for team members is, 'Assume constructive intent' on the part of colleagues, particularly when things go wrong. Adherence to this in a particular situation ensures that an otherwise instant negative reaction is replaced by a positive attempt to explore what actually happened and why, and it is generally revealed that, although someone may have been mistaken (and to err is human), his intentions were honourable, and trust is not damaged.

Confidence in a person's judgement or wisdom may be damaged, but confidence is not the same thing as trust. You can send me out to play golf with Jack Nicklaus and *trust* me to give everything I've got, but you should not be *confident* that I will win!

How much teamwork?

It is easy to assume that because a number of executives report to the same boss, that group automatically constitutes a team and should behave like one. This assumption has been challenged effectively by Bill Critchley and David Casey, who take the view that 'there is a very *large* proportion of most managers' work where teamwork is not needed (and to attempt to inculcate teamwork is dysfunctional). There is at the same time a very *small* proportion of their work where teamwork is absolutely vital (and to ignore teamworking skills is to invite disaster).*

They go on to distinguish three modes of working which call for different kinds of interaction and different degrees of sharing, as follows:

*'Second Thoughts on Team Building', *Management Education and Development*, vol. 15, pt 2, pp. 163–75, 1984.

— Unshared certainty, applicable to most routine work in which issues are independent of each other. The 'mind your own business' principle applies, and the only interactions are polite social processes.

— Co-operation, for dealing with more complex issues that impinge on several members of a group. Here the interactive problem-solving methods described earlier, and the open-minded communication skills that go with them, are particularly appropriate. I would call this 'functional' teamwork, in which individuals still restrict their judgements to their own area of action responsibility but engage in interactive problem-solving to resolve conflicts and reach compatible solutions.

— Shared uncertainty, for major problems, perhaps concerning strategy, about which nobody knows what to do. A group is dealing here with the future and trying to create something new. There are no future facts (because it has not yet happened); past experience and expertise are of doubtful relevance. Personal feelings (which do not normally enter into management discussions) become highly relevant, if only because people are most likely to achieve what they most *want* to achieve. How to voice these feelings (and to what extent it is desirable to do so) is a crucial issue which I address below. This mode of working might be labelled (with some hesitation) 'emotional teamwork'. (Casey and Critchley, as well as other professional teambuilders, feel this is the only mode they can accept as 'real' teamwork!)

Distinguishing between these three modes of working is valuable because it enables us to apply the appropriate processes and techniques to the task in hand. Most management groups move between all three modes, though there is a tendency to avoid shared uncertainty by resorting to such ploys as appointing a consultant or setting up a task force. Furthermore, each mode finds its precise counterpart in the concepts of action responsibility and 'mind your own business' described earlier. Unshared certainty corresponds to the individual's area of autonomy; co-operation corresponds to interactive problem-solving; shared uncertainty is the characteristic of team objectives and strategy meetings.

My experience is that these meetings can be run very successfully using creative problem-solving techniques, with emphasis on creative techniques such as metaphor, analogy, scenario-writing, imaging and vision-building. These methods elicit the expression of feelings indirectly, and most managers can handle this comfortably. In fact, they can choose how far they will disclose their personal feelings, and I believe it is right that this should be a matter of personal choice.

The alternative approach, much favoured by professional psychologists and psychotherapists, is to *start* with feelings, to engage in what Casey and Critchley appropriately label 'soul-searching'. As they point out, 'Some people will argue that management groups cannot even begin to engage with each other in any kind of serious work . . . until they have first built a degree of openness and trust.' They go on, rightly in my opinion, to reject this approach, on the grounds that most management groups are likely to be task-centred and work at an intellectual rather than an emotional level. 'Approaching such a group suddenly at an emotional level will either generate shock, pain, distrust and confusion, or produce a warm, cosy, euphoric one-off experience', neither of which achieves anything of lasting value.

I believe that building openness and trust is a slow, patient and essentially gradual process, founded on a high level of interpersonal skill and supportive behaviour and regular, participative team meetings. The shared experiences of business successes and setbacks, reviewed and discussed constructively, create the bonds of trust gradually over the years.

Trust created in this way can in fact bring its own problems. It is clearly strongest among the longest-serving members of a team, who tend to develop an almost telepathic understanding of each other's views and reactions. This closeness can be resented by newcomers, who cannot belong to the charmed circle because there has not been time to develop the same kind of bond. They can easily feel excluded, and this feeling can have a divisive effect on a team.

I know of no easy solution to this problem. The inner group needs to be aware of the effect their cohesion can have, and try to remain open to the contributions of newcomers and sensitive to how it feels to be in their position. I have tried the 'soul-searching' approach with intra-group problems of this kind, using a skilled psychotherapist. On balance I believe the team benefited from it, though it certainly did not resolve all the problems and the team eventually decided to discontinue it. Certainly our business improved during that period, which suggests that the soul-searching was beneficial, but it has also continued to improve since we discontinued it!

3. Interpersonal relationships in the team

I referred at the beginning of the book to the correlation between team performance and team 'climate' or culture, the link being the amount of personal energy each individual had to use to protect himself from being hurt. Analysis of group behaviour from video-tapes has convinced me that individual self-esteem is fragile and easily damaged by any experience that is perceived as negative or punishing.

How team members manage their interpersonal relationships is a major factor affecting team climate (although not the only one – the quality of leadership, considered in Chapter 4, is also critical). In this chapter, I want to describe some guidelines and techniques I have found helpful in developing a code of practice for building sound personal relationships in a team. They represent 'work in progress'; I do not claim they are complete, but they might provide a starting point from which your own team can build a code of practice.

Some of the points raised (such as the 'mind your own business' principle) have been mentioned elsewhere and are repeated here for completeness.

Direct dealing

The principle of direct dealing is that any problem which arises between two team members is best dealt with directly by those individuals themselves, without the involvement of a third party, unless both are of the opinion that the presence of an agreed third party would be helpful. If they cannot resolve the issue on their own, it is the responsibility of *both* of them to refer the issue to their leader, together. (To have to do so reflects negatively on their interpersonal problem-solving skills and it should be very much a last resort.)

In day-to-day practice, this principle means that if Tom starts to complain to Dick about Harry's behaviour, Dick's most constructive response is, 'Talk to Harry about it, not me.' The worst thing Dick can do is to listen sympathetically and then go to see Harry himself and to reproach him with his behaviour towards Tom. Unfortunately there are a lot of well-meaning interfering busybodies who do just that!

Contrary to what Dick may think, it is *not* his business to act as a mediator between the two (unless they *both* ask him to, and they are in a bad way if they need to do that). It is *Tom's* responsibility as the aggrieved party to take the matter up directly with Harry; if he shirks that responsibility, Dick does nobody a favour by assuming it himself.

Moreover, Dick's intervention introduces 'noise' and distortion into the communication between Tom and Harry. Tom at least has first-hand knowledge of what he is upset about; Dick's information is necessarily second-hand and almost certainly not strictly accurate. By the time it reaches Harry, via Dick, it is third-hand and further distorted by Dick's interpretation of what he heard.

Interpersonal communication is difficult enough at the best of times; I have suggested elsewhere* that the typical success rate of face to face communication is 25 per cent, perhaps rising to 50 per cent among the more skilful. When the subject matter is emotive, the success rate falls. Communicating through a third party reduces it dramatically – it becomes 25 per cent of 25 per cent, i.e. 6.25 per cent! (Or at the very best, 50 per cent of 50 per cent, i.e. 25 per cent.)

The principle of direct dealing is simple in concept but more difficult in practice. It conflicts with the urge to gossip (i.e. to talk about someone behind his back and say things you would not say to his face). Gossip seems to be prevalent throughout society (hence the popularity of TV soap operas). It seems to bring drama and excitement into otherwise dull and boring lives. I believe it is wise to regard all gossip as potentially malicious in its effect, if not in intent; it has no place in a good team.

I will entertain, reluctantly, one possible exception to the direct

* In the companion volume, *Communication*.

dealing rule. It may be that Tom is so incensed by Harry's behaviour that he needs to let off steam to someone before he can talk rationally to Harry about it. He uses Dick as a sympathetic shoulder to cry on, before taking the matter up directly with Harry. If Dick restricts himself to listening sympathetically and calming Tom down without accepting the validity of his complaints (because he only has Tom's version of events), no harm is done. Dick has acted supportively, as a good team member should.

But who says that Tom has to talk *rationally* to Harry? Maybe it would be good feedback for Harry to experience at first hand just how upset Tom is? That depends on Harry's ability to cope with Tom's feelings without getting upset himself and the whole incident escalating into a blazing row. (Some would argue that the occasional blazing row does no harm to a team and should be seen as a sign of emotional honesty. This is not borne out by my experience, but perhaps that merely reflects on me – I hate emotional upheavals and would rather get on with the job.)

If Tom needs emotional support and a sympathetic ear, perhaps he can find it outside the team, at home, for example, or with a close friend or confidant. Here he is dealing with primarily emotional relationships, whereas relationships within a team, I believe, are primarily functional (albeit with an important emotional element). Not everyone agrees with this view, and I accept that there are grey areas between the concept of a team as a functional unit, with emotional dimensions, and the concept of a team as a therapy group existing to satisfy the emotional needs of its members (with which I have no sympathy).

Constructive feedback

In addition to dealing direct with interpersonal problems as they arise, team members also need to provide feedback on how they relate to each other on a more general basis. It would be unfortunate if they only discussed relationships when these were suffering, though too often this is what happens. When things are going well, we tend to take it for granted; as a result, all we ever get is the bad news.

Regular periodic reviews, on a semi-formal basis, keep a relationship in perspective and provide good learning opportunities for both parties. It requires some discipline to make sure they take place; the pressure of day-to-day events always seems more urgent, but putting in the relatively small amount of time required for a review is a necessary and rewarding investment.

For a team leader, a review at least annually with each team member constitutes a major part of his responsibilities. (It is probably required by the corporate appraisals system, though the kind of review I have in mind is very different from the traditional appraisal.) For other team members, the need for, and frequency of, review meetings depends on the extent of their interaction; it may make more sense for them to review specific shared experiences rather than their general relationship.

The format I favour for a review is that of a mutual problem-solving meeting. It starts with each individual delivering a detailed and balanced statement of his experience of working with the other, preferably prepared in advance to give time for sufficient depth of thought. The statement is in the form of an itemized response (in problem-solving jargon), i.e.:

— these are the things I appreciate, enjoy and admire in my experience of working with you – the positives;
— these are the aspects I wish we could change – the negatives, but expressed as directions for improvement and alteration.

This format is essential for feedback to be perceived as constructive. It is expressed in terms of information about the person giving the feedback; it is not meant to constitute , and is not expressed in terms of, objective information about the recipient. Consequently, it is likely to be accurate, and can be accepted as accurate – I am the expert on my experience of you, just as you are the expert on *your* experience of me.

It also allows for an exchange on a basis of equality – the same kind of information is given in both directions. This is particularly important when the team leader is involved in a review. He has special responsibilities as leader, but these do not make him a superior human being.

Identification of the positive features of a relationship provides a perspective for any discussion of possible improvements, and is critical to the constructive climate of a review. We all need to know what we are doing well, and we are too seldom told. When we are informed, we have a strong tendency to discount the good news. Why this should be so I am not sure, but I suspect that the massive amount of negative feedback we receive as children results in low self-esteem and a highly developed internal self-critic. The positives need to be heard, and it is useful to have the recipient paraphrase his understanding of them, without discounts.

The negatives are framed as wishes for improvement, i.e. problems to be solved. They are not criticisms (though they can easily be interpreted as such, given the tendency to self-criticism). They are concerned with the future, not the past, and they invite ideas for action by either party to improve the situation. Maybe there are things that I could do to help solve the problem I have identified. Unlike the conventional appraisal, there is no assumption that the responsibility for change lies only with the recipient of the feedback.

In fact, the problem areas identified by the two individuals are likely to be related – they are often both conscious of the same difficulties. Once identified, they can frequently be solved by applying relatively simple ideas. The solutions adopted should be written down in the form of a mutual contract, adherence to which it is hoped will ensure the desired improvement in the relationship. This provides a starting point for the next review – how far have we achieved what we agreed to do?; what still remains to be done?

A good review meeting is a win–win experience. (Compare this with the conventional appraisal!) Afterwards both parties feel better understood and better appreciated and they have agreed on what to do to improve their relationship. As the relationship develops, reviews become quicker and less formal. Eventually a level of trust and confidence may be reached at which formal reviews become redundant. As stepping-stones to that end, I have found them invaluable.

Incidentally, if you do have to carry out a standard appraisal, be assured that this sort of review meeting gives you all the information you need, at a much higher level than any other procedure I know!

Coaching/learning

The same feedback principles can be applied to the processes of learning from and coaching each other within a team. In my own team, in which we frequently have occasion to work in pairs and one person has the opportunity to observe another in action, it is standard practice for the observer to write 'coaching notes'. These represent his view of what happens and are accepted as such, without consideration of whether he is 'right' or 'wrong'. The subject's experience may well be different, and that is accepted too. We all see the world differently, and it is not unusual for two people to experience the same event differently.

Feedback is much more acceptable and useful if it is presented as information about the observer rather than a judgement about the observed. Differences of view then become interesting areas for exploration and learning on the part of both parties. Conversely, the same information presented as a judgement, e.g. 'The right way to do it is . . . or 'What you should do is . . .', is likely to provoke a defensive reaction, e.g. 'I did it that way because . . .', which can lead to argument and debate about who is right and who is wrong. On the other hand, the judgement may be apparently accepted but resented. Either reaction tends to close the mind to learning and diminish the value of the feedback.

Presenting a judgement has this effect because it sets up a superior–inferior relationship, leaving the recipient in an emotionally 'one-down' position, which is damaging to his self-esteem. His mind is likely to close as a means of protection against the pain.

Even though a coach may be vastly more experienced and knowledgeable than his 'student', he must bear in mind that the student's way may be right for him. Equally, a student is foolish to ignore his coach's greater experience and knowledge, but he does not have to behave as though his coach is infallible. A good sense of a productive relationship between coach and student is captured by Al Huang's definition of a master:

A master is someone who started before you did.*

A good coach provides a model of the learning process and must therefore be open to learning himself and demonstrate that this is the case. Again, therefore, feedback needs to be two-way. The observations of the less experienced person provide important information concerning his own learning process, indicating what points are registering with him and what are not. They also provide the coach with a mirror which reflects the effectiveness or otherwise of his coaching. They may also stimulate additions to the coach's own knowledge and awareness.

Conflicts

Just as a chain is only as strong as its weakest link, so a team is only as strong as its weakest interpersonal relationship. Where there is animosity and hostility between two members, or even mere

*Quoted in Gary Zukov, *The Dancing Wu Li Masters*, Hutchinson, 1979.

personal dislike, there is potential for divisiveness and a threat to team cohesion.

Warring parties tend to disagree almost automatically about everything, taking opposing points of view almost out of habit. They seek to recruit allies and in so doing extend their division through the team. Their antipathies close their minds to each other's ideas, blocking the way to the creative problem-solving needed to resolve substantive issues. Their animosity casts a shadow over the team climate, embarrassing other members and generating a state of 'psychic contamination'.

The frustrating thing about a situation like this is that nobody can really do much about it except the contestants themselves, and they may be unwilling or unable to do so. The team leader and other team members can offer to help or mediate; professional external help, perhaps from a psychotherapist, can be enlisted; work can be organized to minimize interaction between the parties concerned. At the end of the day, however, none of these remedies works unless the individuals want them to.

In the end, there is no course open to a team leader but to bang their heads together, tell them (preferably together) that their behaviour will no longer be tolerated and make it clear that they will *both* have to leave the team if they cannot settle their differences within a reasonable time. This at least gives them something in common – imminent departure from the team – and an incentive to sort themselves out!

A leader should not, in my opinion, allow either of the protagonists to drive the other out of the team. Nor should he allow himself to be set up as judge of which party is guilty and which innocent. It is up to each of them, as responsible team members, to manage their relationship constructively. They do not have to *like* each other, but they must develop a satisfactory way of working together and refrain from destructive behaviour. Failing this, they must leave.

Humour

By their jokes you will know them. A healthy team is a good-humoured team, one in which smiles and laughter are the order of the day. But the *quality* of the humour is all important.

Among the groups I work with, I frequently encounter a lot of leg-pulling and jokes at everyone's expense. It is perceived by group

259

members as a healthy, normal interaction – even a sign of good teamwork – and they are astonished when I challenge this view.

Over time, I have begun to see a correlation within groups between the prevalence of this kind of 'sharp' humour and of cautious, guarded behaviour when it comes to discussing work issues. Team members are reluctant to risk putting forward new ideas, or say what they really think or feel, for fear of being the butt of a colleague's wit. Though there may be laughter, it has an uncomfortable feel to it.

Undoubtedly this kind of humour sets up 'revenge cycles' – you make a crack at my expense and I am sure to get you back at the earliest possible moment. All good clean fun, I am told by the protagonists, but I am not convinced. At the very least, these revenge cycles take up energy that could be more usefully deployed on the job – I have to be on the alert to spot my opportunity to get back at you, and keep my guard up against your next thrust. It is certainly a distraction.

More seriously, it is a win–lose activity, and therefore contrary to the win–win approach that a team must adopt if it is to be a healthy one. Win–lose rapidly becomes lose–lose, as the loser of the first round sets up a return match on his own ground which he is sure to win.

I am aware that my view runs counter to much of our national culture, particularly that of the north of England (including my home town of Liverpool!) in which the ability to give and receive sharp knocks is prized as a sign of maturity. (It is even more pronounced in Australia.) But there are other societies, in Europe, America and the East, which do not seem to need this kind of humour and, I suspect, get on better without it.

My reason for asserting this is quite simple: however good-natured the *intent* of the joke-maker, the effect on the recipient is very likely to be negative. He may not be aware of the hurt he receives, and consequently not acknowledge it, but watch his subsequent behaviour (preferably a few times on videotape) and you can see his guardedness and desire to get his own back, resulting from the blow to his self-esteem.

With some reluctance I have tried to curb my own tendency to make fun of others; I have decided it is too dangerous and too costly. There is enough to laugh about in the world around us without laughing at each other!

'Mind your own business'

In voicing this apparently 'hostile' expression I am in fact urging respect for the autonomy of team members. It means making sure a colleague wants to hear your ideas and opinions concerning what he is doing before you actually offer them, i.e. not interfering without permission, however helpful you feel your interference is going to be. It is up to him to decide whether he wants his work to be interfered with or not!

An important corollary of this principle is to speak for yourself. You are the expert on you and can speak with authority about yourself. The same applies to all individuals. It follows that I cannot speak with authority about what anyone else is thinking or feeling; I can only speak about *my perception*, of these things, a very different matter.

It is also dangerous to presume to speak for someone else by classing them under the collective 'we'. It must be clear who 'we' represents in addition to the speaker. Have the other parties mandated the speaker to speak for them? If not, he is only entitled to speak for himself, to use 'I', not 'we'.

The use of 'we' (and its close associate 'one') can cause a lot of subtle trouble in working groups. It creates situations in which members of a group are conscripted by a speaker to a view he is expressing, without their consent. They are faced with the choice of going along with it or voicing their opposition, neither of which they may want to do. This can happen so quickly they are not aware of what is going on and suddenly find themselves identified with a position they do not support.

Of course there are times when 'we' is appropriate – for example, in the expression of agreed corporate policy ('We only give refunds on production of a receipt.') But many people say 'we' when they have the right only to say 'I', and in so doing muddy the waters of team relationship.

Assume constructive intent

Any transaction between two individuals is not one event but two – it represents a different experience for each of the individuals concerned. Looked at in this way, many misapprehensions and breakdowns in interpersonal relationships become readily understandable. Two people's experience of the same event can differ enormously, in a manner quite unanticipated by the initiator of that event.

When intent and effect are uncoupled in this manner, it is common to find that positively intended actions have a negative effect. Maybe they are undertaken unwisely or carried out clumsily, or maybe the recipient misunderstands or is hypersensitive. My experience is that people seldom set out to hurt each other (unless they are already locked into a long-standing feud). Damage is the result of clumsiness rather than malice.

Once this hypothesis is accepted, it is possible to place a negative experience in a different perspective. Suppose the initiator of a particular transaction, the effect of which is perceived by a recipient as destructive, had in mind something constructive, what might this have been? Such an approach is a positive response to the assumed constructive intent, not a negative reaction to the apparent negative effect.

If, for example, you say to me, 'Your idea won't work. We tried it a couple of years ago and it flopped', I can reply, 'That's only because you bungled it.' (i.e. get my revenge). Conversely, assuming constructive intent, I can say, 'It sounds as if you had an experience a couple of years ago that you consider relevant. I'd like to hear more about it.' The door is now open to constructive discussion of how my idea might be modified to avoid the fate of two years previously.

To be able to manage immediate emotional reaction (sit on it, in fact) long enough to explore the probable constructive intent behind what causes it, is an invaluable skill in a team. It creates a calm and positive emotional climate and saves endless time and energy otherwise wasted in unnecessary wrangling. Its effective exercise calls for a high degree of emotional maturity, and it is a leader's responsibility to set an example. However, he probably has less need of recourse to this skill than other team members; he is, after all, less likely to be the subject of attack on account of his position as leader. Rather, older and more experienced members of a team might be better placed to set an example, although in my experience there is no necessary correlation between age and emotional maturity!

4. Team leadership

The concept of team leader

Almost implicit in the idea of a team is the assumption that it has a leader of some kind, a captain, manager or coach, to name but a few commonly employed titles. (A football team may have all three of these, each assuming a distinct role.)

What is involved in taking on the role of leader varies according to a team's activities. A cricket captain makes, and takes responsibility for, strategic decisions, such as whether or not to bat on winning the toss, or whether to declare an innings closed rather than continue batting. He also makes tactical decisions, on such matters as which bowlers to use, from which end they are best deployed and when it is most expedient to change them, and in which order his players go into bat.

A football captain, on the other hand, can do no more (on the field of play) than lead by example and cajole, encourage and exhort those within earshot – an altogether less powerful role.

In a work context, a team leader usually bears the title 'manager', and his immediate team consists of those who report directly to him. His leadership responsibilities extend beyond this, however, to all the sub-teams in his part of the organization. Each member of his immediate team may well lead their own team, the pattern continuing up and down the hierarchy. Every manager (except the chief executive) is both a team leader and a member of another, higher level team.

Like Janus, therefore, a manager faces two ways, and his two roles may call for quite different behaviours. He is confronted with the difficult task of looking in opposite directions without appearing two-faced (or developing a split personality!). His responsibilities are likely to cover *all* the functions of sports captains noted above, and a few more besides. Typically, he is responsible for:

— making certain specific decisions;
— maintaining team morale;
— leading by example;
— team selection;
— allocation of responsibilities and resources;
— coaching, i.e. developing the skills of team members;
— stimulating a sense of purpose and excitement about the future — the feeling that his is a great team to belong to because it is going to do great things.

It is a formidable and possibly daunting list. Consideration of these responsibilities can easily create the feeling that they are beyond the scope of the average manager and call for a special kind of supermanager. There do, of course, exist some specially gifted individuals who take to them like a duck to water (the action profiles described in Chapter 5 can help to identify them). But I believe it is well within the scope of the averagely gifted manager to fulfil the role of leader competently, once he is aware of the nature of that role and what it requires of him.

A number of considerations, however, can ease the burden. A team leader is not alone. He can look to his own boss for guidance and support, unless he happens to be the chief executive, in which case he may turn to a trusted external confidant, perhaps a non-executive director or consultant.

His team members can also be a source of support, given a relationship between him and them that is based on mutual respect *and* a mutual recognition and acceptance of his distinctive role and authority. To establish such a relationship in the first place is one of his primary tasks.

When a team leader takes his place within a large organization, major strategic decisions have (it is to be hoped!) been taken already. A company, assuming it is reasonably well led from the top, has already defined its corporate mission, and devised the strategy by which this is to be fulfilled. It has also articulated its value system (although, as we have seen, this tends to be a blind spot for many British companies!).

Assuming a company has done a reasonable job in these areas, an individual team leader's strategies become a subset of the corporate strategy, and the strategic decisions he has to take are fairly straightforward and need only be checked out with his boss.

Under these circumstances, and assuming he has the technical competence to handle the job, neither the strategic nor the tactical decision-making aspects of his work should cause him much difficulty. He is free to concentrate his energy on the development of interpersonal relationships within his team, the area in which success or failure as a leader is ultimately determined.

If, however, there is no corporate strategy, a team leader must take on the role of the entrepreneur – the leader of an independent team – and seize the opportunity to develop his own strategy. This is the ideal vehicle for creating an exciting vision of the future which mobilizes the energy and commitment of a team.

Recently I worked with a team of educational psychologists employed by a local education authority. One of their problems, they complained, was that the authority had no clear strategy for the role of educational psychologists in the education system. To me this seemed to be the ideal opportunity for *them* to work out what they believed the strategy should be, and start putting it into practice. At best, they would have the strategy they wanted; at worst, they would provoke a reaction which would lead to the development of an alternative strategy, thereby filling the vacuum of which they were complaining. Either way it would be an exciting project with shared risks and shared benefits, a perfect way to build a high-performance team.

Developing your leadership skills

If you are one of nature's born leaders, this section has nothing to offer you; you do it all, intuitively, and no doubt more besides. However, before you move on, it might be worth answering the question, 'How do you know you are a born leader?' I have known a few people who prided themselves on their leadership skills, but their team members told a very different story!

It might be worth getting some objective feedback before concluding that your leadership style has no scope for improvement. One way of doing this is to ask an independent observer, like an external consultant, who can talk to team members individually and report back the collective view while preserving the anonymity of individual comments. Alternatively, you can use a structured questionnaire, such as the one developed by Roger Harrison and

David Berlew of Situation Management Inc. in connection with their Power and Influence Programme.

Not being a born leader myself, I cannot claim to know the precise formula of leadership, but I think it is worth sharing the conclusions I have formed from my own experience of leadership and observation of a wide variety of leaders at work. The following principles seem to me to be important:

— *Be yourself:* you can only lead in ways that come naturally to you. It is fatal to keep in mind an image of what you think a leader should be and to try to live up to that if doing so involves putting on an act. Your team members are not stupid; they know when they are being conned (even if they do not know *how*). Your personal integrity is your most valuable asset and the basis of the trust you need to build with your team. Do not put it at risk by acting a part.

— *Know yourself:* if you have a clear idea of what you do well naturally, and where you are vulnerable, you can structure your activity as leader to exploit your strengths and get help where you need it. I find that knowledge of my own action profile is a great help in this respect, and I imagine that other forms of psycho-metric measurement would serve the same purpose if they were reasonably accurate.

— *Define your role as leader:* your team needs to know what kind of activities you are going to engage in as leader, and what decisions you are going to make. They need to know in which areas they have the autonomy to make their own decisions, when they need to get your approval for what they want to do, and when you reserve decision-making for yourself. Similarly, they need to know which of your policies are fixed and non-negotiable, and which are open to discussion and change. People need to know where they stand; to know that, they need to know where *you* stand, and it is your job to tell them.

— *Provide a model of behaviour you want practised in the team:* you are the architect and the guardian of the team's style of working, and the team takes its cue from the example you set. If you believe it is important that meetings start on time, for example, you have to be on time yourself (normally — you are allowed some human frailty, too!)

— *Come clean:* you have to disclose what you are thinking and planning to do. If you do not, your team members only waste their energy guessing and adjusting their behaviour accordingly — and they can easily guess wrongly. Of course, there are times when you have information you are not at liberty to disclose because it has been given to you in confidence, but your need to acknowledge the fact ('This is the way it's going to be, for reasons I'm not in a position to disclose.') Your personal honesty is essential to the building of trust, and if you want honesty in a team you have to set an example yourself.

— *Give constructive feedback:* I have already emphasized (see Chapter 3) the critical importance of feedback being given in ways that recognize the sensitivity of the recipient and enable him to do something positive with it. In particular, be generous with your appreciation: it costs you nothing, but is of inestimable value to the recipient in building his self-esteem. Some managers work on the opposite principle: 'He is a professional. Why should I praise him for doing the job he is paid to do? I will tell him only when he falls short.' As well as being mean-spirited, this is a short-sighted, self-defeating approach. It assumes that a leader and team members have identical views on what the requirements of a job are (a dangerous assumption) and means that all news is bad news (the most effective demotivator imaginable!)

— *Give honours judiciously:* 'What is honoured in a country is what is practised there.' Any promotions, commendations or other awards you hand out are interpreted by team members, quite rightly, as evidence of your value system. They adapt their behaviour accordingly. If a team member is rewarded for successful performance achieved by dubious methods, the message is, 'Dubious methods are okay as long as they bring results.' That may be the message you want to give, but it would be a pity to give it inadvertently!

— *Be consistent:* few things are more demoralizing to members of a team than to find that the goal posts have been moved without warning. They have been working to achieve success by one set of criteria and find themselves being judged by a different set. The criteria by which you judge people need to be explicit and stable.

I am conscious that the whole philosophy of leadership underlying these principles runs counter to what might be called the 'tough management' school of thought. This is based on the belief that people at work are motivated primarily by fear, and is expressed in such maxims as 'Divide and rule', 'Keep them guessing', 'Make them compete against each other.' It has to be said that some exponents of this philosophy have successful track records to support it.

The issue for me is whether these people are successful because of their philosophy or in spite of it. I believe they would be even more successful following my principles, but we have no way of testing who is right. However, I do not accept that my way need be any less 'tough' than theirs; on the contrary, objectives can be just as demanding and standards just as high. The difference is that these matters are out in the open, and everyone knows where they stand. For me, that in itself is a huge benefit; it is the way I prefer to live and work, and I would be willing to trade some commercial success for it if that were necessary. But I do not believe it is!

I am convinced (though, again, I have no proof) that the more the environment a team works in requires innovation, and the greater the extent of external change, the more team members need a style of leadership that is open, honest and constructive. In conditions of great uncertainty, there is no way of knowing whether a particular initiative is going to be successful or not. Team members have to have the confidence that they can take sensible (i.e. affordable) risks without being penalized if they are not successful.

If they lack the confidence to do this, they refer all risky decisions to their team leader, who is probably less well placed than they are to take them because he is further from the action and therefore less well informed. Then the leader complains of being overloaded and burdened with unenterprising subordinates!

Team members should be encouraged to check with their leader before taking serious risks, and the leader, while having the right of veto, should share responsibility if he decides these risks are to be taken. An environment which prompts such behaviour is created only through trust and mutual respect.

Leadership and democracy

There is a widespread belief, especially among younger people and in the public, as opposed to the private, sector, that teams should be 'democratic'. What is meant by 'democratic' in the context of a working team is not too clearly defined, but it seems to imply everyone having the right to have a say in every decision that affects them. If there is disagreement, as is almost inevitable, decisions are presumably taken by vote!

I believe that this view is based on a false notion of democracy; it also happens to be unworkable in practice. Political democracy champions the principle of one man, one vote. Having elected a government, the electorate has to accept that the government will make its own decisions without consulting it further until the next election, as a result of which it may be replaced. Even in that most democratic institution, the sports club, members elect the team captain. Once elected, the captain makes his own decisions, with as much or as little consultation as he sees fit, until such time as the members decide to elect someone else to the job.

Similarly, in a workers' co-op or common ownership company, members, in their capacity as owners of the business, appoint or elect the management (in the same way that shareholders theoretically elect the directors of a limited liability company). Once appointed, management leads the business in the way it sees fit. This includes taking unpopular decisions because it believes them to be right for the success of the business. Whether it is re-elected or not should depend on the performance of the business under its leadership, not on whether it interprets correctly the wishes of its constituents on every issue!

I recently worked with a team leader who told me that he saw himself as *primus inter pares* ('first among equals', he translated, to make sure I got the point). He refused to give a lead on anything, complained about poor standards of work, criticized his subordinates and refused to take responsibility for anything himself. Not surprisingly his team ran around in circles like a bunch of headless chickens, making a lot of noise and achieving very little. Where they needed leadership there was a vacuum.

'First among equals' is a helpful concept if it is taken to mean that everyone in a team is equal in terms of deserving the same degree of respect and identical treatment (analogous to 'equal before the law' in a democratic society). But members of a work team do different jobs, and a leader has a unique job that only he can do. 'First among equals' is not an excuse to abdicate the responsibilities of leadership.

Situational leadership

'Situational leadership' is the label given by management researchers Paul Hersey and Ken Blanchard to the unsurprising assertion that 'there is no single all-purpose leadership style. Successful leaders are those who can adapt their behaviour to meet the demands of their own unique situations.' As a general proposition, this is hardly news to practising managers. (It is more of a surprise to management academics, who have apparently been involved in a search for the 'best' style of management for some decades!) However, the Hersey–Blanchard model usefully goes on to identify three variables which provide some clues as to *how* a leader should vary his style according to his situation. Two of the variables relate to the leader's style and the third to the capacity of the 'follower' (the party that is led).

The two leader variables are called 'task behaviour' and 'relationship behaviour', and are defined by Hersey and Blanchard as follows:

Task behaviour is the extent to which a leader engages in one-way communication by explaining what each follower has to do as well as when, where and how tasks are to be accomplished.

Relationship behaviour is the extent to which a leader engages in two-way communication by providing socio-emotional support, 'psychological strokes', and facilitating behaviours.

These are identified as two independent variables which can co-exist in a leader's style to any degree, as opposed to either–or elements which exist only in a single continuum (so that a manager is described as either predominantly task-oriented *or* relationship-oriented). In the Hersey–Blanchard model he can be both (or either!) – a breakthrough for common-sense!

This distinction allows the authors to draw one of those quadrant diagrams beloved of management writers, dividing leadership style into four categories:

— high task and low relationship;
— high task and high relationship;
— high relationship and low task;
— low relationship and low task.

('High' and 'low' relate to the *degree* of each type of behaviour exhibited by a leader, rather than its nature!) Any of these styles may be effective, depending on the 'situation'. This is defined in terms of the degree of 'maturity' of a follower in relation to a specific task. Someone new to a task obviously needs more direction and guidance than someone familiar with it. More controversially, Hersey and Blanchard suggest that a newcomer needs less 'socio-emotional' support than an established follower (or is it that a leader, in spelling out to a newcomer what a task entails, has no time or energy for supportive behaviour?)

Be that as it may, the four leadership styles are mapped on to the degree of task-relevant maturity of followers in order to ascertain which of them has the highest probability of carrying out success-fully which particular jobs, as follows:

— *Telling* (high task/low relationship): leader simply issues instructions;

— *Selling* (high task/high relationship): leader still makes the decisions but tries to persuade his followers to support them;
— *Participating* (high relationship/low task): leader and followers share decision-making;
— *Delegating* (low relationship/low task): leader lets followers do the job their own way, because they are willing and able to do so.

Thus, the situational leadership theory calls for a high degree of flexibility on the part of a leader. He may need to vary his approach with the same individual on different tasks, with different individuals on the same task, and with the same individual over time as his maturity and competence in a particular area increase. This is a disturbing proposition for a leader who has evolved a style of his own which he uses all the time!

I would say that if you have a personal style that works for you, stay with it until you come across a situation in which it does not work. Then look to this model for some clue as to where you may be going wrong and how you might usefully modify your approach. You may find it particularly relevant when you move into a new job or get promoted (remembering the Peter Principle, which states that people tend to be promoted to their level of incompetence, i.e. the level at which their habitual style is no longer appropriate and they fail to modify it).

While a model of this kind is a useful tool to clarify the issues involved and provide a common language for their discussion, I have reservations about some of the implications of this particular one. There is potential for conflict with at least two of the leadership principles put forward earlier, viz. 'Be yourself' and 'Be consistent.'

If it does not come naturally to you to engage in high relationship behaviour, do not try to force it. If you do, it will appear insincere and possibly patronizing, and will do more harm than good. Paradoxically, a *small* move in that direction may well have a powerful impact if you are known as habitually reserved. People will be aware of the effort it has cost you!

The demand for consistency may well be met by telling your team that you intend to operate on the Hersey–Blanchard principles. The only issue then remaining is that of securing agreement on individuals' levels of maturity as regards particular tasks, which is a subject for discussion between you. In the last analysis, it is your judgement as leader that counts, since you carry ultimate responsibility for the performance of the team as a whole.

At a more fundamental level, the model fails to take into account the *quality* of relationships between a leader and his team members.

If the level of mutual respect and trust is sufficiently high, the varying degrees of competence in respect of different tasks present no problem. A team member actively seeks help and welcomes guidance and direction when he is working on something new or something he finds difficult.

When his task-relevant maturity is low, a team member is at his most vulnerable and therefore in need of the maximum socio-emotional support his leader can lend, as well as the maximum direction and guidance. As he becomes more competent he may need less of both in purely quantitative terms, but the quality of relationship must be sustained at the highest level right across the spectrum.

I am also suspicious of the idea of a leader 'selling' a decision to a team. It smacks of manipulation and phony consultation. It is his privilege to decide which issues he settles on his own, with or without prior consultation, and which he tackles in a participative manner. In many situations he may be well-advised to consult first and obtain feedback on a proposal before coming to a final decision. He is also well-advised to give his reasons for reaching a particular decision whenever possible. At the end of the day, of course, a decision is his; team members who do not like it must either accept it or leave the team.

There is one other situational variable that has a major bearing on the appropriateness of leadership style. This is the nature of a team's activities, broadly classifiable as 'operational' or 'developmental'. In an operational situation a team operates in real time, and many decisions have to be made instantly; the situation is probably a routine one for which there are known solutions and drills. Developmental activity is concerned with the future: there remains time for consultation and for exploration of a variety of options, and there is likely to be a call for a high degree of original thinking.

In general, an operational situation calls for a decisive leadership style (and a corresponding instant response from team members). In developmental activity, a consultative style is more appropriate – no one knows the answers, and there is time to search for them.

The same team may operate in both kinds of situation at different times. Thus a fire brigade crew fighting a fire is in operational mode and autocratic leadership from the captain is called for. On the following day, the same crew might discuss ways of improving its firefighting techniques for the future, and a highly participative mode is then appropriate.

Perhaps the ideal leadership style is one which is flexible and allows a leader to adapt his approach according to the precise demands of a situation (within the natural limits of a leader's personality), with both leader and team members being clear about the basis on which the flexibility is being exercised. I hasten to add that I have not yet reached this nirvana myself!

The leader as coach

It is fashionable nowadays to view the development of a leader's subordinates as one of his principal responsibilities, so that as well as being a manager he is also a coach. Because a leader is usually older, more experienced and it is to be hoped, wiser than those he leads, the idea has immediate appeal. Moreover, if a leader sees himself as a coach, he is less likely to interfere to the point of doing a job himself. Even so, because the perception of a leader as a coach is so fashionable, it is worth taking a critical look at it.

Why *should* a leader take responsibility for the development of team members? What benefit does he, the team or the organization gain from his doing so? How about team members taking responsibility for their own development? What about the role of the management development manager in the personnel department?

The answers are different for an independent team and a team that is part of a larger organization. In the case of an independent team, the growth of the people in it drives the growth of the business itself, or at the very least limits its capacity for growth. For the leader, investment of his time and energy in the development of his team members is an investment in the future of the business – assuming they stay in the business. And they are more likely to stay if they feel they are improving their skills and amassing relevant experience. The coaching relationship inevitably brings the leader and individual team member into close personal contact, and this helps the leader keep his finger on the pulse of team morale.

Many of the same benefits can be reaped by a team within a larger organization, but space for expansion of its activities cannot be taken for granted. If this is lacking, the development of team members can lead to frustration on the part of the individuals concerned and the temptation on the part of the team to empire-build or encroach on other teams' spheres of activity.

Moreover, there is often a trade-off between developing people in a team and achieving short-term results. Development takes time and energy and involves risks in giving tasks to inexperienced

273

people that would be done quicker and better by someone already experienced. If a team leader is to be judged by short-term results, he needs to think hard about investing in the long term – he may not be there to enjoy the rewards! (An ambitious team leader may not intend to be there – his strategy may be to get himself promoted by achieving visible short-term results without regard to the long-term consequences! Being a coach has no place in such a strategy!)

For the leader of a team within an organization, the extent of his responsibility for developing his subordinates needs to be worked out explicitly and agreed with his boss. It cannot be taken for granted. Maybe the organization wants to use his department as a training ground for future managers of other parts of the business. If so, it must be made an explicit objective.

Furthermore, a leader's ability to be a good coach cannot be assumed. A person is often appointed leader because of his success as a performer of his team's activities (or one of them), but the best performers tend not to be good coaches. They may not know how they achieve their results; they may just do it instinctively. It probably comes easily to them, so they have little understanding of, or patience with, the difficulties of the less gifted.

It is, in fact, unreasonable to expect any team leader to be an effective coach without providing him with relevant training. A coach is, or should be, a facilitator of learning. This is a very different concept from that of the traditional teacher, on which most managers unconsciously model themselves in tackling their coaching duties. A teacher is perceived as a source of knowledge (often information) which is to be passed on to pupils; the criterion of success is often the pupils' ability to regurgitate the same information in an examination.

The role of coach is one of helping pupils develop their ability to do new things. It is a process of skill development, in which the active role is that of the learner, not the coach. The coach facilitates this process by setting up the learning opportunities, ideally in a series of graduated steps of increasing difficulty, and by giving feedback at each stage in a helpful way. In the real world, as opposed to a training environment, it is not so easy to provide a series of suitably graded steps. The approach has to be much more opportunist, and a team leader has to judge when to throw someone in at the deep end, and when he does so, what support to provide. If his team operates in an environment of innovation, circumstances often make these decisions for him; when no one has previous experience of a situation, it provides an opportunity for everybody to learn!

Ideally the steps should be so graduated that each one is a stretch, but can be accomplished successfully, and if it is not, the consequences are acceptable. (It needs a stable environment to be able to get close to this ideal – where innovation is taking place it is unlikely to be possible). The aim is to build confidence through successful achievement of progressively more difficult tasks. The experience of these achievements is the essence of the learning process; feedback provides reinforcement of the experience.

For feedback to be experienced as reinforcement, it must be positive, constructive and forward-looking. In the process of experiential learning, any experience is received in a positive fashion, in that it is recognized as providing the material for learning, regardless of its consequences. Indeed, the more unexpected the consequences, the greater the potential for learning.

A leader's reaction to what goes wrong is all-important. If he reacts to every setback as to a major disaster, his feedback is experienced as negative and punishing. Consequently his team develops an aversion to risk-taking and innovation, and ceases to learn.

'We have a monumental cock-up on our hands,' said Fred, the international production director of a multinational company. The occasion was his annual conference of production directors from subsidiaries around the world, being held this time in Madrid. The monumental cock-up? Fred had discovered that slide projectors in Spain take a different sized slide from those he had brought from the US! He can choose to see this as a challenge to his ingenuity, and tackle the question of how to get his message over without his slides, or how to adapt his slides to fit the projector, or how to find an American-sized projector in Madrid! He could also have seen it as an interesting learning experience for himself, the discovery that American slides (like American stationery sizes, weights and measures) are not standard with those elsewhere in the world. But Fred chose to see it as the result of a blunder by the Spanish production director, who was hosting the conference – an unfair and demotivating reaction, in my opinion.

When something goes wrong, there are only two things you can usefully do – find ways to put it right and learn from the experience for future reference. To learn from it you may have to conduct an inquiry into what went wrong and why, but if an inquiry turns into a witch-hunt with the object of apportioning blame, it generates a cover up and nothing is learned. Apportioning blame is only worthwhile if a disaster is so serious that you have to get rid of the people responsible for it.

Not long ago I was comparing experiences with my opposite number in the US. I mentioned that it was some years since we had had a client session that went seriously wrong. Their experience had been the same, he said. There was a pause, then he went on: 'I'm not so sure that's such a good thing. It probably means we're not taking enough risks. When a session did go wrong, we used to research the hell out of it, and we learned a lot from it!'

By adopting this sort of attitude, a leader really does establish an environment that is conducive to learning, and in so doing establishes his role as coach. By inviting and welcoming feedback (provided it is positive, constructive and forward-looking!) and acting upon it, he demonstrates his own readiness to learn, thereby setting an example to his team. The two-way appraisals described in Chapter 3 provide an excellent opportunity for a leader to engage in mutual learning with team members and to demonstrate his own willingness to learn and change.

'Followership'

A great deal is said and written about 'leadership', yet 'followership' is rarely mentioned. The existence of one implies the existence of the other: it would be an odd sort of leader who had no followers!

Intuitively and emotionally I (and, I suspect, others in the field) back away from the notion of 'followership', because it suggests subservience and loss of dignity – it has a sheep-like ring to it. But the issue cannot be fudged; quite simply there are many more followers than leaders, and as we have already seen, every leader in a hierarchical organization (except the chief executive) is also a follower, a member of a higher level team than the one he leads. How can he fulfil these two apparently opposing roles without detriment to his own consistency and integrity as a human being?

I remember sitting talking to Arthur, the chief executive of the UK subsidiary of an American-owned multinational company, when a call came through from the company president in the US. Instantly, the powerful, authoritative, even dominating personality I had been talking to was transformed into a crawling, subservient creep! I was astonished, and began to see why his subordinates did not hold him in the same high regard as that in which I had been inclined to hold him!

The paradox resolves itself if we go back to the concept of action responsibility (see Chapter 2) and the notion of a contract between an individual and an organization. By joining an organization, or by moving into a particular job within it (and so joining a particular team), an individual enters into a contract with the organization – he is bound to carry out certain tasks and accept certain constraints. This contract defines the space within which he exercises his action responsibility; it is his area of autonomy.

In an organization there is a hierarchy of activities, in that the higher level activities constrain the lower level ones. A leader is responsible for higher level activities and in fulfilling his responsibility constrains his followers. If he is skilful, he does this without diminishing the motivation of team members; ideally this is enhanced through a process of consultation and mutual problem-solving.

Obviously a leader cannot please all his followers all the time, particularly when it comes to the allocation of scarce resources or necessary but unpopular chores. (It is a fortunate cricket captain who has eleven players who each prefer to occupy a different place in the batting order!) Even when it is possible to give everyone what they want, a good leader may decide that an alternative, and less popular, decision is in the best interests of the team. He will be wise to explain his rationale, so that his decision does not appear arbitrary and irrational. But it is his right to make his own decision, in his area of action responsibility; team members may feel that they would make a different decision if they were leader, but any expression of what this would entail can be treated merely as the voicing of a second opinion and ignored if desired.

Within this framework, the relationship between leader and team members becomes one of interdependence. Team members need a leader who does his job well, who provides them with the environment in which they can best get on with their own jobs effectively. A team leader is dependent for success on his team members doing their jobs well, because he is judged on their performance.

This is not a relationship of subservience; it is a relationship between equal human beings doing different jobs, one of which is the creation of a context in which the others can be successfully carried out. The person whose job this is might be perceived as more powerful than his colleagues, but his power is actually dependent on the performance of others. Looked at in this way his position can be seen as one of weakness!

It is only in quasi-military operational situations that instant obedience to a leader's instructions is required from team members. Even this cannot be called subservient behaviour if a contract has been entered into which explicitly demands it. Every cricketer knows that he must change his position on the field in response to his captain's signals – it is part of the game.

To carry this attitude into all business situations, however, is nonsense. 'I always do what my superior officer tells me,' said Walter, an ex-RAF wing commander colleague of mine, when doing something we both knew to be stupid. I am sure his boss would have liked to have had the opportunity to reconsider his decision in the light of the information Walter and I had. But Walter's unquestioning obedience deprived him of that opportunity.

We are right to resist the notion of followership; it has no place in the teamwork of the intelligent and autonomous. But a responsive and constructive attitude to leadership is an essential part of the role of team members.

'The first responsibility of a manager', according to Sir Nigel Foulkes, when he was Managing Director of Rank Xerox, 'is to educate his boss.' The same can be said of any team member in relation to his leader. A team member has first-hand knowledge and experience of what he is doing: his leader depends on *him* for his knowledge. A well-informed leader will make better decisions than an ignorant one.

Equally important is a team member's mentality, in particular the assumptions he makes concerning his leader. If he is suspicious and mistrustful, he interprets his leader's actions and decisions negatively, and his suspicions are reinforced – a case of self-justifying expectations. A willingness on the part of both the team members and the leader to give each other the benefit of the doubt – to 'assume positive intent' – is a good basis on which to build a secure relationship.

Team members must also be careful not to impose excessive expectations on their leader. He is as human as they are, and probably (hopefully?) on a learning curve too, so he is just as likely to make mistakes as they are. Tolerance of human fallibility, again extended by both parties, also helps in the building of understanding and trust between leader and team member.

The success of a relationship is indeed a mutual responsibility, a concept far removed from that of team members following their leader like sheep. The Leadership Trust use the term 'teammanship', and while this may be a little clumsy, it comes much closer to expressing what is appropriate than does 'followership'.

The leadership of the chief executive

The chief executive is the leader of the macro team, made up of many sub-teams and involving possibly thousands of people. He has special problems of leadership arising from the scale of the operation and the many channels and levels through which he must exert his influence.

He is also unique, as we have seen, in being alone; he is not a member of a higher level team with a leader to refer to for guidance and support. That might seem to be a blessing to a team member with an unsatisfactory boss, but it can leave the chief executive isolated. He is well-advised to seek the help of external advisers (corporate staff, consultants, non-executive directors, chief executives of other businesses, retired chief executives or simply wise friends) with whom he can share in confidence the problems he cannot, or chooses not to, discuss with his own immediate team.

He has a major communication problem, both in transmitting his message to the organization at large, and in keeping informed of what is happening. If he communicates down the hierarchy, there is a real danger that his message will be altered at each level as it is passed on. I have argued elsewhere* that the typical success rate in the average unstructured face-to-face communication is no higher than 25 per cent. Even if this is raised to 50 per cent by improved communication skills, the chances of success are down to 6 per cent after three transfers!

The setting up of briefing groups, which attend regularly scheduled meetings operating from a written brief, goes some way towards overcoming these problems, but in addition I believe a chief executive needs to communicate directly to all members of his organization periodically so that everyone knows where he intends the organization to go and how it should get there.

Probably the best way to do this is to address them directly at a series of meetings; if this is not feasible, a videotaped talk, with provision for everyone to see it, is probably the next best thing. A letter or newsletter is a poor substitute, because it loses the tone of voice and non-verbal dimensions of the message.

Everything a chief executive says and does is likely to be scrutinized for its significance by the organization. I suggest to chief

*See *Communication* in the Sphere 'Innovative Management Skills' series.

executives I work with that they imagine they are permanently plugged into a poor quality public address system. Everything they say comes over loud and indistinct or garbled.

The same principle applies to their actions, as one of them pointed out to me recently. He had just been appointed chief executive, and I phoned to congratulate him and arrange a meeting. He received the call warmly and then said, 'You weren't thinking of coming here, were you?' I was. 'Let's meet for dinner, instead,' he said. Over dinner he explained: 'If I were to be seen talking to you, all sorts of rumours and speculation would be flying round the organization before you left. They know what you stand for, and they would immediately draw their own conclusions – probably wrong ones. I don't want that happening.' Every action has to be assessed for its symbolic significance.

There is a similar problem with information coming up the organization. Of necessity it is summarized and filtered as it moves from one level to the next. In addition to the normal risk of faulty communication, there is the extra hazard of deliberate editing and window-dressing. No one wants to be the bearer of bad news; if it can be glossed over, it probably is, particularly if the prevailing management style is punitive. (One great advantage of a non-punitive style is that it increases the chances of accurate and honest reporting).

A chief executive, then, must supplement the formal information system with his own direct observation carried out on a sample basis, by 'walking the job' and talking to people at all levels in an informal, friendly way. He must make it clear that he is doing this for his own benefit, and to make himself known and visible in the organization. He must be scrupulously careful not to cut across the authority of sub-team leaders. When he encounters complaints (as is only inevitable) he should note them for future discussion with the managers concerned, in the course of which he will hear the rest of the story. (One chief executive of my acquaintance has an unfortunate habit of reacting with instant decisions to complaints he picks up on his walkabout, thereby infuriating and undermining the authority of the managers directly responsible, and making bad decisions at that. Any malcontent in the organization uses him when he wants to stir up trouble!)

The combination of a feel for the business as a whole and an ability to keep in touch with the nitty gritty, at least on a sample basis, is decribed by Dr Muller as the 'helicopter' quality, which he sees as the outstanding quality of a successful chief executive. It is a delicate combination which it takes considerable adroitness to maintain.

However, it is through his leadership of his own immediate team – the managers who report directly to him – that a chief executive sets the tone and direction of the business. Whatever messages he gives to the organization as a whole, they must be reinforced by the actions and behaviour of senior managers.

'You may think I have power, Vincent,' a chief executive said to me sadly, 'but I don't have power to change men's minds.' The chief executive is only as powerful as the team that supports him. If its members are not of one mind with him, either he or they must change, or he or they must go.

Leading for innovation

'If you love sausage and respect the law, do not be present when either is made.' This saying is quoted by George Prince in an unpublished paper, 'Managing Yourself for Innovation'. However desirable the end product – sausage, law or innovation – the *process* by which it is produced is messy and not for the squeamish. The innovation process is full of mistakes, anomalies and surprises.

For a team leader who wants his team to be innovative there is a serious dilemma. If he is a good manager, he is supposed to be in control of what his team does. Yet if he engages in controlling behaviour, he *inhibits* enterprise among his team members. 'Many of the actions and attitudes that are essential if subordinates are to maintain an innovative posture are for you, the manager, *counter intuitive* and *counter to your conservative training*. Counter, in fact, to many of the expectations transmitted to you by your boss. Yet failing to recognize and be in synch with the innovative process of subordinates sends a loud clear signal to stay mundane and keep you comfortable.'*

One solution for a team leader is not to look too closely – to exercise the Nelson touch, you might say, and to do so in both directions, down as well as up the organization! (In other words, don't be present when the sausage is made.) Alternatively, as George puts it, 'Shield your boss, and to some extent yourself, from the messier aspects of innovation.' It is an uncomfortable notion for me – it suggests almost an abdication of leadership – yet I find myself increasingly behaving in this way, and lo, innovation is flourishing in my team!

Ideally, a team leader and his team (and his boss!) need a

*George Prince, ibid.

common understanding of the innovation process, so that he can behave, and be perceived to be behaving, in a manner appropriate to the current stage of the process being carried out at any particular time – permissive and supportive in the experimental stages, hard-nosed and controlling when far-reaching, high-risk decisions have to be taken.

The innovation process is an iterative cycle, progressing from speculative thought which generates new ways of dealing with a problem or opportunity, to specific actionable ideas that can be tested in some form of pilot scheme or experiment. An experiment provides data, which may prompt fresh directions of thought and new ideas which are in turn subjected to test, until an idea is solid enough to be implemented as a solution. A leader and his team members need a common understanding of this process, and to be in agreement as to what stage they are at with any particular innovation, so that they think and behave in the appropriate way at all times.

The duty of a leader in promoting innovation in his team is to create an environment which encourages innovation, rather than do all or most of the innovating himself. Although one of the ways he can create such an environment is to set an example of innovative behaviour by taking on new challenges himself, thereby encouraging others to do likewise, the area within which he does this must not take in those tasks properly carried out by his team members, only those which it is his responsibility as leader to attend to.

To stimulate innovation in the area of team tasks, he needs to find 'champions' from within his team. If he sees an opportunity for innovation, he must offer it to a team member on the understanding that he is free to tackle it in his own way and should not feel compelled to employ methods which he himself would choose. A leader's own ideas and opinions should be offered as a resource to the champion: whether he adopts them or not is up to him.

A champion should check with his leader before taking any action that might represent an encroachment on his leader's area of action responsibility, i.e. action which might put substantial team resources or the team's reputation at risk. If a proposal is not acceptable to a leader, he must give feedback in a constructive way: 'These aspects are acceptable and these are the problems we need to overcome before going ahead.' *How* problems are overcome is for the champion to decide (and remains subject to his leader's approval). Again, his leader's own ideas are available to him, if he wants them.

By delegating opportunities for innovation to team members, and by encouraging team members to come up with their own proposals for innovation, a leader mobilizes the innovative capacity of his whole team – a much more effective approach than attempting to do all the jobs himself. Innovative activity is usually the most interesting, stimulating and exciting part of a job, and carries the highest potential for learning. Ideally, all team members should have some share in it.

It is equally a part of a leader's job to keep innovative activity in balance with the routine work of his team. Businesses succeed in the short term through the efficient implementation of well-tried, solutions; they survive and grow over the long term through the process of innovation. Neither activity must crowd out the other; each has its proper place and calls for its appropriate style of working. It is a leader's responsibility to create an environment in which a suitable degree of innovation co-exists with the efficient performance of routine operations.

5. Team composition and formation

EXIT

Introduction

How do you put together a group of people who will work well as a team? Or, given an existing group, how do you arrange the mix (assuming you have some power to do so) to ensure the maximum chance of it becoming a successful team? Given that some highly successful teams come together spontaneously, is it possible to emulate that phenomenon through the conscious choice of team members?

There are no guarantees, but I believe you can weight the odds in your favour by selecting a mix that is both complementary and compatible. To the extent that these two partly contradictory characteristics co-exist, you have a team that is functionally effective (assuming, of course, that the individuals concerned are sufficiently technically competent to carry out their jobs). What cannot be guaranteed is that they actually *like* each other; to the extent that they *dislike* each other, you carry a potential for the development of seriously disruptive emotional problems in the team.

There exists a variety of approaches to the systematic selection of people who will form a balanced, complementary whole. They all start from a recognition that people differ in their aptitudes for and in their desire to undertake a given activity. If individuals' aptitudes and desires are identified and matched with the requirements of a team, the best of all worlds is had — round pegs in round holes, all the necessary holes filled, and the individuals blending into a harmonious, mutually supportive whole.

Differences in approach arise over how the aptitudes and desires of individuals are described and measured, and how they are translated into roles in a team. Certain psychometric tests are applied in the interpretation of individuals in terms of 'personality factors'; other methods are employed to describe people in terms of the team roles to which they appear most suited.

In my experience, there is one approach that is unique in its key methodology for the assessment of individual aptitudes. This is the method of Action Profile developed by Warren Lamb, Pamela Ramsden and their associates in Action Profile International. It is based on observations of elements of non-verbal behaviour in an individual, whereas all the other approaches rely on verbal data, either gathered by means of questionnaires or recorded during group discussions.

Non-verbal behaviour strikes me as a source of uniquely reliable data. It is involuntary and cannot be faked. Through it, a person exhibits a constant mix of behavioural elements, be he acting or drunk. A questionnaire can be invalidated by false replies (though a well-designed questionnaire does have internal checks for consistency).

The use of non-verbal data also accords with our intuitive approach to forming impressions and making judgements about people. Many of the adjectives we use to describe people relate to physical aspects — 'deliberate', 'ponderous', 'agile', 'quick', 'alert'. It would be unheard of to hire someone without meeting them. We can get verbal information through correspondence and phone conversations, but we know we have to meet a person to find out what he or she is *really* like. When we meet someone the impressions we form of them are stimulated by our experience of their non-verbal behaviour. This process can only take place when people are face to face with one another, hence the knowledge that it is essential to meet a candidate for a job before deciding on his or her suitability. Action Profile performs the same task of recording and analysing non-verbal behaviour in a systematic and disciplined way.

I have used Action Profile as a tool in team formation and analysis for over a quarter of a century and have found it invaluable. I propose to discuss my experience in depth, with little reference to other methods (of which I have no experience as a user).

The disadvantage of Action Profile is that it needs a trained practitioner to make the observations and is therefore more expensive than questionnaire-based systems. However, given the importance of the issues at stake and the cost of a wrong decision, the differences in cost seem to me to be unimportant. In this field, it pays to buy the best quality without regard to relatively minor differences in price!

Action profiles

The following description of action profiles is based on material supplied by Eddie Bows, one of the principal UK practitioners. Fuller treatment can be found in *Top Team Planning*, by Pamela Ramsden; *Management Behaviour*, by Warren Lamb and David Turner; and *Body Code: The Meaning in Movement*, by Warren Lamb and Elizabeth Watson. The best simple introduction is *Executives in Action*, by Carol-Lynne Moore.

Action profiling, unlike many other assessment techniques, is unique in its methodology. Unlike those techniques which rely on the answering of questions and the ticking of boxes, some of which can be applied by a subject to him- or herself, action profiling is carried out entirely independently of a subject's conscious behaviour. Comparisons with the 16 PF, Costic, Miers Briggs and other tests are meaningless because an action profile is concerned with that aspect of motivation which is believed not to change significantly over time under normal circumstances. (Abnormal circumstances are constituted by, for example a nervous breakdown or some form of brainwashing – in fact, any experience sufficient to induce a significant change in personality.)

In action profiling the assessment of motivation is based entirely on information which the subject provides unconsciously. It is entirely non-verbal in origin. It is not, however, what is commonly referred to as 'body language'. Body language, which has many interesting applications, is to do with those aspects of non-verbal communication which are usually transitory and which may be used in role play or to create a particular impression.

Action profiling relies on the analysis of a highly specialized form of non-verbal behaviour, described by Warren Lamb (the pioneer of the technique) as 'integrated movement'. Every individual has a particular repertoire of integrated movement which has been shown to reflect his or her unique way of thinking about decisions and problems and the way this thinking is perceived by those with whom he or she comes into contact. *Integrated movement cannot be faked.* A subject cannot influence his or her action profile through any conscious effort.

Action profiling is essentially a technique which describes the way people prefer to make decisions, solve problems, drive cars, buy houses and do whatever else requires a degree of initiative. An action profile is, in fact, a measure of intrinsic motivation. It is not in any way a measure of ability, skill, intelligence, experience, education or, indeed, anything else.

Consider decision making as a three stage process, as follows:

(a) *Attending* e.g. giving attention to the situation, defining what you mean, surveying, analysing, researching;
(b) *Intending* e.g. forming an intention to go ahead, making a case for what you want to do, building resolve, making the issues clear, weighing up the pros and cons;
(c) *Committing* e.g. committing yourself to action, progressing your decisions, seizing opportunities, timing and staging your actions.

Most of us like to believe that our decisions are balanced in some way, that they reflect pertinent research and thorough preparation, are purposeful and realistic, and are implemented at the right time and according to a plan. In action profile terms, a sound decision reflects a balance between attending, intending and committing, appropriate to the context in which it is made.

We can all think of situations in which so-and-so 'didn't do his homework', 'gave up too easily' or 'missed the boat'. Such situations reflect particular motivational imbalances between the three action profile stages. The first suggests a low attending motivation, the second a low intending motivation and the third a low committing motivation. We can just as well think of situations in which a high attending, intending or committing motivation applies. For example, someone who is a stickler for detail has a high attending motivation, and so on.

In action profiling, the three stages of decision-making together carry a total score of 100 per cent. Each stage is divided into two individual action motivations, as follows:

Attending – investigating (analysing, establishing method);
        – exploring (looking for new ideas and alternatives);
Intending – determining (persisting against difficult odds);
        – evaluating (weighing up the pros and cons);
Committing – timing (taking the opportunity);
        – anticipating (having objectives, planning ahead).

A score for one of these six action motivations of 20 per cent or more indicates high motivation in that area. Any score below 10 per cent indicates low motivation. Theoretically, an ideal balance is represented by six scores of 16⅔ per cent. In reality, the most effective teams seem to be those which consist of people with both high and low individual motivations, but which carry an average score of around 16 per cent for each motivation.

Clearly, the most appropriate balance for a particular team, company or situation depends on the context and the environment in which decisions are taken. According to Eddie Bows there are three main types of situation represented by strength in each of the three stages of decision-making. Taken in turn these are as follows:

Attending Strength in this area is most appropriate when a company is breaking new ground and the environment is constantly changing.

Intending Strength in this area is of most value when a company has reached rock bottom and it is essential that considerable strength, determination and realism be brought to bear in order to pull the company round.

Committing Strength in this area is needed when a company's main concern is to be competitive and to stay ahead of the competition.

It follows that since all chief executives have action profiles, some conclusions can be reached about their particular styles of decision-making. They may, of course, have balanced action profiles but this is very unusual. They are much more likely to have profiles or decision-making styles which reflect strength in some areas and weaknesses in others. Those who are really successful seem to have an intuitive feel for those of their colleagues who are strong where they are weak. They are also able to modify actual behaviour for short periods to meet the needs of a particular situation.

An action profile provides a framework in which a chief executive can consider his own style and the style of his colleagues. It shows him at a glance who can support him in his weaker areas and, equally importantly, it highlights the areas in which each subordinate needs support.

An action profile also describes 'interaction motivation' – the way a person's action motivation is perceived and experienced by those around him. It reflects the extent to which others are invited to share in, or to be excluded from, his or her attending, intending and committing processes. The sharer generates an environment in which colleagues are consulted about decisions being taken. The private interactor prefers independence and generates a more autocratic style of management. Some people are versatile, in the sense of being able to include or exclude others as they wish. Others are neutral – their willingness to interact exists but needs to be activated by another's initiative.

A high motivation is not necesarily a strength or a low motivation a weakness; there are positive and negative aspects of both a high and a low motivation. People have a tendency to over-indulge the activities for which they have a high motivation. This is only natural, because these are the kinds of activity with which they are most comfortable, but it may not be appropriate to a particular situation in hand.

Conversely, a low motivation provides a freedom from the need to spend much time and energy on an activity, and in some situations this can be an advantage. There is no such thing as a 'perfect' profile; a profile is more or less appropriate for a job, which means that an individual tends to do a job in a particular, individual way.

For example, my own strongest motivation is in evaluating (weighing up pros and cons), which is great for deciding between strategies, policies and priorities. The downside is a tendency to pre-judge and rule out options because they seem to be impracticable or otherwise unsuitable. I have a colleague who has a particularly low score in the same area. For him all options merit serious consideration: quite often he attempts a course of action that I would judge quite unfeasible – and succeeds!

Such a difference indicates enormous potential for synergy in a team – and an equally enormous potential for disruption. On the positive side, my colleague can open my mind to possibilities that I tend to ignore if left to myself; I can learn from his achievements that more opportunities for action exist than I generally take into account. In addition, owing to my powers of evaluation, I can provide him with assistance in ordering his priorities. He can then use his energies in a discriminating fashion, pursuing those opportunities most likely to bring success or deliver the highest payoff.

For this synergy to work, we need to understand one another's very different ways of working and appreciate the value of each other's approach. Our action profiles provide us with sufficient data, and a common language, to identify our differences and to work out how best to use our combined strengths to our mutual benefit.

Without this data, it is all too easy for me to consider my colleague undiscriminating and irresponsible and for him to dismiss me as restrictive and controlling. (Even with the data we still have our problems! But at least we know what is causing them, which makes them easier to deal with.)

When the action profiles of all of a team's members have been prepared, a comprehensive team analysis and report is presented to the team leader in preparation for a joint meeting or seminar with the entire team. The report describes the current balance or imbalance which exists individually or collectively and makes recommendations according to the context in which the team operates. The context might embrace such elements as the company's organizational structure, its standing in the market, its products, its profitability or its diversification programme. A particular motivational balance is neither good nor bad in itself. It is simply more or less appropriate to the circumstances prevailing.

The seminar is used to provide each team member with a new perspective on the decision-making styles of his colleagues and how these styles relate to his own. Each member is viewed as a dynamic part of a whole. He can influence others and be influenced by them. For the first time, perhaps, he is given a structure in which to proffer influence. More importantly, he knows when and under what circumstances he should seek the influence of a colleague with a strength in his own weaker motivational areas.

Selecting people to fill vacancies in teams can be a problem because there are often two potentially conflicting forces at work. On the one hand, an attempt is made to improve the balance of an existing team by bringing in someone new to the organization. The intention here is not necessarily to create balance such that the six average scores of the team are roughly equal. It may be deliberately to create a certain type of imbalance in order to fill a particular need, e.g. to introduce a higher level of committing to bolster up the company's selling activities.

On the other hand, a vacant position may require someone with a profile strong in certain areas of motivation, but whose appointment, precisely on account of his or her particular strengths, would produce an undesirable imbalance within the team.

That either the filling of a team's particular functional needs or the maintaining of an otherwise desirable balance within a team be to an extent compromised is often inevitable, but the decision as to which of these should suffer can be taken before an appointment is made. Whichever view prevails, it is possible to exercise control before, rather than after, the event.

It is clearly possibly to plan 'ideal' teams using action profiles. Some companies use them for precisely this purpose. Mr Ian Marks, Managing Director of Trebor, was quoted in the *Financial Times* are saying he used action profiling to 'balance continually' his management team.

A team leader must be prepared to allow his subordinates' motivational strengths to make good his own weakneses. For example, a chief executive may recognize his weakness in, say, exploring, a deficiency which makes his approach to decision-making rather narrow. Despite his recognition of the problem, however, the motivational urge not to adapt to new ideas is overriding. Experience suggests that the most effective way to compensate for such a weakness is to employ a highly motivated 'explorer' to provide new ideas and to encourage lateral thinking. This releases the chief executive to be himself while recognizing and using the strengths of his colleagues.

At a more philosophical level, I believe it is essential to appreciate that different individuals achieve their results in quite different ways, and that those ways are 'right' for them. There is no one right way. I see many managers (especially successful ones) operating on the unconscious assumption that there is one right way – the way they do things themselves! It's understandable, because that way has been successful for them, but it cuts them off from appreciating and using the potential of people with different ways of achieving results.

I have found action profiles very valuable as a means of creating awareness of different styles of working. They encourage tolerance of differences and ultimately a willingness to seek help from colleagues with high motivations in areas where one's own are low.

Applications of Action Profile

The data from an action profile can be used in several ways:

— to fit an individual to a job (and vice versa!);
— to inform team members of their own and their colleagues' preferred working styles;

— to build balanced teams;
— to identify areas in which an individual or a team need to be supplemented by systems, structures or external support by way of compensation for a bias or weakness in profile.

Fitting an individual to a job. The most obvious application is to recruitment, but equally important are transfers and other changes in team composition. In principle, it should be possible to specify, in broad outline at least, the action profile required for a particular job, as a guide to recruitment. Maybe a market researcher or a research scientist should have a high attending motivation, a salesman a high committing and sharing motivation, etc.

Unfortunately jobs are not as simple as that, and job titles can be misleading about the job content. A corporate planner, for example, does not 'plan' – his job is to devise planning systems and to ensure that the managers in an organization produce plans according to a format and timetable which allow him to combine them in a single corporate plan. A research and development director is unlikely to engage in either research and development (though he should probably have experience in both).

To the best of my knowledge, no systematic research has yet been carried out to identify the action profiles of the people who are most successful in different types of job. Intuitively, I would expect there to be some clear correlations between motivations and successful performance, but it is by no means certain, because people in the same kind of work may achieve success in quite different ways.

An action profile can demonstrate that performance in a job can be drastically affected not by the job itself, but by the way the individual is asked to work. A dramatic case, from my own experience, was Richard, a young OR analyst, who was hired by his previous boss, Alan, when Alan came to work for me, because Richard's experience exactly fitted a field of work we were developing.

After a few months, Alan said to me, 'I think I've made a mistake in hiring Richard. I put him straight into Project X because I knew he had experience of that sort of work, and he made a mess of it. So I switched him to Project Y, which he should have been able to take in his stride, and he's made a mess of that. Either he's not the man I thought he was, or we're doing something wrong.'

We decided, with Richard's agreement, to have his action profile assessed. The profiler (Warren Lamb) told us: 'Richard is the kind of person who needs always to start at the beginning. If you pitch him into something ongoing in midstream, he will try to fight his way back to the source before he can contribute effectively.'

'So I've been using him in exactly the wrong way,' said Alan, 'pitching him into projects that were already in progress.' He took him off Project Y and gave him Project A to start up. Richard did so with conspicuous success; when I bumped into him twelve years later, he was still working happily for the company, long after Alan and I had left. (Today, incidentally, I would not normally hire someone without seeing their action profile first.)

Team understanding: When all the action profiles of a team's members have been prepared and dicussed with the individuals, so that each person has a good understanding of his own profile, the results are usually presented to the team as a whole. Team members can relate their experience of working with colleagues to their own and their colleagues' profiles.

Problems in working relationships can often be explained in terms of differences in profile. A high attender would probably see a high committer as impetuous – he would seem to be taking action without giving due attention to finding out the facts and exploring the options. ('Due attention' for a high attender is the amount of attention *he* wants to give it – a lot!) Conversely, a high committer would find a high attender dilatory, perhaps theoretical, and reluctant to get on with the action.

Similarly, a high intender can be perceived as resolute; equally, the same characteristic can be experienced as stubbornness or bossiness. These are all judgemental and emotive terms which are unlikely to be helpful in discussing relationships.

Action profiles provide a neutral, factual basis for discussing the different styles of different people, and the likely interaction between them. People who are having difficulties can discuss them in the common language of Action Profile while sharing an understanding of each other's preferred style of operation.

The same information can be used in deciding what type of activity (in action profile terms) is demanded by a situation and in making a conscious decision to get into that mode of operation. Firefighting in a crisis, for example, needs everyone working in the committing mode; high attenders and intenders know they must switch out of their preferred mode into committing. Developing a strategy is more a matter for the attending mode – committers need to curb their impatience. These are differences in degree of course, and most people can operate successfully in their areas of low motivation for short periods when they know that is required of them.

We have found, in fact, that many people can 'flex' their profiles when asked to. At a meeting at which roles and responsibilities are clearly defined and an explicit structure is imposed (like a Synectics meeting), each individual knows what kind of contribution is expected from him at each stage of the meeting. Under these conditions, and for relatively short periods of time, it seems that most people can behave in ways that are not typical of their profile. This is an important quality and enables a team of diverse personalities to pull together.

Perhaps the greatest single benefit accruing to a team from the use of action profiles is a marked increase in the level of mutual tolerance and appreciation. Without realizing they are doing so, many people act on the assumption that 'the person whose decision-making process is different from mine is wrong, i.e. those who think as I do are right and those who think differently are wrong'.*

Action profilers stand that assumption on its head: it becomes 'because our decision-making processes are different, we are in a position to enrich each other should we feel this desirable; he represents a valuable resource to me, as I do to him, and provided we get our act together we can both benefit.' 'Getting our act together', in this context, is a matter of recognizing which dimensions of an action profile are appropriate to the task in hand, and working through them one at a time.

In this way the irritation and even contempt that can easily be experienced as a result of a colleague's very different way of working can be replaced by understanding and appreciation — a big step forward in internal team relationships.

Building a balanced team: One of the great temptations for a manager is to recruit in his own image — if I believe I am a capable person, people like me must also be capable, so I hire people like me! Usually it is not a conscious or explicit policy; it tends to be followed unconsciously through the selection criteria that are applied.

The result is likely to be a skewed or biased team, with most members showing the same predominant characteristics. Such a team tends to get along well, but tends also to be rather unsuccessful. Team members become puzzled by their lack of success, because they are proud of their teamwork (they are great friends, socially as well as at work). In fact, they are a great club, but a poor team.

A team like this lacks some essential dimension — it doesn't fire on

*Carole Lynne Moore, *Executives in Action*, Macdonald and Evans, 1982.

all six cylinders of the action profile! Moreover, any individual who is brought in to provide the missing elements has the greatest difficulty fitting in. He is perceived as an outsider, a maverick, not 'one of us', and tends to find his contribution rejected. He, too, ends up feeling frustrated and rejected and probably leaves even before he is asked to!

A well-balanced team, in action profile terms, is one in which the average score for each of the six motivations lies between 12 per cent and 20 per cent. (I think it is pedantic and unrealistic to try to get close to the theoretical ideal of 16⅔ per cent for each quality.) Usually the effect of a new recruit on team balance is unlikely to be so critical as to determine whether or not he should be hired; it is generally sufficient to be aware of his effect on the team mix.

However, I have on three occasions made recruitment decisions almost entirely on the basis of the effect on the team profile. One was negative − I turned down a well-qualified, experienced and likeable candidate solely because his profile compounded an existing bias in the team. (Fortunately, he was also an action profile user, and understood the reason for the decision!) It is impossible to know whether it was a good decision or not, but neither of us has had reason to regret it since.

In the other cases, my colleagues and I set out deliberately to fill a deficiency in our team profile. In each case, the best candidate in action profile terms turned out to be someone without relevant qualifications or experience for the job. Taking a deep breath, we went ahead and hired the individuals on the basis that the jobs could be learned but that action profiles could not! Their respective appointments have turned out (after stressful learning periods) to have been entirely justified. Both the individuals and the team have benefited.

Going for a balanced team creates its own problems in terms of interpersonal relationships. Just as a biased team tends naturally to be a cosy group which gets along, so a balanced team has built into it the seeds of conflict because of the diversity of natural styles.

To some extent, understanding each other's profile reduces the problem, individuals coming to see colleagues' different ways of working as a resource which can supplement and complement their own. (As a low anticipator, I find it great to work with someone who orders tomorrow morning's taxi the night before − it does not normally occur to me to do such a thing!)

At the rational level, such mutual understanding works well, though it does call for an investment by everyone concerned in learning what profiles mean. However, in my experience, it does not seem to be sufficient to deal with deep-seated emotional difficulties between team members (neither, incidentally, is anything else that I know of!)

I have at times wondered whether deliberately building a biased team and finding other ways to compensate for missing qualities might make life simpler by reducing the potential for emotional problems in the team. So far I have not needed to experiment in this direction, but ways in which an individual and a team can compensate for missing qualities are discussed below.

Complementing the action profile: The information from an action profile identifies areas where an individual or a team is vulnerable because of low motivation. While it seems unlikely than an individual profile can be changed (and possibly undesirable to attempt to do so), there are a number of ways in which support can be provided to minimize risk.

A profile itself creates awareness that a problem or need exists, an essential first step. People who lack a particular motivation tend to be unaware that such a thing exists, and therefore do not realize that they lack it! (They may find that information from a profile explains problems they have experienced; for example, when I discovered that I was a low anticipator it explained my tendency to be late for appointments and miss planes and trains!)

One way to compensate is to provide colleagues with the missing qualities, i.e. build a balanced team, but this is not always possible, and there is no guarantee that a complementary colleague will always be available to help. A team as a whole has to operate with some degree of imbalance, and it is important to have means of supplementing areas of weakness.

For both an individual and a team, training in the techniques of providing assistance in weak areas is worth trying. (For my low anticipating, a time management system is an obvious aid, like spectacles for the short sighted!) Note that this is a different *kind* of training from that which an individual spontaneously opts for. He usually wants to learn more about the things that interest him, and these generally lie in the area of his strongest motivation. Consequently, training tends to reinforce his strengths and do nothing for his weaknesses.

Equally, an individual struggles with the compensating kind of course. (I did a time management course, did not enjoy it much, and even now do not make much use of the techniques I was taught, even though I know they are 'good for me'!) Even so, the effort is worth making. Equally valuable are any disciplines or routines an individual can develop for himself – today, I work out a timetable for myself in order to ensure I get to the airport on time and no longer miss planes!

In the case of a team imbalance, it is helpful to employ external specialists in areas of weakness as both consultants and trainers. A good example is given by Carole-Lynne Moore.* A team she describes as The Achievers had a management of individuals recognized as outstanding talents in their fields but were not meshing as a functional team. The team action profile showed a 34:66 imbalance between the 'perspective' components (exploring, evaluating and anticipating) and the 'effort' components (investigating, determining and timing). 'This meant that although the team tended to be aggressive in its actions, decisions were made without a sense of what the company mission was, or what the long range implications and results of a decision would be.'†

Their solution was to use a consultant in strategic management (an individual with high perspective motivations) to run a series of seminars on strategy formulation. As well as successfully developing a strategy for the company (thereby filling an important vacuum), the exercise enhanced the team's understanding of their individual collective profiles, on the strength of which they drew up a set of operating guidelines in order to capitalize on their strengths and safeguard them where they were vulnerable.

In this particular case, the group not only hired an outside consultant to supply missing elements in their profile; they also made a massive commitment in terms of time and energy to working in an area (strategy development) in which they had little spontaneous interest. This willingness to work against the grain of its natural inclinations is required of any group which wants to compensate for low levels of motivation in any area.

Another method of compensating for low levels is to use a 'horses for courses' approach to particular tasks, even when this might cut across normal functional responsibilities. In the case described above, the production director was given responsibility for a new products project, because he was the highest anticipator in the group. The marketing director, to whom it would be assigned conventionally, was quite happy to pass the responsibility to a colleague who was temperamentally more suited to it.

*op. cit., pp. 115–21.
†ibid.

Other assessment methods

I have concentrated on the use of action profiles because this is the area in which I have experience, as well as confidence in the basic assessment technique. In principle, alternative assessment methods should yield many of the same benefits, namely:

— the ability to build a balanced team;
— awareness and understanding of individuals' different ways of achieving results (an increase in the level of mutual tolerance);
— 'horses for courses', in the sense of fitting an individual to a job and using the most suitable individual for a particular task;
— compensation in known areas of team and individual weakness;
— provision of a common language in which people can discuss their own and their colleagues' styles of working.

My impression, however, is that most psychometric techniques focus on the development of the individual rather than on team development, although there is one approach, the Margerison–McCann Team Management Index, that is geared specifically to the composition and operation of teams. This index is calculated using a self-completion questionnaire, of sixty items which takes about ten or fifteen minutes to finish.

A completed questionnaire is used to produce a detailed personal profile covering a number of key areas fundamental to the work process. These include:

— team role overview
— work preferences
— interpersonal relationships
— decision making
— team building
— leadership preferences
— self organization
— information management
— personal profiling summary'*

(A lot to ask of such a short questionnaire, you may think!)

A profile thus derived is related to the following classification of work functions involved in team management:

*Charles Margerison and Dick McCann, *How to Lead a Winning Team*, MCB University Press, 1985.

- Advising
- Innovating
- Promoting
- Developing
- Organizing
- Producing
- Inspecting
- Maintaining

The first four are described as diverging activities and the second four converging, corresponding to the traditional staff and line distinction in management theory. There is also a ninth function, Linking, which co-ordinates and integrates all the others and also deals with relationships with units outside a team.

The authors go on to apply a behavioural label to each of the functions, coming up with role descriptions such as 'thruster organizer', 'creator innovator', etc. Classification of an individual under one of these headings provides his 'major profile'.

I have not used this approach myself, so I cannot comment on it from experience. I believe any system that encourages members of a team to understand their own and each other's preferred mode of working is of value. Discussion of the key areas and work functions is likely to have a sort of Hawthorn effect, by making participants aware of the issues, emphasizing the existence and value of diversity and developing a common language for yet further discussion of team working styles.

I am, however, suspicious of the tendency to classify people in convenient boxes, and of the apparently arbitrary allocation of behavioural labels to these boxes. (The urge to classify seems to be a characteristic of academics!) I am also concerned that the basic data used are 'work preferences' as expressed in the answers on the questionnaire. People have preferences based on their own experience, but they may not have experience of situations likely to bring out the full range of their capabilities. And I am not sure that my preferences are for what I am best at – a lot of clowns want to play Hamlet!

6. Training for teamwork and leadership

Introduction

If the quality of teamwork and team leadership is critical to the performance of an organization – and personally I believe it is more critical than any other single factor over the long term – it makes sense to work at developing it to the highest possible degree. Investment in team training and other team development events becomes a high priority, particularly for an organization seeking to achieve significant change in its style, culture and performance.

There is inevitably a plethora of approaches available in the market place. A useful booklet published by the Coverdale Organization* summarizes, in its 1979 edition, no fewer than twenty-five different selected approaches; anyone who wanted to could no doubt come up with a further twenty-five today.

I do not propose to offer any kind of comprehensive review of the field, still less attempt an assessment of those which represent the 'best buy'. Not only am I not qualified to do so, I am positively disqualified by being an active practitioner in the field with a strong bias in favour of the type of training my own company provides! The following exposition is therefore limited to those activities of which I have some knowledge and which I believe have something useful to offer.

There is a sense in which any time a team takes to examine, reflect on and improve its methods of working together is bound to be beneficial. The mere fact of stopping to think, in the hurly-burly of everyday activity, is as valuable for a team as it is for an individual.

*Susan Scott (ed.), *Behavioural Theories*, 2nd edn, Coverdale Organization, 1979.

Being together for an extended period of time (typically three to five days) gives team members a chance to get to know one another as people (although it does not guarantee that they will like each other any better!)

Sharing an experience that is different from those typically undergone every day has a bonding effect, even when (perhaps particularly when!) it is a bad one. It becomes a common reference point, maybe a shared and exclusive joke. Moreover, people who are good at learning from experience learn from *any* new experience, which is why the better courses wisely put a lot of emphasis on the conscious learning process itself.

I believe it is essential for teams regularly (once or twice a year) to take time off to take stock of how they are working and how they can improve their ways of operating. Whether this should take the form of a training course, or some other kind of event — a workshop or conference, for example — depends on a team's circumstances.

The benefit to be had from going through a team training process *first* is that it provides some commonly agreed processes and structures, and a common language, which the team can use subsequently, with or without external help.

The time spent is costly in terms of executive hours, quite apart from trainers' fees and residential expenses. If an overhead ratio of 150 per cent is applied, the cost for a £20,000-a-year executive works out at about £1,000 a week (allowing for holidays). It is, proportionately more expensive for higher paid executives. A five day course, then, 'costs' £8,000 for a group of eight before it starts! Alternatively, the expense can be viewed as a straight 'opportunity cost' — think of the value of the work the executives would be doing if they were not on the course (which *ought* to come out at an even higher figure!)

How can you tell whether a course has been worth the time and money invested in it? I know of no other criterion than the judgement of the participants, both at the end of the course and some time later, say three to six months. However, it has the weakness of being entirely subjective, and 'contaminated' by the relationship the trainer will have developed with individual participants — he may even have brainwashed them! There is also, I suspect, a compulsion on the part of course attenders to justify the time they have spent ('I've spent a week doing this. It must have been worthwhile.')!

A more objective measure would be team performance, before and after the course, but this is likely to be affected by many external variables as well. If it were possible to isolate performance in one or two co-operative areas – the efficiency and productiveness of management meetings, for example – we might have a reasonably objective and relevant criterion.

An organization which regularly conducts attitude surveys has an overall measure of the changes effected by training along with whatever other initiatives have taken place over the same time. Again, it is difficult to isolate the training effect. Feedback from 'customers' of the trained group, i.e. the people who have a regular interface with them, is much more specific if obtainable.

For example, the marketing department of a company came to Synectics for training because they had observed the change in the design department we had trained. They had become much easier to work with and more constructive. In the same way, another marketing department decided to take the Synectics course because they had seen the effect of our training on their advertising agency. (I have also to confess that sometimes we have people on our courses who say, 'This would really benefit my boss', and we have to admit that his boss received the same training some time previously!)

In the following sections, I want to explore some of the issues surrounding training in more depth and in the context of three specific types of training:

— Coverdale Training
— The Synectics Innovative Teamwork Programme
— Adventure Training, conducted by the Leadership Trust and others

Coverdale Training

Coverdale Training probably represents the most popular and widely adopted approach to team training in the UK over the last twenty years. It was originally developed by the late Ralph Coverdale within Esso and became an independent company in 1966.

Coverdale's teaching formula provides a structure within which there is freedom for ideas to develop over the years.

The underlying philosophy is that 'in industry and business, the emphasis must ultimately be on getting things done'. The two-fold aim is 'to enable people to learn from experience and develop skills which are relevant to co-operating with others in getting things done'. Practical activities provide a vehicle for both kinds of learning.

A course is based on practical activity. From the very start, clients are involved in a series of short activities which involve them mentally and physically. The physical involvement is not military-styled physical exercise, rather the performing of unusual mental tasks in public.

Tutors set tasks according to the emerging needs of clients and conclusions reached in the frequent review discussions. Printed summaries of the house-message are given after these reviews, but they are considered to be no more authoritative than the personal notes of those taking part.

Courses are hotel-based and much of their spirit is generated by the need for each course to create its own environment. Tasks may be simple and short, even silly and frantic. As indicated above, individuals are sometimes required to go into town to do unusual things – carry out interviews, undertake research, etc.

In order to develop the ability to learn from experience, Coverdale stresses the sequence of Plan, Do, Review (as does the Synectics course). Planning involves specifying the aims of an activity, recognizing that several aims may be involved at once and that they may be individual or shared. It also involves specifying criteria of success in specific measurable terms, in order that the question 'How will we know whether we have been successful?' can be answered.

Course participants are trained to observe the process of what is happening, i.e. *how* things are being done, as opposed to what the task is – to develop an awareness of the kinds of activity that contribute to success or failure in the attempt to achieve objectives. Observation is the necessary means of providing data for review meetings, out of which the learning is drawn for the next experiment.

Co-operative skills are developed by encouraging supportive behaviour such as listening, building on ideas and putting forward creative proposals, and deliberate planning for co-operation.

In summary, the themes running through Coverdale training can be described as follows:

— use of the naturally occurring stages of thought and action in an orderly sequence – a systematic approach to getting things done and achieving objectives;
— identification and co-ordination of purpose, success criteria and objectives;
— gaining people's commitment to their work, their team and their organization;

— setting measures of success and self-monitoring of performance;
— overall awareness – observation – necessary for the implementation of improvements appropriate to a situation;
— recognition and use of personal strengths and skills;
— listening, building on ideas and making creative proposals;
— deliberate planning for co-operation;
— responsive use of authority appropriate to the demands of a situation;
— trial and success learning.

It could be argued that all the above are matters of common sense and do not need a training course to inculcate them. I disagree. If you observe people at work you will find that the principles represented above are ignored more often than not. 'Common sense' is not common practice!

My own experience of working with Coverdale trained people is that they are significantly more receptive to the methods I want to introduce than those who have not had training of this kind. They already have an awareness of process and the need for positive and supportive behaviour. They take readily to additional techniques and structures that increase the probability of constructive behaviour.

My one reservation about Coverdale Training is a suspicion that it might encourage the avoidance of conflict rather than its resolution. People are so concerned to be nice to one another that they sweep disagreements under the carpet rather than rock the boat. I remember observing a meeting in a Coverdale trained organization (and Coverdale insist that *all* members in an organization should be trained) in which every time a topic looked like becoming controversial, the chairman said, to the agreement of all present, 'I think we should deal with this outside the meeting.' It was an organization with many unresolved but submerged conflicts.

It may be unfair to attribute this characteristic to Coverdale Training; it may well have existed in the organization long beforehand. Coverdale, however, had certainly not dislodged it, and there is, too, a very English quality to the Coverdale approach that is consistent with the view that it is not gentlemanly to disagree, at least in public! I prefer the more direct and open American approach, which brings conflict out in the open. It can then be resolved, provided the skills exist to do so constructively. Unskilled attempts to resolve conflict can, of course, be destructive, although no more so than leaving it to fester underground.

The Synectics Innovative Teamwork Programme

The Synectics Innovative Teamwork Programme (ITP) shares with Coverdale the focus on process awareness, the systematic approach of Plan, Do, Review, and the necessity for constructive feedback and good listening and supportive behaviour. It differs in its emphasis on the innovative dimension, through the development of creative problem-solving skills. It also focusses attention on the unique responsibility of each member of a team through the concept of action responsibility (see Chapter 2). The combination of creative problem-solving skills and the action responsibility concept provides a particularly effective structure for the resolution of conflict (see Chapter 3).

There are also significant differences in training methodology. Participants are asked to bring real tasks from their actual work, and these are used as vehicles for learning in group and individual working sessions. (An incidental benefit from this approach is that participants probably make some progress in these tasks, which reduces the 'opportunity cost' referred to earlier.) I believe that working on real tasks increases the relevance of learning. If artificial tasks are used, it tends to leave unanswered the question, 'How does this relate to the real work, if at all?'

Group sessions are all videorecorded and analysis is conducted using the tape – a review is literally a 're-view'. Used in this way, video is an enormously powerful learning tool. It enables people to see themselves as others see them, and the experience is always a surprise if not a shock. They see how easily their well-meant actions can have the opposite effect to that intended. At the same time they are offered alternative techniques which they can try out in subsequent sessions. Video makes it possible to carry out a microscopic examination of incidents, going back over them as often as is necessary in order to understand what actually happened.

Video is such a powerful medium for learning that its use requires special skill and discretion on the part of a trainer. It is all too tempting for him to focus on what goes wrong as the area for improvement, without putting it in the context of all that goes well and the positive intent behind unsuccessful efforts. The videotape can be left to speak for itself; course members are far more critical of themselves than a trainer is ever likely to be. It is his job to make sure they balance their self-appraisal by appreciating their achievements as well as their shortcomings.

Because at Synectics we train internal company trainers to carry out the Innovative Teamwork Programme, we have spelled out in some detail the role of a Synectics trainer, as follows:

The function of a Synectics trainer is to facilitate the learning of course members. He/she does so by:

1. Creating an environment conducive to learning – relaxed, non-threatening, encouraging of risktaking, positive;
2. Modelling in his/her own behaviour the Synectics principles – good listening, clarity about his/her action responsibility and respect for the action responsibility of others, open-mindedness, responsiveness to the needs and wishes of others, good teamworker;
3. Providing feedback which is constructive, positive, and 'timely' in that it connects with the current learning needs of course members;
4. Providing input from the Synectics body of knowledge, and his/her experience of using it, as and when he/she judges it will contribute to course members' learning – and not otherwise!
5. Designing and setting up learning experiments to provide a sequence of learning steps that are easily understood and absorbed (these are largely provided in the course design, but the trainer has some discretion in deciding the exact sequence, pace, selection of exercises, etc.).

This description of the trainer's role has implications for the way a trainer operates. First and foremost, he is not a teacher in the conventional sense of the expert 'jug' pouring out its knowledge of a subject into empty 'mugs'. (Many course members come with the unconscious assumption that this *is* the trainer's role, having as their model their own school and university experiences.)

To correct this assumption, a trainer must behave at all times in ways which respect the autonomy and self-respect of course members. They are experienced and successful managers who already know a lot, from their own experience, about the subject matter of the course (human behaviour at work). They must be treated as equals and never put in a 'one-down' position on account of their trainer's superior knowledge of his speciality. A trainer's role is that of a specialist coach, or a master in the true sense – one who set out on the road before the pupil did, and has therefore travelled further along it than the pupil.

Secondly, a trainer must model in his own behaviour those kinds of behaviour he recommends – particularly by:

— recognizing what is his own action responsibility (items 1–5 above) and what is the action responsibility of course members (their own learning);
— listening attentively to course members, and paraphrasing his understanding of what they are saying;
— accepting the opinions of course members as truths about them and valid for them (he doesn't have to agree);
— assuming constructive intent as regards course members' behaviour (both in sessions and in discussions).

It's what you *do*, not what you *say*, as a trainer that has the greatest impact.

It is, of course, quite contrary to Synectics principles to ask questions without saying why you are asking. This immediately rules out the use of questions in the way that teachers often use them, either to test knowledge or to elicit a point that they want to make. If you already know the answer, do not ask the question. Doing so puts course members in the position of having to 'guess what you have in mind', a potentially 'one-down' position.

Equally, do not get into arguments of the 'I'm right, you're wrong' variety, which are potentially punishing: accept a person's view as valid for him, and if you have a different view, say so, as a truth about yourself.

Participants on a Synectics course learn primarily from their experience of the things they do (the sessions and exercises), secondly from the video feedback, thirdly from their colleagues, and *lastly* from their trainer. A trainer's role is a relatively humble one: to set up learning experiments and allow the learning process to take place. It follows that it is not necessary to do a lot of talking; in fact the less talking a trainer indulges in, the better a course turns out. I suspect that most of us talk too much; it's a great temptation when you are enthusiastic and knowledgeable about a subject, but it inhibits learning!

There is one other, rather comforting, implication of this view of a Synectics trainer's role: you do not have to be perfect! You do not have to know the answers to all the questions course members may put to you. It's quite adequate to say, 'I don't know', 'I've never thought of it in that way', 'That's an interesting new angle', 'I'll check with my colleagues to see if they know', etc. By doing so, as well as taking the pressure off yourself, you model for course attenders the key quality of being open to learning. If you are perfect, you cannot have anything to learn! It is possible, and necessary, to combine being professional, competent, prepared and confident, with being human, fallible, liable to make mistakes and willing to learn from them!

Adventure Training

This generic label covers a wide variety of Outward Bound type courses which have in common the use of outdoor activities as the medium of development of both individual and team skills. The underlying assumption is that by engaging in very different activities from those normally undertaken at work, participants become aware of the personal and internal processes involved in the completing of the exercises set.

Terry Simons, an independent consultant who has been engaged in this field for most of the post-war period, puts this type of training into an historical perspective:

Coming as it did, in the 1950s, many potential buyers were ex-service senior officers who were looking for a civilian replacement for military methods.

The problem was that organization theories which specified job descriptions in terms of reporting relationships said very little about the human being who filled a particular role. At the same time there was a reaction against institutionalism on the part of the smarter potential young executive.

So the old warriors took on ex-service trainers to devise ways to legitimize forced marches and physical deprivation because 'it never did me any harm'. These trainers looked for help not only from the biographies of great leaders but also from the emerging behavioural sciences. Simple formulae began to appear.

The new formulae seemed not to work without the physical hardship, and ways of turning this hardship into 'skills training' began to appear. Managers were persuaded of the necessity to tie figure-of-eight knots, to ford rivers, and to stay awake for long periods.

With the admission of T-group training into the rules of the game it became okay to replace much of the received theory with mutual 'feedback'. At the end of the physical torment it was said that honest discussion would become even more honest because it was based on mutual experience, even though participants may have had to travel hundreds of miles from their mutual workplace to do it.

Out of all the experiments in the alchemy of leadership a few emerged as successful long-term programmes. Some religion-based programmes were offering independent views and opportunities for meditation and counselling These still exist, but serve quietly and are only found by recommendation. Others found a simple formula that a growing organization could use as a ready-made common culture. The latter would print their gospel on plastic reminder cards that, while still gathering dust in corners of offices, remind the manager of good intentions.

Good leaders emerged from the programmes, and sometimes did lay the credit at their doors. But the courses provided a more important service to the training/development manager who hired them.

All of these programmes were part of a wider programme in the company. Although occasionally there would be a single representative from a company, mostly there was a planned campaign. By having the keys to an external experience that not only was personally beneficial as a physical holiday but also was a necessary rite of passage into the 'in' group in the company, the nominating manager had great power. Sometimes the company changed its politics, and usually if the training manager went, his 'leadership' course went with him, and some new magic replaced it. This, more than anything else, demonstrated the shibboleth nature of the training.

Personal feedback, disinterested opinions, having to get things done outside one's familiar territory, all might have an effect on leadership potential. Most of all, they tend to separate the leader from the follower, and to show the follower how to respect and follow leadership. True originality and creative leadership usually play mayhem with leadership courses.

To varying degrees in different programmes, there is provision for explicit review and learning after each exercise, the quality of which depends heavily on the skill of tutors. The Leadership Trust stresses to its tutors that 'the real learning takes place in the appraisals and reviews. It is essential to dig deep and identify underlying factors, strengths (and how to exploit them) and weaknesses (and how to cope with them). There are several opportunities for the participants to appraise and this is where self-awareness leading to self-realization really starts.'

There is no doubt that programmes of this kind are highly popular with the majority of participants – and hated by others. They seem to generate extreme reactions – love or hate. My own experience is limited to a long weekend (it seemed *very* long) and a single day, so I do not claim to be an authority on the subject.

There was certainly for me exhilaration in discovering in my mid-fifties that I was able to learn to rock-climb and abseil down a rock-face (albeit in very safe conditions set up by expert tutors). Equally, I was not amused by being put in the situation of having to build a raft from barrels, planks and rope at four o'clock in the morning in order to cross an estuary and finish acting out a complicated scenario devised by the course designer.

Some of the general influences noted earlier – the bonding effect of shared strange experiences, the potential for learning from any experience, the whole Hawthorn effect of focusing attention on teamwork issues – work in favour of this kind of programme. Certainly the strangeness of the experiences, the contrast of physical outdoor activities with the normal sedentary cerebral routines of managers in business, can have a mind-stretching and unblocking effect which opens the participant's mind to learning.

But I still have reservations about the whole cult of Adventure Training. I am suspicious of its armed services origins and its association with the authoritarian traditions of the military. There is a strong flavour of the Boy Scouts, and part of the enthusiasm of participants seems to come from reliving happy scouting days (and nights) of their youth (not that I see any harm in that!).

More seriously, I doubt the *relevance* of these activities to the work of managers, especially senior managers and others working in an innovative environment. (They may be more appropriate for managers in a high pressure operational environment, with complex choices to be made under time constraints. With increasing automation, planning and computer control, the number of environments of this kind is likely to diminish substantially.)

Essentially, the tasks involved are what Professor Revans calls puzzles as opposed to problems – a puzzle involves discovering an already known solution, a problem requires the development of a solution where none exists. By definition the process of innovation deals with problems, not puzzles. The senior management of businesses of any size ought to be busy creating the future of the company, leaving day-to-day operations to lower levels of management.

If we return to the Critchley Casey model (described in Chapter 2), we see that it is *only* when dealing with true *problems* that a high level of teamwork is actually needed. To practise teamwork on puzzles, where simple co-operative skills are all that is required, seems superfluous.

Thus, 'to get both barrels and the fluid in them, all your team and yourself past the finishing line in forty minutes, without any person, equipment or barrels touching the ground' is clearly a puzzle with a solution known to the trainer, and calling for expertise in the use of ropes, pulleys, planks, scaffolding and other equipment provided. How it relates to the work of a manager in business (assuming he is not running a construction site!) escapes me, though I have no doubt connections could be made.

Similarly, on the overnight exercise I found myself trapped in, one of the teams came up with a simple and elegant solution to one of the 'problems' posed. It was immediately ruled out of order by the course tutor because it did not fit in with the planned course of the exercise – which immediately lost much of its point as far as I was concerned.

Perhaps the greatest single objection to the use of puzzles in this way is the effect it produces on the relationship between the course tutor and participants. It puts the tutor in the position of saying, 'I know something you don't know, and you have to find it out', leaving the participants feeling 'one down' and 'set up' – not a good state of mind for learning. (It was for this reason that my company discontinued the use of a sort of puzzle at the beginning of its courses, even though it was open to alternative solutions.)

However, rather than leave you with my own rather jaundiced view of the subject, I will give the last word to Terry Simons, who has been a tutor on a number of these programmes:

Some of the activities retain a military flavour – climbing, diving and foot-slogging; getting wet is normal. These are a small part of the learning experience. Most of the tasks are highly stylized problems with a given kit – poles, planks, ropes, and yet more water. These problems punctuate a continuous tutor-led group development that is unique to each team.

A large number of courses are designed around a facility. A new hotel decides that it will attract a regular clientele by working with a training team. This team is usually part of the outdoors sub-culture of climbers/canoers/mountain leaders who just want a living in the open air. The legitimization can be done by process consultants who would be just as effective anywhere.

Adventure centres that were originally built for children have found that the scale of charges that they can make to industry gives them a better return, and most of them offer some sort of course.

Longer business school courses have now realized that they are looked upon by active young executives with greater favour if they can offer a couple of weeks in the middle at a more romantic place, and some of them have combined with the PE departments to put something on.

In summary, they all tend to be 'followership' courses with a measure of self-revelation on influencing skills and guts. They tend to be an extension of company culture, to be used as rites of passage for intending managers. They pretend a magic to be got at the peak, so long a you get there the hard way, and that submission to the gorilla in gym shoes compliantly will transform you into 'officers and gentlemen'.

Psychological approaches

From the T-groups of the sixties, through the Gestalt Therapy and Transactional Analysis of the seventies, to today's Neuro-linguistic Programming, there have been a host of psychological/psychotherapeutic approaches which have been applied to a greater or lesser extent to the improvement of teamwork in the business environment. I have experimented, cautiously, with a few of them, and I take a guarded and restricted view of their suitability or desirability in this field.

There seem to be two assumptions behind this type of training. The first is that if people have a better understanding of the psychological factors at work in group processes, they are able to handle them better. To the extent that they have a common language in which to talk about them, I agree with this proposition, simply because I believe it is more constructive to talk about interpersonal problems than to act them out.

I have to admit I observe a paradox here: the people who are most knowledgeable in these matters seem to be the ones who cause the most emotional problems in a team, while the cheerful, uncomplicated ones who are a pleasure to work with often know very little about psychological theories! (Perhaps it's like physical health: the naturally healthy are not very interested in diseases!)

The second assumption is altogether more questionable. It is that if team members experience some kind of group therapy, they emerge a better team, more understanding and more trusting. They may indeed, but this depends a great deal on the skill of the therapist and the existing level of trust in the team. A team that works reasonably well together may in fact shift to a higher level of trust under the guidance of a skilled therapist. But most of the teams I observe greatly improve their performance by much simpler and less risky steps, of the kind described in this book, before venturing into such deep waters.

I am also concerned about the possible invasion of personal privacy. Group therapy can open up some highly personal aspects of an individual's life which he may have no wish to share with his working colleagues. Certainly no team member should be forced to go into such a session, either directly or by peer group pressure; and if one team member declines, for the rest of the team to go ahead would be divisive.

The practice of psychotherapy is far from being an exact science, and therapies come and go with a frequency that is rather alarming. Richard Bandler, the guru of Neuro-linguistic Programming (the current vogue), has some scathing comments to make about both Transactional Analysis and Gestalt Therapy. Of TA he writes, 'Not everybody in the world has a parent, adult and child that argue with each other. You won't find much of that in Tahiti. You have to go to a therapist to learn to have those problems.' And of Gestalt Therapy, 'People learn repeated *sequences* of behaviour, and not necessarily the content. The sequence you learn in Gestalt Therapy is the following: When you feel sad or frustrated, you hallucinate old friends and relatives, become angry and violent, and then you feel better and other people are nice to you. Take that sequence into the real world without the content . . . How's that for a model of human relationships.'*

I cannot wait to read what the authors of the *next* breakthrough in psychotherapy have to say about Neuro-linguistic Programming!

Team and management conferences

Increasingly, business organizations are feeling the need to get the entire management team together for a couple of days each year for a company conference. I believe the instinct is soundly based; it is potentially extremely valuable for a whole team to reaffirm its purpose, clarify the direction in which it is going, and create and renew links between those of its parts that do not frequently come into contact with each other. A good conference can send its delegates away with batteries recharged, confidence renewed and enthusiasm rekindled.

But results like these do not automatically flow from simply having a conference. Quite apart from the cost of a conference (both

*Richard Bandler, *Using Your Brain – for a Change*, Real People Press, 1985.

in terms of financial expenses and the diversion of management time from current operations), a poorly run conference can do more harm than good. It can strengthen cynicism and spread dissatisfaction through an organization; the management of a conference reflects the management of a business as a whole.

To structure the proceedings to ensure that fifty or one hundred participants have a worthwhile and rewarding experience is a complex task. Often it is tacitly avoided; the formal proceedings are treated as mere ceremony, benefit actually accruing from informal contact in the bars, over meals, and so on.

Such an attitude represents, in my view, an abdication of responsiblity. The formal aspect of a conference provides a major opportunity to achieve worthwhile results, informal contact being enriched by high quality formal sessions.

The key to a successful conference is active and meaningful participation by all its delegates throughout the greater part of the proceedings. This cannot be brought about by a simple series of presentations, however skilfully they are given and even if they are followed by questions and discussion. The amount of 'air time' available to the individual delegate is minimal; he is asked to spend 99 per cent of the time listening. Listening effectively is hard work, and I believe it is unrealistic to expect conference delegates to maintain attention over long periods without active participation. (I know that political parties run their annual conferences in this way, which is almost a good enough reason in itself for *not* doing the same!)

The simplest way to provide for participation is to split a conference up into working groups or syndicates (preferably not exceeding eight persons per syndicate, because this seems empirically to be the maximum number for an effective participative meeting). Syndicate-working of itself, however, does not guarantee that discussions are meaningful and rewarding. It is not enough to say, 'Break up into groups, discuss the presentation you have just heard and report back to the plenary session in forty-five minutes.' Participants need to know why they are discussing it, what they are expected to achieve, and what will be done with their output. (Too often managements seem to expect syndicates to regurgitate the presentation, and syndicates set out to tell top management what they think top management want to hear!)

Syndicate sessions provide a good opportunity to find out what participants really think and feel about a business, and to collect their ideas on how that business can be moved forward – assuming top management wants to know these things! To get these results

313

sessions need to be correctly structured and run by somebody with at least a modest understanding of how to conduct such a meeting. My own preference is to appoint facilitators/moderators to run syndicate sessions, giving them some training in how to do this before the conference.

One of their duties is to record the ideas generated and conclusions reached by groups. Usually these are reported back to the full conference. Alternatively, information sheets can be pinned up round the conference room, and everybody given the chance to wander round and study the output of all the groups. This creates an interesting 'street market' atmosphere and is a refreshing change from sitting in serried ranks in the conference hall.

The output of the groups needs to be taken seriously, and be *seen* to be taken seriously, by top management. It is worth the effort to get the sheets typed and circulated as a conference record. Along with this report, there needs to be a statement from the top team of the initiatives it intends to take as a result of the conference output. It may well decide to set up some task groups or working parties to pursue further some of the issues raised. These post-conference activities provide a natural link to the following year's conference, which can begin with a review of what has been achieved since the previous one.

One of the most difficult tasks of a conference designer is to vary the design over the years so that it does not become stereotyped. One of my clients, for example, decided after two years of successful conferences on the lines described above, that they wanted something different – less business related, more light-hearted, but still a worthwhile use of time. They opted to run a management game on personal computers in syndicate teams; it worked extremely well, providing a high level of involvement, new experiences and potential learning about teamwork.

The social aspects of a conference are also worth giving some thought to. It may be that unstructured informal contacts are all that is needed, but a conscious decision should be taken that this is the case – it should not be assumed. There is a risk that people will only talk to those they know already and miss the opportunity to make new contacts.

The alternative is to put some structure into the social events. I have on occasion set groups to work on such tasks as writing and performing a company song, with impressive results in terms of the energy, wit and creativity that is revealed. Other forms of internal cabaret have a similar effect. On the other hand you can call in

314

professionals to stage-manage a murder mystery (preferably with the chief executive as victim.)

It is a matter of judgement whether or not these kinds of activity are appropriate to a particular organization at a particular time. (It would be highly insensitive to organize a cabaret just after a wave of redundancies, for example!) I am sure that an enjoyable and memorable experience is good for a team, but I know no way of guaranteeing that an experience is viewed in this way by everyone. There is usually somebody who objects to being involved in what they see as 'silly games', and if that is a widely held view, it is probably better not to push them.

7. Assessing the teamwork

How do you know how well your team is doing? Is there any way, however qualitative, in which it is possible to measure something as intangible as teamwork?

However difficult it may be, people do make judgements of this kind, both about teams they belong to and teams with which they interact. And professionals in this field (myself included) cheerfully pontificate on the subject to anyone who will pay them to do so. It is, in fact, necessary to make such judgements (explicitly or implicitly) if there is to be a basis on which to decide how to go about improving the quality of teamwork in a given situation.

In this chapter I present the factors that I take into account, and suggest ways of going about making a judgement.

Task performance

Improving teamwork is not (for a business, at least) an end in itself (it could be for a religious community or a boy scout troop). It is a means of achieving higher performance in those tasks that a team exists to carry out. Since performance in most cases is relatively easy to measure, it may seem that we have a simple answer to our question: a team that is working well is a successful team, and vice versa.

I believe this is broadly true, with a couple of important

qualifications. The first concerns the criteria according to which performance is judged; they may be set misleadingly low or misleadingly high. A low-performing team which is allowed to set its own objectives sets them at a level it feels can be achieved comfortably, way below its potential. Likewise, a team that is working well may have objectives set for it (or even set them itself) which are so far out of reach as to be meaningless as a measure of performance. It is important, therefore, to look critically at objectives and the way they are set, before using performance data to judge how well a team is working.

Environmental factors also need to be taken into account. It is easy to look like a team of heroes, for a year or two, if you happen to be in a market that is expanding rapidly (like that of home computers in the recent past). How you perform in the period subsequent to the boom is the real test of your teamwork. Equally, developments like the Falklands War or the year-long coal strike can blow the best teams off course if they happen to be directly affected.

There can also be a significant time-lag in a business environment between completion of an activity and its results. Companies can continue to prosper for years on the advantages gained by initiatives made in the distant past, almost without regard to the quality of current work. (When I worked for Rank Xerox in the late sixties, the technical and commercial leadership established in earlier years almost guaranteed continued growth and rising profits independently of the current activities of the people in the business!). In reversing a decline, many years of good work may have to be put in before an improvement begins to show in the performance figures. Similarly in a new enterprise, some years tilling the soil and sowing will probably be needed before the harvest becomes visible.

Ask the team

Part of a team leader's job is to keep his finger on the pulse of his team's (and individual team members') morale and motivation. He does this by talking to team members singly and in groups – and particularly by listening to them sensitively. Formal review sessions, such as the feedback and appraisal sessions described in Chapter 3, provide one means of collecting data, the informal day-to-day contact of normal operations another.

Team meetings can (and should) be used to pose the question,

'How well are we doing as a team?' Information is best collected in the form of a group 'itemized response', in which team members are asked to identify all the aspects of the team working they are pleased with, and those they wish to change. Each individual's view is accepted as true for him, without argument as to whether it is right or wrong, justified or unjustified. The aspects members wish to change are then the subject of group problem-solving, to find generally acceptable ways of making desired changes without losing the good features.

Unfortunately, these direct methods only work successfully when the team climate is such that members feel able to express their views openly and honestly and say what they really mean. A team that is not working well talks in coded generalizations that mean very little and provide no specific starting point for problem-solving. If a team is in a really bad way, members remain silent rather than say what they think.

Attitude surveys conducted by questionnaire provide a way of collecting data anonymously. They can also be repeated on a regular basis in order to measure changes in the state of a team. In my view, they are an essential feature of any long-term programme of change. They are most commonly carried out on complete organizations rather than individual teams, though there is no reason why they should not be carried out on individual teams, if there is felt to be a need to collect information in this way.

As with any questionnaire-based technique, there is always a risk that questions may be misunderstood or that answers may not be given honestly. You do not need to devise your own questionnaire from scratch; you can start with a tested questionnaire (e.g. the one provided in *Beat the System!* by Robert F. Allen*) and adapt the wording to your own precise needs.

If you decide to use an attitude survey, you have to be prepared to publish the results and act on them. There can be a backlash if the expectations raised by conducting it are not met by subsequent action. People feel disgruntled: 'They asked for our opinions and then ignored them.'

There is also a danger that managements react against findings when they turn out to be unpalatable. They claim either that the survey is in some way inaccurate or misleading, or that the respondents 'don't understand' what the management is doing. That gap in understanding is precisely what a survey is intended to reveal, highlighting the need for better communication on the part of management.

*McGraw Hill, 1980.

For a quick snapshot of how a team's members view the quality of their teamwork, you can ask each of them to write down a score, in strictest confidence, on a scale of 1 to 10, which you then collect. You can publish the result as an average (mean, mode, median, or preferably all three), or more meaningfully as a complete listing, without names. The danger of the complete list is that it may highlight one or two malcontents. Their discontent needs to be known about by the leader, but it may be preferable to deal with them privately rather than in a full team meeting.

Ask an outsider

There are a lot of consultants (myself included) who happily talk to team members individually and report their findings without identifying individual contributions. (This approach is similar to depth interviewing in qualitative market research.) A consultant may also conduct group discussions with or without the team leader present.

The value of this approach rests heavily on the skill of the consultant, particularly as an interviewer. He needs to establish quickly an environment which encourages a respondent to open up and speak freely. Having done so, he needs to be a superb listener, picking up what is *not* being said, as well as what is, and to be attentive to nuances of tone and non-verbal signals – at the same time capturing the essence in his notes, or recording the conversation on tape if a respondent agrees. He must probe for more depth without interposing his own views or asking loaded questions.

Having amassed all this data, he has to make sense of it. If he is lucky, it falls naturally into a manageable pattern. The great danger is that he imposes on the data his own preconceptions, and the more experienced he is the more likely he is to have them! The experience that makes him a skilled and perceptive interviewer can lead him into hearing what he expects to hear!

Other outsiders interact with a team in the normal course of its operation, particularly its 'customers' – i.e. the recipients of its output – and specialists such as staff of the company's personnel department. Their impressions are worth canvassing, discreetly, since they are formed as by-products of everyday transactions rather than a special enquiry, and will not be contaminated by the enquiry itself.

Characteristics of a good team

Many years ago I was travelling with a colleague much older than myself. We were to stay at an unknown provincial hotel. As we approached it, but still at a distance of two hundred yards, he said, 'My god, I can smell it already', and went on to describe graphically the odour of stale food, damp and cigarette smoke that would assail our nostrils the moment we stepped inside. He was absolutely right – years of travelling in the UK had taught him the warning signs.

I have a similar way of anticipating the quality of teamwork in the many different organizations I work with. I believe I can 'smell' it almost as I walk through the door. I have tried to identify below the characteristics which seem to me to be indicators of good teamwork:

— People smile, genuinely and naturally.
— There is plenty of laughter – genuine belly-laughs as opposed to nervous, embarrassed laughter.
— People are confident, a 'can do' rather than 'can't do' group.
— They are loyal to their team and to each other – they do not denigrate colleagues or the organization.
— They are relaxed and friendly, not tense and hostile.
— They are open to outsiders and interested in the world about them.
— They are energetic, lively and active.
— They are enterprising, taking the initiative rather than reacting to events.
— They listen to and do not interrupt each other (or me!).

This is a highly personal list: you may like to draw up your own. And then score your own team against it.

Conclusion

On re-reading my manuscript and reaching this point, I felt the need for some concluding remarks to tie it all together. It was then that my colleague, Terry Cooke-Davies, handed me a paper he had just written about project management and project teams.

'I wish I had written that,' I said, as soon as I had read it; 'It's just what I need to conclude my teamwork book.'

'Use it anyway you want,' replied Terry, and after some hesitation, I decided to do just that.

Before I quote him, however, I would like to reflect on the teamwork implications of the incident. To get (and to give) the help that is needed precisely *when* it is required is the essence of good teamwork. So why did I hesitate before taking up the offer?

I think it was because of a feeling that this occasion was too one-sided – there was no *quid pro quo*. Then I realized that in the give and take of teamwork there are times to take as well as times to give. In a supportive environment, you have to be prepared to be supported as well as to support.

So, with thanks to Terry and also to another colleague, Barre Fitzpatrick, whose ideas are quoted by Terry, here are some concluding words about teamwork.

'The key to success is deceptively simple, and surprisingly obvious. In a word, it is energy. Energy, both individual and collective, both human and natural, is 'the difference that makes the difference'.

In a team which consistently wins, it seems as if each individual performs to the peak of his or her own performance, and the team as a whole achieves a greatness which is more than the sum of the individuals. It is as if the team has a life of its own, and by 'tuning in' to this 'being', each individual can raise his own game for the good of the team. You could almost say that the energies of each member of the team somehow match, complement and augment each other, to produce a team energy which is greater than the sum of the individuals'.

The team manager, therefore, can see his role as focussing the energy of individuals and separate groups towards winning the game, even though they are scattered and separated.

It was a Synectics colleague of mine, Barre Fitzpatrick, who first drew to my attention the behaviour of a strange organism, or rather an accumulation of organisms, called cellular slime mould (*Dictyostelium discoideum*), and just how much it resembled the performance of teams.

Dicky, as I shall call this rather endearing being, lies in a kind of evolutionary no man's land, somewhere between the single-celled amoeba and the true multi-cellular organism.

Most of the time, the separate amoebae of which Dicky is made up roam around old bits of wood and dead leaves, looking for their favourite kind of bacteria to feed on and every now and then multiplying like all other amoebae. If food begins to run a bit short, however, the separate amoebae begin to cluster into small groups of perhaps a few dozen individuals. These clusters then congregate into a single blob, called a 'grex', which might contain thousands of amoebae.

Having got himself together, as it were, some of Dicky's cells begin to climb up over the backs of their colleagues, until they form first a hemispherical dome, and then a cone with a nipple on top. At this point, Dicky topples over onto his side, and becomes a small 'slug', able to move across the forest floor in the direction of light. The nipple is raised and leads the way.

When Dicky finds another source of food, he is likely to dissolve again into thousands of individual amoebae, each going their separate way.

Barre, who is Irish and a scholar of philosophy and psychology, had been describing how he kept the energy constructive in a problem-solving group by recognizing certain patterns of interaction as likely to lead to problems. It seems that one way of looking at the leader's job is to regard him as there to direct the group's energy towards harmony and achieving group goals. In this respect, he is performing a similar function to the conductor of an orchestra, bringing out the best in each of the players, but also keeping an eye on the score.

If this is right, then the role of a process leader in projects becomes critical at those times when Dicky has got himself together and needs to go off looking for another source of food.*

If the process leader does his unobtrusive job well, then Dicky manages the transition from cluster of amoebae to mobile organism smoothly, and finds nourishment somewhere else. Then it becomes safe for the individuals to go off on their separate ways again, finding new food supplies for themselves, thanks to the performance of the group as a whole.

On the other hand, for most of Dicky's life he is either a widely scattered colony of individual amoebae, or a series of small clusters.

This is where the team leader/project manager comes in. He or she is that invisible sensory organ by which the being that is Dicky keeps in touch with the separate constituent parts. It is the project manager's job to be sensitive to the needs and energy of all the individual amoebae and small clusters, so that groups can begin to form when the food supply begins to run short. How he does this is unique to each individual, but some of the elements which are common to all high-performing managers are now becoming clear.

The first is a range of highly developed communication skills. This is not surprising, in view of the separateness of the different elements of the team. The range of skills, however, includes not only the obvious, such as listening, speaking, and writing, but some much less common ones such as the ability to communicate complex concepts using image, metaphor and analogy. In this wider sense, it seems to me that communication is a whole body activity, not just a function of the ears, eyes and mouth. One very important aspect is the ability to 'tune in' to the messages which are being transmitted to you (and by you) outside your normal level of awareness.

In every day language, this kind of whole body communication is often labelled 'intuition'. People will tell you that they 'sense something is wrong' with what they are being told, even if they 'can't quite put their finger' on what it is. The most successful project managers I have ever met have all told me how much they rely on their intuition. In a similar vein, when I ask groups of experienced project managers to think back to projects which have gone wrong, they invariably identify some point in the project at which they 'sensed something was wrong', long before the wheel actually came off and the project crashed.

*i.e. at times of innovation.

The project manager, then, sets up and maintains communication channels between the individuals and clusters who are working alone, and the being which is more than the individuals – in essence, Dicky himself. To do this, there are all kinds of tools which he can use, but these are of no use unless he can tune in both to Dicky's wavelength and to the wavelengths of the individuals in their separate states. These communication channels are essentially two-way, so that the team is aware of each individual and each individual is aware of the team.

When there is evidence that the team and an individual, or several individuals, are drifting apart, or even worse directing some of their energy against other members of the team, then the project manager needs to call the team together again. This is when his skill as a process leader will once again evoke the sense of group identity, and raise the level of the team's performance.

You can see what effect this can have on the project by looking at a kind of 'energy curve' representing the amount of energy, enthusiasm, or optimism exuded by the team throughout the project's life. After the initial enthusiasm and optimism, there is a kind of 'honeymoon period' which can last any time from a few hours to a few months. During this period, the team members seem to be bolstered by their common vision of the benefits which the project will bring.

The next phase is often a kind of progressive awareness that things aren't going to be as easy as was hoped. The team energy seems to drop off during this phase, sometimes relatively slowly (if the team is closeknit and members are on each other's wavelengths), and sometimes relatively quickly (if the energy turns inwards against members of the team). In the second case, certain characteristic phrases begin to be heard: 'Why weren't we told?', 'Who allowed that?', 'Don't look at me, that's not my responsibility.', and in the most dangerous instances, 'What are we doing this for, anyway?'. Perhaps one rule of thumb for the project manager who notices phrases like this becoming commonplace is 'Get the team together, and fast!'.

But whether the decline in energy is slow or fast, there seems to come a time when the original food supply is insufficient to sustain the team's life. This is a time of crisis for both the team and its leader. What is needed is a new source of energy for the team as a whole, and we have already talked about how a skilful project manager can help the team to provide that. In a long project lasting for months or even years, this cycle is likely to repeat itself many times, with the project-workers feeding separately in one area until the nourishment becomes scarce, then congregating and moving to a new level of team awareness before re-separating.

It isn't too much of an exaggeration to term this period the 'zone of crisis' for the project, since at any time, if the energy falls below a certain critical level, the project will die.

In addition to monitoring the energy curve of the project, another valuable indicator of the health of the project team is what the energy is being focussed on. One useful model in this context is the triple circle of task, group and individual. We have already seen that in teams which persistently win, the amount of group energy seems to be very high, so that the team focusses very effectively on the task.

If we look at the opposite situation for a moment, in a team which is losing, there is often very little energy available for either task or group needs. On the contrary, the available energy seems to be directed towards sustaining and even protecting the individual. In many companies this same focus is widely recognized as 'cover your arse' behaviour, with all its trimmings – the oft repeated 'Don't blame me for this mess.' and memos sent by anyone who feels that the 'shit-coloured spotlight' might be turned on them next.

Each of these three different kinds of energy, if it becomes the primary focus of an individual member of the team, will make itself felt in its own characteristic way. A member of a project team performing a specific task will behave rather differently, and communicate his or her progress in ways which are subtly different, according to whether he or she is doing the job in order to get results (task focus), make a helpful contribution to the team as a whole (group focus), or serve his or her own interests in some way (individual focus). Paradoxically, in a high-performance team, it seems as if all three areas complement each other effortlessly.

So it rather looks as if a team which wants to win can learn something from Dicky. If the team as a whole can stay healthy, vigorous and full of life, there will be plenty of energy available for the task of winning. In a healthy body, each cell contributes to the overall quality of life, while being fulfilled in its own specialist function. An effective project manager monitors the health of each cell, while a skilful process leader takes the body to places where there is sufficient nourishment for the whole being.